# THE LAWS OF COMMUNITY

**The Handbook
for Safeguarding
the Family of God**

# THE LAWS OF
# COMMUNITY

## The Handbook
## for Safeguarding
## the Family of God

MICHAEL B. KNIGHT, DSL, B.C.C

# DEDICATION

To the 1,200 members of Covenant Community Church

who have stood by me all these years.

Thank you for exemplifying the laws of community.

# CONTENTS

# Acknowledgments

I wish to express my sincere appreciation to those who have worked on this book to help it come to fruition.

- I wish to thank Nellie Keasling for doing the copy-editing.

- I also wish to thank Lonna Gattenby for doing the design work and layout for printing.

These ladies have been a living example regarding the principles of this book. May God's richest blessings be upon them.

—Michael Knight

# FOREWORD

When I was a sophomore in high school, I remember like it was yesterday, when I took a geometry course by Miss June Cappell. She was determined to teach her students the axioms and the postulates surrounding all the elements of geometry. If the student did not understand the basics of geometry, then his or her future was unlikely to be successful at it. I remember seeing a number of students who began with excitement in taking the course, but eventually dropped out of it. Miss Cappell made it clear to us when she would say: "As we progress through the various levels of geometry, each level will be built upon the previous one. If you fail to comprehend the basic axioms and postulates, you will find it extremely frustrating to ever master its laws."

One of the foundational axioms is: "The shortest distance between two points is a straight line." I used to believe that this basic law is always true in life. However, even though this may be true in geometry and in geography, it is not true in relational community. The shortest distance between two points is a close relationship, for in reality, there is no distance at all. The closer the relationship, the shorter the distance between these two people. In fact, I have come to learn, when I have an extremely close, biblical relationship, there is no distance between a fellow leader and me, no matter where we may be on the planet.

In his latest book, *The Laws of Community*, Dr. Michael Knight articulates carefully the biblical foundational laws to be observed in order to birth, build, and broaden Christ-centered and life-giving communal relationships.

In an era, when people would rather text than talk and email instead of converse, Dr. Knight shows us the path to biblical communal success. It is one thing to talk the path; but quite a different thing to walk the path.

It is with great joy that I highly recommend *The Laws of Community* to you. I have seen firsthand how Dr. Knight has lived his life among friends, family, and foes. Your life will be both wider and deeper as a result of reading and studying the pages contained within this valuable resource!

James O. Davis
Cofounder/Billion Soul Network
Greater Orlando, Florida

# Introduction

The last words of Christ are the most revealing and often, as a pastor, the most haunting for me. You would think that Christians everywhere who believe in life after death would want to hang on to the last words of any dying man, not to mention the last words of Jesus Christ. I can't help but think about Him in His last hours. The supreme intelligence hanging on a tree He created, then coming out of a rock that He spoke into existence. He was resurrected and standing erect, having accomplished all that He was sent to earth to do. The grave could not hold Him, and the ground from which He created man had to yield its dust to His power once again. It must be a great feeling to be preparing to leave this earth, knowing that you are leaving, having accomplished your mission. Yet, before His ascension, He spoke a few last words. I would suspect He would have given great thought to what He would say near the end of His stay here on earth. I know I think deeply about my last words to my wife, children, parents, staff, or church family. I do this for several reasons. I know what it is to say goodbye to my sixteen-year-old brother, Dustin; start for a Teen Challenge graduation in Missouri; only to receive a phone call upon my arrival that he had been taken tragically in a car wreck. I know the power of last words. As calculated and focused as Jesus Christ lived His life here on earth, I suspect He gave grave thought to the last words He would utter. My question to you is this: "Do you know what the last words of Christ are?"

I can't wrap my mind around all the things He must have had on His mind that day. He could have used His last earthly syllables to warn against the "yeast of the Pharisees," the "pride of life," or the "deceitfulness of riches." But, no, He did not speak a word about those things in His last few sentences—no mention of church building programs, evangelism outreaches, deacons, elders, or the importance of full-time clergy. He looked up to heaven and said: "May they all be one as You, Father, are in Me and I am in You. May they also be one in Us, so the world may believe You sent Me" (John 17:21). Please notice, He didn't mention government, politics, religion, or natural disasters. He did not utter one word about commerce, spiritual gifts, or styles of music. The last words His disciples heard Him pray composed a prayer for community. These were the same lips that uttered, "A house divided against itself cannot stand" (see Mark 3:25). Mission is no match for disunity, and He firmly knew it. He was the one who told the Pharisees that Beelzebub could never cast out Beelzebub, because a house divided against itself could not stand. There is a reason that an ant can accomplish all that it can accomplish; it never works alone, and it never works in disunity. So, like an army of ants, the church must have a clear focus and a unified objective in achieving its mission on earth. The last words of Christ give us the key to achieving our mission—unity.

It's every pastor's worst nightmare; it's a heartache that only a parent can know. Hearing one's children arguing and fighting is a sound that brings deep grief to any mother or father, because parents know that this old world is rough and full of enough enemies, disappointments, setbacks, and tearful nights on its own. God forbid that families fight among their own blood—the very ones who will be the most likely to stand with them when the times and days become tough. As a pastor, there is nothing that makes me happier than to see my congregation at peace and fellowshiping. Why? Because I know they are safe when they are unified. A wolf can take any one of them when they wander from the fold; but if they are together, even the strongest lion will think twice about trying to devour them. Your adversary roams about like a roaring lion, seeking whom he may devour (1 Peter 5:8). The one thing a good shepherd knows is this: Isolation brings death, but "two [can] put ten thousand to flight" (Deuteronomy 32:30).

The Christian life was never meant to be lived alone or even apart from deep love, respect, and commitment to one another. I will never forget the haunting words of a denominational leader when I made the statement that we should ask for the complete trust and commitment from a group of leaders to keep confidentiality. He sadly let me know that this was not only impossible, but also I should never be so naïve as to expect it. Well, I do expect it from my elders and staff from Covenant Community Church, and I receive it the majority of the time. This raises a great question: Is it possible that we are experiencing a great disloyalty among those who work in the kingdom of God because we accept poor community skills? Anything permitted increases. We have lost more than Jesus' last words; we have traded trust for suspicion and commitment for politics. God help us, when we who are supposed to love each other with deep trust and radical loyalty play our cards against each other so we can get ahead of one another. That world was never the plan of God. Jesus Christ knew that money, the power of Domitian, fame, lies, the fires of Nero, martyrdom, lions, the hot iron chairs of Ephesus, the armies of Persia, nor the powerful seat of Rome could topple the church. No, the only enemy with that ability would be the enemy within.

I have studied extensively the science of social change, and, to me, there is one book that far exceeds any others ever written on this topic. It's a book written by two homosexual men titled, *After the Ball*. These two brilliant scholars from an Ivy League school make Saul Alinsky look like an amateur. They not only understand the science of social change, but also the power of movements. They mobilize the ground troops with the sting of a queen bee and the instruction of a fire ant. What we know today and believe about homosexuality in the twenty-first century is from their plan to unify the LGBT community and change societal views about their community. My point is this: Unity works when millions refuse to break rank for their own individual agendas. My prayer is that you and I and the billions of Christians could return to Christ's last words. If we do so, we can save the world.

What are the laws of community for the body of Christ? What are their foundation stones? If you have ever toured any archaeological site, it won't take you long to realize that ancient civilizations knew that the protection of any community begins with the right foundations. As it relates to the laws of community, the foundation stone is often underestimated in any attack. When the Greeks were attacking Troy, they assumed, because of the way the wall looked, that the weakest point was (as it was in most ancient walls) the corners. The Trojans outwitted the Greeks by placing extra strength in the corners of the walls, thus placing the weakest spots in the walls of Troy in the middle. The foundation stone is a protective stone.

There are actually ten strong stones in building the laws of community.

1. The law of unity is the foundation stone, which teaches us that unity begins with love.
2. The law of discipline helps us to protect the walls of community.
3. The law of support and care teaches us to care for our own.
4. The law of judging gives us wisdom to administer the community Sunday through Sunday.
5. The law of humility protects the hard work of community.
6. The law of leadership guides the community.

7. The law of followership gives the individual the ability to actively follow a leader.
8. The law of speech guides our every word.
9. The law of loyalty builds a garrison around our walls.
10. The law of hospitality gives us tangible ways in which to show our commitment to love and unity.

Only two institutions were ever created by God—the family and the church and these laws of community reinforce their original principles for living life with each other. I can think of no better way to protect the most important work on earth than by abiding by the precepts found within each one of these laws. When we know the laws and understand the precepts, then we can live by the rules that protect our church and lives.

Our God has made a covenant with each of us, and because of this covenant, we faithfully want to live our lives in a way that pleases Him. The answer is not only found in the words of a dying man, but also in the very root of the Hebrew law where He said: "Love your neighbor as yourself" (Matthew 22:36-40). While many may think that the term *law* is crude and old covenant, let me remind them that the same Hebrew laws that spoke of threads in our garments, and how to prepare a table for the Sabbath, also taught the laws of *tzedakah* and *Tikkun Olam*—the laws of charity, justice, and repairing the broken world.

As we begin, remind yourself that love is the foundation of revelation and our highest calling on earth. If we who are called by His name would ever humble ourselves and pray, deeply commit to each other by long-term loyalty, keep a strong allegiance to one local church and to each other, we would see Him heal our land, because those who didn't know Him can at least now have a possibility of knowing Him when they see Him through the way we actually treat each other (John 13:35).

—Michael B. Knight

## CHAPTER ONE

# The Laws and Their Precepts With Wisdom

"Delight in and meditate upon the laws and precepts of our Lord" (Psalm 1:2).

## The Knowledge Box

**Laws:** God's instructions concerning the moral, social, and spiritual behavior of His covenant people.

**Precepts:** General rules intended to regulate behavior or thought.

**Wisdom:** Insight.

In the second Book of Timothy, Paul informs the young pastor of the church at Ephesus that in the last days "lawless times" would prevail (see chapter 3). I see it everywhere, just like you do. It's in the mall at Christmas, and it's happening in the halls of Congress and the Senate. In the last ten years, we have watched "lawlessness" unfold in the United Nations Oil for Food Programme, the IRS scandal with conservative groups, Benghazi, and in the streets of our cities as our children play "knockout" with an innocent bystander. Whether it is a pastor in Iran or an American hero in a Pakistani prison, we can find lawlessness. But stop and think for a moment: Is it possible that "lawlessness" is prevailing, not just on the streets of New York, but also in the sacred confines of the church? Honoring Christ's laws is a source of freedom. We don't obey the laws of God so we can obtain righteousness, but because we are already right with Him. We obey them out of a love for Him. There is a difference in trying to obey God out of fear that He won't accept you and in obeying God out of love because He has accepted you. As the psalmist said to us, "we delight in his law" (see Psalm 119:77).

**What Is a Law of God?**

The law is God's instruction concerning the moral, social, and spiritual behavior of His covenant people. His Law is reflective of His nature. A law is a commandment. Now, His grace has made possible what the law could not do for us—set us free (Romans 8:2-4). However, He also made laws to govern the universe with beauty and order. Any created thing in the universe is governed by a set of laws. The universe obeys certain rules—laws to which all things must adhere. These laws are precise and mathematical in nature as the Book of Jeremiah describes them as "ordinances of heaven and earth" (Jeremiah 33:25). If God built order into the universe so that it might operate appropriately, then why would we not believe that He has built order into the church as well? After all, would He not want it to operate appropriately also?

Laws are developed to bind the behavior of a community of people. They protect our safety and ensure our rights. They arise out of shared values and morals. They bring us peace in a chaotic world. In science, there are many laws. If we look into scientific laws, we can see how God uses even the laws of nature to protect our freedoms and way of living. One such law is a word called *biogenesis*. It means "life must come from life." When a church is dead with trespasses and sins, one cannot expect life. When people argue, fuss, and fight over the style of music, one cannot expect life. Life comes only from life. There is another law called the law of chemistry. It simple states that life requires a specific chemistry. This law is called the center of science, because it is the bridge to other scientific laws. In other words, unless there is chemistry in your church, you are not healthy enough to produce the order you need to succeed. Nothing works together—no plans, no missions, not even an outreach. Among the many laws God created, He also created the law of logic. This means that His truths are transcendent. This law says that God has set the ability to reason within the universe. The early church father, Saint Augustine, wrote:

> The validity of logical sequences is not a thing devised by men, but is observed and noted by them... it exists eternally in the reason of things, and has its origin with God. For as the man who narrates the order of events does not himself create that order....and as he who points out the stars and their movements does not point out anything that he himself or any other man has ordained.

Man did not make these laws, but man can observe that these laws do exist. It's logical to conclude that if we have no chemistry, we can never become a commissional community. It is, therefore, our job not to invent these laws, but to discover them. Even the universe has a special set of laws to govern its order and design. The Bible contains relational laws that protect humanity's desire for community, and these laws teach us how to love each other through tough times and troubled days. Also, the Bible contains many laws, telling us plainly how to live effectively with one another. Church splits and fighting among elders and deacons are weapons used to break the heart of God. After all, unity was the subject of Christ's last words.

The uniformity of nature reminds us that His laws are uniform; they do not change. An atheist cannot account for the laws of nature, because they go against the laws of naturalism. If the world is full of so many practical, mathematical, prudent laws to develop order out of chaos, then why do we live life together in the local church like there are no laws for us? If the local church is the hope for the world — and it is — then its health is as important as the laws of Kepler. God has established the universe with a certain sense of order through laws, because the purpose of the law is to establish order. The law by its very nature gives us the idea that someone has legitimate, binding authority to institute and establish certain regulations. The Old Testament is called the Law. Its Hebrew word is Torah. It comes from a word that means "to indicate, to direct." The law gives us direction, instruction, and guidance. It is the regulatory instruction of God. Jesus said plainly,

> "Don't assume that I came to destroy the Law or Prophets. I did not come to destroy but to fulfill. For I assure you: Until heaven and earth pass away, not the smallest letter or one stroke of a letter will pass from the law until all things are accomplished. Therefore, whoever breaks one of the least of these commands and teaches people to do so will be called least in the kingdom of heaven. But whoever practices and teaches these commands will be called great in the kingdom of heaven" (Matthew 5:17-19).

It's my desire to see your church have uncommon success. Laws set all of the earth, and these laws produce penalties or rewards. While we are living under grace, the law still serves as our primer for education in righteousness (Romans 7:7; 2 Timothy 3:16). Keep in mind that grace (Romans 8:29-30) is never promoted over obedience (Acts 5:32; John 14:15). It is a joy to keep His commandments (Romans 7:12; 1 John 5:3). It's a joy to live in obedience to His everlasting Word. Don't forget, heaven and earth will pass away; however, God's Word and His laws shall never pass away. So, I encourage you to live them, not out of fear, but out of obedience and love.

### Why Do We Need Laws to Guide Our Community?

In the Bible, it was through community that a law was established. Laws ensure the proper order of society. They keep us safe and give us the guidelines in which to live peacefully among others. For this reason, a law is actually based on a national covenant. A covenant is an agreement between two parties. This covenant or law establishes the boundaries for a nation's actions, and dictates what a people can or cannot do. It takes not only a law to bring order to a society, but also adherence by a community to establish the law of order. Gerald Borchert says it this way: "When you establish community, one of the principle factors of success is the establishing of boundaries for action for which we call laws."[1]

If we are to see order in the house of God, it is going to require a deep commitment from the body of Christ to adhere to His laws. Laws bring order. First Corinthians 14:40 tells us, "Let all things be done decently and in order" (NKJV). The half-brother of Jesus said in James 3:16: "For where envy and self-seeking exist, confusion and every evil thing are there" (NKJV). Darkness thrives in disorder. When our hearts are dark, disorder often prevails. This darkness often affects how we relate to the people with whom we attend church each week. Take a moment and notice the list of sins recorded in Galatians 5. However, when our hearts have been touched by grace, we want to obey His commands. As believers, we believe that we owe a debt because of this grace. It is this debt to Christ that leads our hearts to desire obedience. We have this inner motivation to please Him. This means if we love Him, we will obey what He has commanded us to do (John 14:15). When we realize—truly realize—the price that Jesus Christ paid for our redemption, we will have a change of heart. And the proof of this change is seen through obedience to His laws. Christians today have an obligation to live according to His laws for three reasons: (1) They provide us with a protective boundary; (2) Grace demands it; (3) They identify those people who do not work for the common good.

*First, these laws provide us with a protective boundary.* There are good and solid reasons for having laws. The absence of laws is not freedom from their bondage. If you say to yourself—*I am free, so therefore, I will run every red light I see as an expression of my freedom*—it won't be long until you suffer the bondage of death. However, when you submit to the law that says, "You should stop at a red light," then you are actually protecting your freedom. The power of a law then is not in the law, but in the collective obedience to the law. You see, covenants lie behind the laws. When people recognize the price of redemption, they also recognize the responsibility to obey the divine commands. We owe it to our Lord to morally obligate ourselves to be obedient to His laws.

Obedience to the law has not been removed from the new covenant. Matthew 5:17-20 essentially is saying to us, "Look, if you thought the law was tough, wait till you see this: If you really want to be My disciples, give Me your hearts without reservations" (*The Message*). It seems that this passage is actually suggesting that if you are an uncommitted believer, than you are not a believer at all. Jesus Christ always, and very clearly, demanded obedience to the Scriptures (Matthew 5:18-19). But now we get to the clincher: Obeying the laws is not enough. Even the Pharisees obeyed the Law. It's not just about how you behave, but who you really are as a person. That is why in Matthew 5: 20 Jesus tells us that unless our righteousness surpasses that of the Pharisees, we won't enter into the kingdom of God. Obedience is a heart issue. The Matthew passage here is followed by two other passages telling us that murder and adultery begin in the heart. The Book of Romans 7:1 says, "The law has dominion over a man as long as he lives (NKJV). Paul told the church of Galatia in 3:24-26 that the law was our schoolmaster. Is it possible that in your local church you have forgotten how to play well with others? To bring back order to the house of God, we should go back and take a serious look at the laws that He enacted for us to use as we live out our faith in a local church. While the Law is a primer for righteousness, no one can live it out perfectly. We have all failed and come up short in trying to meet all the requirements; therefore, grace enters the scene. The writer of Hebrews wrote in 10:11-12, 16-18:

> Every priest stands day after day ministering and offering the same sacrifices time after time, which can never take away sins. But this man, after offering one sacrifice for sins forever, sat down at the right hand of God…This is the covenant that I will make with them after those days, says the Lord: I will put My laws on their hearts and write them on their minds.

*Second, grace demands it.* In the New Testament culture, there was a certain cultural understanding that is far removed from Western theology today. In the New Testament, grace was not just unmerited favor; it was more than "God's riches at Christ's expense." The word *grace* carried with it a sense of reciprocity. When you received grace in the first century, you were fully expected to pay it back through honor. Not to do so was considered being the height of social disrespect and public disgrace. It was a disgrace not to give back to the one who gave you grace. "An act of favor must give rise to a response of gratitude— grace must answer grace, or else something beautiful will be defaced and turned into something ugly."[2] So, with this understanding, I am asking you in light of His gift to you, "What is your responsibility to God?" He asks in return, not for similar sacrifice but for obedience (1 Samuel 15:22). When we have truly been given grace as a free gift, we know and accept fully the responsibility to live our lives in a way that pleases Him and honors Him. It's simple; we owe Him—*big time.*

*Third, when there are sets of laws, the community will iden- tify those people who do not work for the common good.* Laws are written under the harm principle that protects people from being harmed by others. Have you ever been hurt by the church? Laws help all of us to protect a loving and caring society.

### A Law Is Powerless Unless We Live It

A commandment or law is meaningless if the people of the community forget it, or worse yet, refuse to obey it. Rules must be contextualized to have meaning, and laws must be obeyed to bring meaning. The whole earth and all that is within it is full of laws. This earth abhors imbal- ance. Even the tree and its fruit know this truth. But what would happen if once again the church began to learn the laws of relationship set by God in the Scriptures? It would, I assume, possibly produce a better family, Sun- day school class, Ladies Ministries, or Music Department. What could happen if we learned these laws of commu- nity? How many churches could it save? How many new

Christians would it protect? How much more would your church grow if its chemistry were balanced? This would take not only a law but also a precept.

## What Is a Precept?

There is a difference between a law and a precept. The word *precept* comes from the Latin word meaning "to teach." You can't understand His laws without living by its precepts. In early Christianity, a precept was a command respecting moral conduct. In the Roman Catholic canon law, which was based on Roman law, it makes a distinction between law and precepts. "A singular precept is a decree which directly and legitimately enjoins a specific person or persons to do or omit something, especially in order to urge the observance of the law." A precept is an order emanating from authority. It imposes a standard of conduct like a law of individual behavior. A precept is a directive as it gives us rules for actions. This is very important, because as we discussed earlier, a law is not a law if the larger community does not act upon it. For example, one city has a law making it a crime to gargle in public. I doubt there have been very many people arrested! Precepts give our morality a pathway to performance. They help us by providing a rule of conduct. Laws and precepts protect both nature and humans. I have diligently searched God's Word to find the "laws of community" and the needed precepts to follow them.

# THE LAW OF UNITY: PART ONE

## The Knowledge Box

**The Law of Unity:** "Unity of spirit is the oneness which subsists between Christ and His saints, by which the same spirit dwells in both, and both have the same disposition and aims; and it is the oneness of Christians among themselves, united under the same head, having the same spirit dwelling in them, and possessing the same graces, faith, love, hope, and peace."[1]

**The Precepts:**
1. All Christians Carry the Responsibility to Safeguard Unity.
2. Love Is the Foundation and Protective Gate of Unity.
3. Disunity Is the Fruit of Sin.

A.W. Tozer, in his book, *The Pursuit of God,* wrote an interesting illustration about unity. "Has it ever occurred to you that one hundred pianos all tuned to the same fork are automatically tuned to each other? They are of one accord by being tuned, not to each other, but to another standard to which each one must individually bow." Nothing wounds a pastor more than the lack of unity. And nothing encourages a pastor more than when God's people dwell together in unity. That is why I love the words of the apostle Paul in Philippians 2:2 where he says, "Fulfill my joy by thinking the same way, having the same love, sharing the same feelings, focusing on one goal."

Why is it that we can build a consensus of unity on a football field over a color, but we can't seem to do the same over the blood of Jesus? It's time for the body of Christ to become the unified force it was created to be in the first place. To do this, there are five precepts which give rise and protection to the law of community. They are:

1.  All Christians carry the responsibility to safeguard unity.
2.  Love is the protective gate and foundation for unity.
3.  Disunity is the fruit of sin.
4.  The framework for unity is found within the theology of "one another."
5.  Unity sets the stage for growth.

These five precepts will lay the foundation for the church to be built upon, and for all other laws to be acted upon as they give us a clear framework for living life together. Every house is built upon a foundation, and ours is no different. Jesus Christ is our Chief Cornerstone, and He and the Father are one (John 10:30). You and I have been grafted into the vine (Romans 11:13-22), and now we are all one in Christ (Galatians 3:28).

## PRECEPT ONE:
### All Christians Carry the Responsibility to Safeguard Community.

The guarding of unity in your church is not just the responsibility of an elder, deacon, or pastor; it is every believer's as well. God was so serious about this commission that He began the mission of unity by placing Himself inside that believer. According to Ephesians 4:1-3, Christian unity starts within us then works its way outward. It does so through the conduit of the Holy Spirit (Ephesians 4:3; Acts 1:8.) Here are some wisdom points about doing so.

### Wisdom Point A

*Unity is organic, according to Ephesian 4:1.* The Holy Spirit births unity in us like the Holy Spirit birthed the earth (Genesis 1:2). This unity is often hard to maintain because sin is a disruptive force. It doesn't unify families; it breaks them apart. It doesn't forgive; it holds a grudge. Sin is most effective when it spreads itself relationally. Paul said in Ephesians 4:1-3, that above all else in your church make sure unity is maintained. The Spirit himself births this organic community and then leaves its stewardship to us.

### Wisdom Point B

*It is your conduct that characterizes the harmony in your church.* In Ephesians 4: 1-6, Paul lists four words as the methodology to walking in unity: humility, gentleness, patience, and loving forbearance. These are the four graces that make unity possible. It is our relationships within the body of Christ, especially our conduct that characterizes harmony. The presence or absence of these four graces characterizes our conduct. We are known as a godly person of unity or a sinful person of Satan. God unifies; Satan divides.

## Wisdom Point C

*Unity requires agreement between body members.* In Romans 12:16, we find a scriptural command that we are to be in agreement with one another. The prophet Amos asked: "Can two walk together without agreeing to meet? (Amos 3:3). What does it mean to be in agreement? It means to think the same thing about everyone. Don't show more respect, honor, or reverence simply based on someone's standing in the community. Associate with everyone. You have to understand once again that it's the Holy Spirit who produces unity in the Body. The Bible even says in Romans 15:5 that God himself, the God of endurance and encouragement, grants us agreement. The word *agreement* reflects the idea of harmony, and once again, like-mindedness, with the idea of receiving other people into your church, because God received you into His. The beautiful thing about this passage is that Paul describes who God is as it relates to relationships. The words, "the God of endurance and encouragement," mean that this God is the One who will enable you to suffer with, and have the patience with, the diversity of people who will come into your church. That is not always easy! Many people will come into your church needing an "EGR: Extra Grace Required" logo on their clothing. But God has already thought through the wisdom of asking what you would need to walk in agreement with other people in your church.

## Wisdom Point D

*Great unity in your church is going to require great submission.* I am somewhat tired of hearing lukewarm saints explain that they don't go to church anymore because of being abused by spiritual authority. A fake Mona Lisa doesn't prove there is not a real Mona Lisa. Satan knows that abuse leads to no use. So, he abuses a gift so that an offense will set up in a believer's life, and they, through their pain and hurt, will not use their gifts again. However,

Scripture does not say, "submit to only your leaders"; it tells you to submit to one another. It's a concept of mutual submission (Ephesians 5:21). However, mutual submission does not mean that there is no authority. Your personal right to be heard does not usurp the corporate health of the church. Spiritual abuse is wrong, but so is spiritual insubordination. We are in a war for the souls of mankind. When we break lines in war, a slaughter is soon to follow. But if we refuse to break allegiance to Christ and one another, Satan's defeat is inevitable.

However, in Jude 1:8, we see where God rebukes those who reject authority. First Peter 5:5 tells us that young men ought to be "subject to the elders," and in Hebrews 13:17, we are instructed to "obey and submit" to our leaders. This is not talking about only when you agree with them. The word for *submit* in Ephesians is actually the word that a military commander would have used in telling his soldiers to line up when he gave the command. Why? Again, every war requires disciplined, subjected soldiers who yield to a commander's words. In the Bible, authority comes from God. God delegates His authority. Here is the bottom line: There can be no unity unless we submit to each other for the greater benefit of the health of the church.

### Wisdom Point E

*Before unity can be productive in your church, alignment is required.* If you can allow the Holy Spirit to birth unity in your church, and if you can place the other person in your church ahead of your needs, and if you can submit to spiritual authority, THEN you may be used by God to win your city. (Assuming that you are in a healthy church where doctrine is safeguarded.) Until there is unity, there will be no possibility of a revival (Acts 1:8). But Romans 5:6 is asking us to do something that we can't do, unless we first have heeded the previous points of wisdom.

Alignment is very important and is required for unity to operate in your church. Alignment requires the direction of an authority. Authority can only operate by submission to godly leaders. Godly leaders are to guard unity, and unity is a requirement for growth (Ephesians 4:16). Until you get aligned, you will not grow. Until you learn how to get along with each other, you will not grow. Until you submit and make yourself subject to ONE local church where you can live a life of accountability with other leaders who are accountable, not only will the church never grow, but neither will you!!! If the God of the universe placed the order of the sun at just the right distance from the earth, and the God of Abraham, Isaac, and Jacob built a nation upon the laws given to Moses, then I can assure you there are protocols and laws within the church He is creating.

**Wisdom Point F**

*Submission may precede alignment, but alignment precedes church growth.* Romans 5:5-6 tells us that it is the alignment of the body that gives God the Father glory so that we can speak with a united mind and voice. It's time for the church to SPEAK! I wonder if one of the many reasons that the world isn't listening to us today is because they can't hear our diluted volume. When our Father speaks, He speaks as One. Even the devil knows that God speaks as One (James 2:19). Every Hebrew child knew the Shema and its direction given to them from Deuteronomy 6:4: "Listen, Israel: The Lord our God, the Lord is One." The word that the Holy Spirit is using for *one* is a word that means "a unified one." It can carry with it the mathematical meaning of the number one. Since we know that God is Trinity and that He is three persons existing in One, then we can safely say that on the day we see God face-to-face, we will clearly be seeing Him speak to us as if one person were doing the talking! He speaks as One. Paul is letting you and me and the church worldwide know that when we have the courage to climb the mountain of wisdom noted from A-E, we then have the opportunity to truly become effective in reaching the world for Christ. We speak with a united mind and voice. It is your responsibility to guard the unified mind and speech of your church.

In the Greek, the former is the source of the later. So, until we get into one mind, we can never speak with one voice. Luke uses this word over eleven times in just the Book of Acts. In Acts 1:14 when Luke writes the word for "one accord" (NKJV), he is using the same word that Paul is using here when he writes "one mind." It does not mean that we always have the same opinions. That is impossible in a world where we are independent and free to think on our own. This passage is implying that your local church should have a unity of love and purpose. It's a basic agreement where we collectively decided for the sake of the gospel and the health of our local church to let fundamental and gospel truths take precedent over our own ideas and views. What does it mean for your church to be of "one mind?" It is "a vivid outward expression of unity and feeling."[2]

When your local church has "one mind" about love and purpose, it is then ready to speak with "one voice." Church unity must be on a verbal level so the lost can know we are His (John 13:35). The unity in your church is proof that grace is present.

## PRECEPT TWO:
### Love Is the Protective Gate and Foundation of Unity.

Unity in a local church requires constant diligence (Ephesians 4:2) and especially hard work. It requires diligence because the Enemy is always looking for an open door in your church. God in His infinite wisdom knew this and thus laid out a few admonishments to help us lock out the Enemy. When you think about how important the church is to Jesus Christ and His sacrifice to build it (Matthew 16:18), you realize the value of unity. Anything that is valuable is usually locked up in a safe place. So one of the most important jobs we have is to guard the unity of the church. So, how do we build the kind of gate to protect those kinds of valuables? In Colossians 3:14, Paul tells us, "Above all, put on love—the perfect bond of unity." The answer is, we build a large, strong, open, and high gate out of love.

## Wisdom Point A

*"Above all else" love and unity are to be the most strategic missions of your church.* There is not one program, one choir number, one pew, one children's class, one elders meeting, one dollar, or one man or woman's opinion in your church more important than the role of love and unity. Colossians 3:14 says that love is the protective gate for the bond of unity. But Paul starts out by saying, "Above all." This means that what I am about to say is of greater importance than anything I have said to you thus far. "Above all, put on love." Love is important for the social well-being of your church. Love protects the relationships in your church. Without love, you cannot attract the lost, because it's our love for each other that lets the world know we are His. Love protects our greater interest in evangelism. Without love in your church, the world will not believe a word you say. Love fulfills the Law (Romans 13:8-10). Christ loved you and paid your debt, so He now tells you that the only debt you have left to pay is the "debt of love" (Romans 13:8-10). Above all else, pay your debts. Above all, let us stay connected to the fact that before Christ loved you, you were in spiritual poverty.

Love is the lubricant that keeps your church running. When love runs out, the gears of the church lock up. Love was created so that it would always overflow. There is no limit to love when you realize there was no limit to the unconditional love in Christ. Love moves your church forward. If you are going backwards as a congregation, it is likely your love gears have become rusty. You or someone else has justified not oiling them, and more than likely, your defense for doing so was rooted in your individual opinion, not the collective consciousness and greater health of the local church. If this is so in your church, you should be living in fear. Proverbs 1:7 tells us that the fear of God is the very beginning of all knowledge. When this fear comes, you realize that love is a product of faith. When there is no love, there is no faith. If you don't have love, you can't have faith, and if you are void of faith and love, let it be perfectly clear to you—you don't have hope (1 Corinthians 13:13). Love is a protective gate for all that your church is, does, has done, and hopes to do, and "above all else" protect it.

**Wisdom Point B**

*Love and unity protect your church from the Enemy within.* Love is the protective gate, because it is the ligament that holds together all other graces in unity. When the Enemy scales the walls of love, your future, as a local church, is not secure. Colossians 3:14 tells us that love is the protective gate for the bond of unity. I have thought long and hard about the possibility of my Enemy scaling the walls of the church of Jesus Christ, and I have come to realize an important truth: He, which is our Enemy, cannot destroy the church. He has been rendered powerless (Ephesians 1:18-23). Jesus himself said that "the gates of hell shall not prevail" against my church (Matthew 16:18 KJV). A demon can't do it (Colossians 2:15). The lack of money, the wrong location, or the need for more space cannot destroy your church (Luke 10:19; Romans 8:38-39)! You and I are the only ones who can destroy the church. It's the Enemy within that we have to keep our eyes on. We are the gatekeepers for the gate of unity, and its bloodstained keys have been made out of love. Love never fails (1 Corinthians 13). But when we fail to love, the protective walls around our church crumble like a Paper Mache airplane flying into tornadic winds. However, when we stand like a solider guarding the gates of our church with love and unity, there isn't a force strong enough to topple us or to defeat our commission. Love protects the unity of your church. Paul admonishes us in Romans 14:19 to pursue peace and edification of our brothers and sisters. Remember, they—our brothers and our sisters—are the only possible weak link in the chain that enables our Enemy. When they are weak in love, the walls that protect your church are weak. Ironically, when you think about it, love is actually a weapon. The stronger we are in love and unity, the stronger the protective gate is that guards our local church.

**Wisdom Point C**

*Love and Unity are eternal issues for you and your church.* The Bible gives us a little insight into eternity in 1 Thessalonians 5:10-11 and Hebrews 3:13. Do you realize that we are told to "encourage one another" and "build up one another" *because* we will be spending eternity with each other? God takes the unity in your church so seriously that He included it into the plan of heaven. Part of the works that last forever is the work we do when we love one another. Good community is practice for the world to come.

**Wisdom Point D**

*There are people in your local church who are emotionally broken and spiritually immature.* Unfortunately, when trouble arises, they are usually in a leadership position. The person, who should be mature enough to know what the Scripture says about how to handle a problem, handles it by the worldly standards in the flesh. They oftentimes do not know that they are broken. Really confused people don't always ask for help, because they think their problems are the fault of someone else. Worse yet, there will be people in leadership who are leading because of popularity, not God's call or wisdom in their lives. What do we do when such an important issue is at stake? Fight? That would be logical since love is a wall and disunity is our enemy, but not here, not now, and not ever. Paul tells us in Colossians 3:13-14 that the way in which we safeguard the wall of love is to be long-suffering with that individual. This fruit of the Spirit is actually a weapon of our warfare. Love is long-suffering (1 Corinthians 13:4), and Paul spells out the graces we need to accomplish being long-suffering with people in our local church.

In Colossians 3:12, Paul says that you are going to need heartfelt compassion, kindness, humility, gentleness, and patience. Notice that Paul says to the church at Colossae: "Therefore, God's chosen ones, holy and loved." He is talking to the church. This is how we are supposed to interact with other believers since we have been redeemed. We accept and forgive one another. Consider how Paul is addressing the way we should act—as loving Christians, not the problem. The problem does not dictate how we should respond to it. Even in dire circumstances, we are to operate within these five graces. This is certainly not easy to do; in fact, unity is impossible without the Holy Spirit's involvement. You see, Christ has set up the church as an organism that cannot live without His involvement. When Paul instructs us to be very diligent in guarding love and unity (Ephesians 4:2), we are told to do this daily (see Hebrews 3:13).

As we guard love and unity, we are to do it in the form of encouragement (Hebrews 3:13); because even when there are immature people in our church, we are to treat them with affection and honor—like family (Romans 12:10). In other words, you have to treat people the way you want to be treated. Yet, there is still deeper wisdom to be found here. No matter how bad it gets in your church, the day you start to belittle your opponent, you lose. You can't fight the flesh in the flesh (Ephesians 6:12). Never stoop to that level. If the Enemy can drag you into the arena of the flesh to do your fighting, he has surely blinded you into walking the plank. It's over for you, because only love never fails (1 Corinthians 13:8). Deal with problematic people with dignity. While many of them will not treat you the same way, you will in the end be the wise one.

### Wisdom Point E

*Love is the foundation of unity.* The entire law is summed up in "You shall love your neighbor as yourself (Galatians 5:14 NKJV). We have already discussed how love binds us together in perfect unity (Colossians 3:14). Here is one more point regarding that statement: The Bible says that love matures us when we love other people (see 1 John 4:12). Christ is our example of how we should love other people (1 John 4:11-12). Because Christ lives in us, He wants to love through us. First John 4:17 tells us that love is made complete among us—*complete* meaning "mature, stable, and consistent." If you want a consistent foundation for your church, love must be matured in your congregation. The only way for love to become mature is for us to go through relational problems, stay planted, and work through our issues in that local church (1 John 4:12). The reason the church is so immature is because we sinfully justify church hopping. We never grow up because we never stay anywhere long enough to grow up. Growing up and maturing is an issue of experience. You can't get experience as a cook until you stay long enough in the kitchen to learn how to cook. You can't mature in love until you have stayed long enough with a group of people to go through days when it was hard to love them. Now that's the kind of foundation love is. It doesn't run off when it doesn't get its way. It is always kind, and it never envies the talents or favor of another believer's life. It doesn't brag or boast about itself. Love acts like a gentlemen and is never selfish. You can't provoke love to be anything other than unconditional love. It never keeps a record of wrongs or shortcomings in another person's life. It doesn't get happy when sin is exposed in the life of its enemy. It loves truth, even when it's hard or difficult to accept. It goes not only the extra mile but also the eternal mile. It naturally believes the best about people. It hopes for successful outcomes, and it has the patience and endurance to wait for them. It simply cannot fail. A stable foundation of unity requires a mature love.

## Wisdom Point F

*Love is proof that we are Christians.* Love is the proof we have passed from death to life (1 John 3:14). Why did God choose loving each other in the church as the sign for being members of the church? He could have said, "You will know those who are My disciples because they feed the poor, relieve suffering, worship Me, pay their tithe, or dance." However, He didn't use any of those terms. He didn't say, "And oh, by the way, you will know who is on My side, because they will be the ones who wear this type of clothing or have this size building." He didn't use that phrase either. He simply said you would know those who are His because they will be marked by their love for EACH other (John 13:35). Ancient Roman emperors wrote about early Christians because they noticed their love for each other. Today should be no different for us. Jesus says that in the last days the love of many will wax cold (Matthew 24:12). The meaning here in the original wording is saying, "In the last days, the love for others will grow cold." Love is a missional word. How does not loving each other endanger the church's protective walls and foundations? The loss of love makes betrayals possible. Love each other and prove your faith. Love each other and speak to the lost through your love. Love each other and lock the gate from disunity.

### Wisdom Point G

*The process protects the foundation of love.* Every time the church I pastor lives by the simple direction of Matthew 18:26, peace is the inevitable outcome. Every time that we find ourselves leaning on man's wisdom by trying to handle a problematic issue any other way, we have deeply regretted the outcome. God does not have a plan B. Love is the way in which we protect unity in our churches. Keep your eye on the love meter in your church more than you keep your eye on the tithing receipts. What Matthew 18:26 gives us is a process in which love should be walked out among difficult people and times. When the process or protocol of Scripture is thwarted, danger is imminent. It is amazing how many Christian leaders know more about handling money scripturally than they do about handling relational viruses in the local church. Sadly, most people are completely unaware of just how much the Scriptures say about relationships and how they are to interact with one another as brothers and sisters. Why do people grab the Scriptures when they are broke financially and ignore the Scriptures when they are broken relationally?

Second Peter 1:4-8 reminds us that love works in our lives through a process as well. It says that goodness must be supplemented by faith with knowledge. Goodness is a starting point, but one day it will need knowledge to continue to do what is right and holy. Knowledge is of no use if self-control is not called upon to discipline our lives into action. Self-control without constant endurance is self-defeating. Endurance is required because we must finish the race, not just start one. Endurance will produce godliness in our lives, and this godliness will evolve naturally into love for our brothers and sisters. James said:

"But endurance must do its complete work, so that you may be mature and complete, lacking nothing" (1:4). But we have to stay together in one local church long enough to evolve into loving people. Then, brotherly affection will give birth to love. Love matures through a process, which in turn increases our effectiveness and productivity (2 Peter 1:7). Don't skip the process of love; stay put in one place long enough to grow some roots.

### PRECEPT THREE:
### Disunity Is the Fruit of Sin.

God will severely judge those who cause trouble and dissension in the local church. Proverbs 6:16 says, "The LORD HATES SIX THINGS; in fact, seven are detestable to Him:
1. Arrogant eyes,
2. A lying tongue,
3. Hands that shed innocent blood,
4. A heart that plots wicked schemes,
5. Feet eager to run to evil,
6. A lying witness who gives false testimony, and
7. One who stirs up trouble among brothers" (vv. 17-19).

This scripture is interesting on several points. First, notice that a body part is associated with a specific type of sin. Second, more specifically, notice that the body part that acts out these sins is representative of the distorted personality behind the sinful actions. Third, notice the word "detestable" used for the last of the seven sins God hates. This word is used to show the intensity with which God hates these specific sins. What is the seventh sin that God not only hates but also detests? Verse 19 says, "One who stirs up trouble among brothers." Verse 16 declares that "seven are detestable to Him." Many Hebrew scholars agree that the phrase "to Him" is literally an interpretation that should read "to His soul." These scholars also suggest that the way this verse actually reads in the Hebrew places an accent on the last line with greater emphasis than the first six things God actually hates.

What does this mean for your local church? It means that of all things that God hates, the thing He hates the most, to the depth of His soul, is the "one who stirs up trouble among brothers." God even adds a preamble in Proverbs 6:14-15 and says, "…he stirs up trouble [constantly]. Therefore calamity will strike him suddenly; he will be shattered instantly—beyond recovery." The Bible clearly says that such behavior will bring punishment from God.

God calls His church to peace (Colossians 3:15). To live in harmony is to effectively spread the gospel. Many of you have a heart for evangelism and want to see the gospel effectively penetrate the darkness in this world. However, if you want evangelism to explode in your church, you have to realize that the detonator for the explosives is unity. Paul tells us that there are to be "NO" divisions among us (1 Corinthians 1:10-13). But the instructions of the New Testament do not stop here; they continue to give us precepts concerning how to address a divisive person.

> I once commissioned a Sunday school class as part of our small-group ministries. Like most pastors, I thought they were "my trusted friends." Little did I know that the leaders of this class had allowed the class to become a "gripe" session every Sunday. They failed not only to live by the laws of community mentioned in Matthew 18; but they also failed to even answer my phone calls to their homes "to work it out." Each Sunday rather than honor and respect the delegated authority that had been given to them, they failed to guard the relationships that gave them the authority to speak into the lives of those people in the first place. I have since learned a few things the hard way.

## Wisdom Point A

*Their secret ingredient is secrecy.* Second Corinthians 4:2 says: "But we have renounced the hidden things of shame, not waking in craftiness, nor handling the word of God deceitfully, but by manifestation of the truth commending ourselves to every man's conscience in the sight of God" (NKJV). If gossiping about the pastor isn't a sin; why do people hide it and wait for the appropriate kind of company to come along that enables them to tell it? If you are hiding something, then you are ashamed of something.

## Wisdom Point B

*The divisive person will be relationally unhealthy.* In the Book of 1 Timothy, Paul talks about "the sound teaching of our Lord Jesus Christ" (6:3). The word "sound" is actually an ancient medical term. The word *sound* refers to being "healthy." The words of a false person are not "sound"; the words of Jesus Christ are "sound." False teachers do not agree with sound words. You can always notice an unstable person by the unhealthy relationships that surround their lives. Their children have restraining orders against them, their spouses are emotional wrecks, and their family members are always contending with them. Healthy people have healthy relationships.

## Wisdom Point C

*Divisive individuals will have certain dysfunctional signs in their relationships.* Don't ignore the smoke. I realize that you can't build a church without trusting other people to lead; however, you must learn the signs of deception. They are obvious. First, look at Proverbs 6:12-14 once again. It tells us that a wicked man stirs up trouble through his mouth, eyes, feet, fingers, and lastly through his heart. Proverbs 6:16-19 gives us the seven things God hates. Proverbs 6:12-15 gives us the seven modes of deceptive action from a "scoundrel"—mouth, eyes, feet, fingers, heart, mind, actions. Dishonest people often communicate nonverbally with their fellow conspirators. This passage points out that deceptive people use secrecy and subtlety to perform their evil duties. The American Psychological Association even says that "Some research links lying with such facial and bodily cues as increased pupil size and lip pressing."[3] Now, another scripture gives us further insight into the characteristics of divisive people.

First Timothy 6:3-5 gives us this direction about "scoundrels" who teach bad doctrine to other people. The word doctrine comes from the codification of beliefs or teaching.

1. **They are proud**: This means they have a "darkened mind" and this clouded mind has produced people who are so prideful that they have a settled state of pride. They often like to call attention to themselves as they convey the false notion that they are really very knowledgeable.

2. **They know nothing**: This implies individuals who cannot concentrate or think reflectively. They are this way because they are caught up in the false sense of their own importance. They literally are teachers who cannot pass their own tests.

3. **They have a sick interest in disputes**: These individuals have an unhealthy interest in controversies. When you crave controversies, you are spiritually sick. They build strife in your church by using words. They engage in word battles over trifle issues.

4. **They are full of questions**: This means that these people are full of words, but they are not interested in the substance of knowledge. You will know them, because they ask a lot of questions that edify no one. They argue about issues that are not real. They have a morbid interest in contention.

5. **They build strife through words**: They love to argue over words rather than deal with the real

crucial issues of the church, like tithing, maturity, and evangelism.

6.  **They produce . . .**

    a.  **Envy:** This kind of person fears a rival. He/she senses internal pain at the sight of excellence or happiness.

    b.  **Strife**: This is contention with words that causes friction in our relationships.

    c.  **Railings:** This is literally the word for blasphemy. It means to blaspheme another believer. It is verbal abuse and considered in the New Testament to be the worst kind of slander. It implies the wounding of another person's reputation. These people are always bringing an "evil report" to the church body about another person.

    d.  **Evil surmising**: They are always suspicious. They whisper and hide their thoughts from and about authority. They are suspect of everyone but themselves. They literally judge any act of kindness with distrust.

    e.  **Perverse disputes**: This means that they have spent so much time arguing with people that atrophy has set up in their own lives. These people waste and misuse their precious time. Ephesians 5:16 says, "Making the most of time, because the days are evil."

Sin is a disruptive force (Galatians 5:19-21). It divides, separates, and tries to splinter the kingdom of God. God is NEVER behind division unless it's a healthy division of multiplication for the purpose of evangelism. Sin does not have the goal of dividing to multiply the Kingdom; it has the goal of dividing to conquer. Division is Satan's chief device against the local church. In Luke, Jesus warned us, "A house divided against itself falls" (11:17). Paul wrote in 1 Corinthians 3:1-23 that both jealousy and strife are proof of fleshly living. The problem at hand is that fleshly living isn't found in the lost, but rather in those who profess redemption. It is certainly an issue of maturity and definitely an issue of sin that has been overlooked.

### Wisdom Point D

*A unified church demands a congregation to be on guard.* Unity is everyone's responsibility. Romans 16:16-18 admonishes us to "watch out" for divisive people. The word for "watch out" is telling us to search out thoroughly, scrutinize, and literally spy out anyone who would bring division to our church. Paul tells us that these people will bring a "pitfall" to our church. The word here is actually where we get our English word for "scandal." Paul is warning us that divisive people are always setting a trap for us. They provide the bait, and then wait for the entrapment. It is an enticement for poor conduct that could eventually ruin the person being trapped. Titus 3:10 tells us to have "nothing" to do with them.

The apostle Paul taught the first-century churches that when you accept a person who is divisive in doctrine or nature, you are part of their wickedness (2 John 1:9-11). He goes further in 1 Corinthians 1:13 when he warns us about our own divisive behavior. Paul suggests that when our local churches are fighting each other over silly issues, the world actually assumes that Christ is divisive.

### Wisdom Point E

*There are biblical rules for interacting with divisive people.* A rule is a principle or regulation that governs conduct or actions. Have you ever noticed that it takes interacting with another person to violate the Ten Commandments? The Ten Commandments are actually the MOST basic laws for governing human relationships. In fact, the list of sins mentioned in Galatians 5:19-21 predominantly require the presence of another individual to violate.

1. **According to Titus 3:10-18, when you come in contact with a divisive person you are to reject him no more than two times.** Then, you should abandon fellowship with this person.
2. **In 2 Timothy 2:23, you are to "reject foolish and ignorant disputes, knowing that they breed quarrels" in your church.** This means that you should avoid "silly" and "uneducated" questions in your church. Stay away from myths and questions that portray nonsense. Your church should be mature enough to stay away from arguing over issues that even the youngest converts should know. Don't argue with an untrained mind. Questions that are without understanding, pointless, and without merit—stay away from them.
3. **Don't fight about words (2 Timothy 2:14).** Paul tells the young pastor Timothy not to fight about words because they are unprofitable and will eventually lead to the ruin of the hearers. Words are creative forces.

**Wisdom Point F**
*In the last days, Satan's chief assault weapon will be division in the local church.*
In 2 Timothy 3:1-5, Paul tells us that in the last days a "form" of religion will try to prevail. Jude 1:16-19 instructs us that in the last days people will come into the church who will specifically come to cause divisions. Peter warned us that in these last days when we see these things, we should love one another fully (1 Peter 4:7-8). Love is the guardian of unity and the antidote to any disunity.

**Wisdom Point G**
*There is biblical wisdom on how to correct divisive people.*
It takes wisdom to know how to correct, and who to correct in a local church. Some people are not sheep; they are

goats. You can correct sheep, because they love their shepherd and they know that their shepherd loves them. But, you can't correct goats, because they won't let you. They are unyielding to your authority, and they do not respect your position. The following will give some insight on dealing with divisive people:

1. Division can be thwarted when we show equal concern for all body members, regardless of social status (1 Corinthians 12:25).

2. While the Word does give spiritual authority the right to rebuke and correct the body where needed, it also tells us that there are times when God allows a divisive person to speak as a proving ground for spiritual leadership (1 Corinthians 11:19; Titus 2:15).

3. We are to correct divisive individuals with gentleness (2 Timothy 2:25). In Colossians 3:16, it mentions the word *admonish*, which means to correct; however, it's the words in Colossians 3:12-13 that give us the spiritual wisdom to do so when we address our brothers and sisters with "heartfelt compassion, kindness, humility, gentleness, and patience, accepting one another."

4. When we have to correct a divisive person (Colossians 3:16), we are to do such a task with wisdom and worship. We are to be wise in every way. We are to be so full of the "words of Christ" that it naturally flows out of our mouths in the form of wisdom. Paul says by "singing psalms, hymns, and spiritual songs." These words are not quickly differentiated in the original language, but their overall meaning certainly can be defined. The article in the Greek here in verse 16 is actually the word "grace." We are to apply wisdom and worship to build an atmosphere of grace. This takes humility with all participants. Grace makes us sing! You cannot admonish

(correct) without "thankful worship." Biblical admonishment is known by its grace and encouragement. To admonish like the world is to correct with no love or hope for change; on the other hand, to admonish biblically requires the Holy Spirit's activity.

5. It takes wisdom of speech to address disunity (Ephesians 4:25). Proper speech is a gift of wisdom in divisive times.

    A. Put off falsehood. Your first duty when coming out of darkness, after serving the "Father of all lies" (John 8:44) is to come clean and be truthful. You are now serving the Truth (John 14:6). You cannot learn the truth and keep up your habit of lying. Unity creates truth.

    B. Speak truthfully: Let what you say be true. Ephesians 4:15 tells us that the reason we put away lying is because we have been saved.

    C. All bitterness, anger, wrath, insult, and slander must be removed along with all wickedness (Ephesians 4:31). We are to correct a divisive person with godly character of our own. We cannot address insults with insults. We do not slander the slanderer. These things are signs of wicked people (Ephesians 4:31)—Paul tells us that "no rotten talk" (corrupt words) should come out of our mouths (Ephesians 4:29). This is true, because you can cause another person to get sick from eating it! Use no harmful language.

6. We must render true and sound judgment (Zechariah 8:16-17). We are to speak only what is good for the building up of other people (Ephesians 4:29).

7. Why should we live this way? Because our fighting and divisive behavior actually grieves the Holy Spirit (Ephesians 4:30).

8. We must forgive one another (Colossians 3:13). Unity requires grace. Healing disunity requires forgiveness, because once you needed grace yourself. Such ending requires submission and repentance among the respective parties.

In Galatians 5:15, Paul warns us that if we keep "biting and devouring" one another, we should watch out, because we are in danger of consuming one another. In other words, we will destroy ourselves. How humiliating!

The antidote for disunity is found in Galatians 5:16, 25-26: "I say then, walk by the Spirit and you will not carry out the desire of the flesh." He says that if we really live by "the Spirit," then we will not be conceited, provoking one another, or envying one another. The addressing of divisive people is crucial to the health of your local church. First Corinthians 1:10 explains that when division is apparent in our local churches, we fail to communicate the gospel message with "one voice." That divisiveness hinders our comprehension of the message and renders us unable to send it forth with conviction. Precious saints, for the sake of the gospel, love one another.

## END NOTES

Chapter Two
The Law of Unity: Part One

[1] KJV Dictionary Definition: "Unity," *The King James Bible Page*, accessed January 1, 2013, www.av1611.com/kjbp/kjv-dictionary/unity.html.

[2] Archibald Thomas Robertson, *Word Pictures in the New Testament* (Nashville: Broadman Press, 1930), Electronic Version.

[3] "Detecting Deception," *American Psychological Association*, December 16, 2013, www.apa.org/monitor/julaug04/detecting.aspx.

## CHAPTER THREE

# THE LAW OF UNITY: PART TWO

## The Knowledge Box

**The Law of Unity:** "Unity of spirit is the oneness which subsists between Christ and His saints, by which the same spirit dwells in both, and both have the same disposition and aims; and it is the oneness of Christians among themselves, united under the same head, having the same spirit dwelling in them, and possessing the same graces, faith, love, hope, and peace."[1]

**The Precepts:**
4. The Framework for Unity Is Found Within the Theology of "One Another."
5. Unity Sets the Stage for Growth.

Precepts four and five provide us with many scriptural commandments regarding our relationship with one another. This chapter will give you many principles to guide your church life effectively, because it ensures peace in the congregation. Precept four gives a framework, while precept five simply tells us why this "unity of the spirit" is so important (Ephesians 4:16).

## PRECEPT FOUR:
### The Framework for Unity Is Found Within the Theology of "One Another."

In Philippians 4:2, we find a plea for life. It's not the kind of plea that you can bargain with in a courtroom. It's the kind of plea that makes a request for the health of the church. It's the plea for harmony. The psalmist said in Psalm 133:1 that it is good and pleasant when the brothers dwell together in unity.

### Wisdom Point A

*Love is a fossil fuel that propels unity forward.* The old song said, "Love makes the world go 'round." I think the author of that song was right. It's like a fossil fuel. You can't get very far without using it, because you are dependent upon its properties. While some people may argue that there is not enough to go around, the rest of us realize that there is more than enough—you just have to dig deep to find it. Romans 14:13-19 tells us that love is the foundation for using the skills needed for protecting unity in your church. It tells us in Romans 12:9 to love without hypocrisy. No matter what distance you are journeying to correct a wayward relationship, remember love never fails (1 Corinthians 13:8).

## Wisdom Point B

*It takes humility and harmony to protect unity in your church.* Some churches need to work as hard on the harmony of the church as they do on the four-part harmony in singing. How do you build harmony in your local church? According to Philippians 2:1-11, harmony is a byproduct of humility. First Peter 5:5 says that we are to "walk in humility" among our brothers. In Romans 12:16, Paul writes, "Live in harmony with one another. Do not be proud, but be willing to associate with people of low position. Do not be conceited" (NIV). This passage tells us to think the same thing about one another. Harmony is rooted in humility. Humility will cut the fights in half in your church. When humility is present, "teachability" is present. When humility is in the room, then ego is not. Humility is an antidote for trying times with difficult people.

First Peter 3:8-9 commands us to live in harmony as the people of God. That means we are to be "like-minded" and sympathetic to our brothers and sisters whom we love with great compassion (Ephesians 4:32). We are not to repay an insult for an insult, but act contrary to divisive people by humbly blessing them instead. Harmony is hard work. Harmony has to bite its tongue. Harmony has to stick very close to the virtue of humility because it takes preferring someone else.

## Wisdom Point C

*Hospitality provides the framework for getting to know one another.* The gift of hospitality has been a precept since the very beginning of Christianity when Christ himself needed lodging in a world that did not have any that night. It was during that first Christmas night that the inn gave Him no lodging. In those days, lodging was considered to be unsafe in an inn. Travelers usually worked out accommodations with family and friends. First Timothy 5:10

tells us that widows were encouraged to participate in this vital ministry. First Peter 4:9 directs us to "offer hospitality to one another without grumbling" (NIV). In the New Testament times, even the poorest person was expected to open his house to guests. The reason was that in the first century there were very few buildings that held Christian worshipers. The local church met in homes. The leaders of the local church traveled extensively, building the foundation of the church. They too needed lodging.

Today, it's dangerous to entertain a stranger in your house and most people would not even think of inviting an unknown person into their home to spend the night. Times and cultures have changed, but the Scriptures have not changed. We are still told to be hospitable to strangers, and especially to other believers who come into our area. The same word for hospitable is used in Titus 1:8, and it too refers to being kind to strangers. While I am not suggesting letting a total stranger into your home, I am saying that our witness must extend to those whom we do not personally know. I am from an area where I still remember my 99-year-old grandmother who would sit on her front porch and invite strangers in the neighborhood to sit down for a glass of homemade ice tea. First Timothy 3:1 says that elders and church leadership should be especially hospitable. I am concerned that the church has forgotten how to honor guests in the ministry. I am further concerned that your church start realizing its role in the marketplace. When I was a young teenager, I started working for the Kmart Corporation. I distinctly remember certain kinds of "Christians" who were cruel to the cashiers at our store. I was puzzled and dismayed at their rudeness when merchandise was wrongly marked. Christians should love other Christians first and foremost (John 13:35). But Christians should love strangers and also be kind to those whom they do not know. Reaching out to a stranger at church or to someone you don't know in a Sunday school class is the basic framework for building unity in your church. We might not open our house this Christmas to a person we don't know who needs lodging, but we can open our hearts to an angel on a tree from a family we do not know. We can show kindness to that unknown person in the name of Christ. The way in which the church practices hospitality may have changed, but the need for it never will.

## Wisdom Point D

*The engine of unity is empowered by how we treat "one another."* If you want to take the air out of your pastor, let him hear that you have been mistreating another human being in your church. Do you want to empower your church to great heights? Then lay a foundation of love, and kickstart unity by guarding and protecting the relationships you have with "other" people in your church. Here are a few examples:

1. "Be kind to one another, tenderhearted, forgiving one another, even as God in Christ forgave you" (Ephesians 4:32). Kindness and forgiveness will go a long way toward building a great church for the Lord. To be kind in the New Testament times meant to furnish someone with what he or she needed. It meant that you were not harsh or did not speak with exasperation. Christ is said to have been kind (see Matthew 11:30).

2. Show concern and promote love for one another (Hebrews 10:24). Love is a verb; it requires action.

> At Christmas, the people of our church have engaged in "The Great Giveaway." It is our goal to show 365 acts of kindness. Kindness promotes love, because we have shown concern. This year one family was given a one- hundred-dollar bill to give away to a total stranger. The family was told to wait and allow the Holy Spirit to direct them

in giving this gift. They were in Wal-Mart, and their little boy ran off into the Christmas decorating aisle. As they were retrieving their child, they heard a lady in a wheelchair telling her children that there was no money to buy Christmas decorations this year. They knew immediately that the Holy Spirit wanted them to give the money to this family. They walked up to her and explained the program and told her that they wanted to give her the hundred dollars. This lady had recently lost her husband. She was left to take care of the children as a single mother; meanwhile she was in the hospital for surgery.

The Holy Spirit is just waiting for you to show concern and promote love. You don't have to go to Wal-Mart; let the Lord guide you to the person who needs assistance.

3. We are to pursue what is good for "one another" (1 Thessalonians 5:15). In this selfish world, we seldom pursue what is more beneficial to another person. But God's Word tells us to pursue what is good for the other person. We are to work hard and be diligent at doing what is helpful to other people. What a powerful antidote for the virus of disunity. It takes a selfish individual to bring disunity. When we pursue doing kind things for another person, it is difficult to be selfish.

4. All of us need to please our neighbors for our own good (Romans 15:2). The Bible says that doing so actually builds up the other person in Christ. In fact, your Christian growth is tied directly to your relationships with other believers.

5. We are to rejoice and weep together (Romans 12:16).

I was recently on a biblical study tour in Asia Minor in Turkey. It was a wonderful week of fellowship with friends as we experienced the beauty of the Mediterranean. At the close of my trip, I received a phone call from my wife telling me that my mother had just had a horrible stroke. The helplessness that I felt that day was indescribable. It's a lonely road to hear your loved one is in pain and be helpless to aid them. Yet, it was my Christian brothers and sisters who wept with me and now rejoice with me at her recovery.

6. There are more than sixty-five scriptures that direct the church in principles regarding how we are to interact and treat "one another."

NOTE: Scriptures numbered 1–67 are taken from the *New American Standard Bible* (NASB).

1. John 13:14: "If I then, Lord and Teacher, washed your feet, you also ought to wash one another's feet."
2. John 13:34: "A new commandment I give to you, that you love one another; even as I have loved you, that you also love one another."
3. John 13:35: "By this all will know that you are My disciples, if you have love for one another."
4. John 15:12: "This is My commandment, that you love one another, just as I have loved you."
5. John 15:17: "This I command you, that you love one another."
6. Acts 7:26: "On the following day he appeared to them as they were fighting together, and he tried to reconcile them in peace, saying, 'Men, you are brethren, why do you injure one another?'"
7. Acts 15:39: "And there occurred such a sharp disagreement that they separated from one another, and Barnabas took Mark with him and sailed away to Cyprus."
8. Romans 12:5: "So we, who are many, are one body in Christ, and individually members one of another."
9. Romans 12:10: "Be devoted to one another in brotherly love; give preference to one another in honor."

10. Romans 12:16: "Be of the same mind toward one another; do not be haughty in mind, but associate with the lowly. Do not be wise in your own estimation."
11. Romans 13:8: "Owe nothing to anyone except to love one another; for he who loves his neighbor has fulfilled the law."
12. Romans 14:5: "One person regards one day above another, another regards every day alike. Each person must be fully convinced in his own mind."
13. Romans 14:13: "Therefore let us not judge one another anymore, but rather determine this—not to put an obstacle or a stumbling block in a brother's way."
14. Romans 14:19: "So then we pursue the things which make for peace and the building up of one another."
15. Romans 15:5: "Now may the God who gives perseverance and encouragement grant you to be of the same mind with one another according to Christ Jesus."
16. Romans 15:7: "Therefore, accept one another, just as Christ also accepted us to the glory of God."
17. Romans 15:14: "And concerning you, my brethren, I myself also am convinced that you yourselves are full of goodness, filled with all knowledge and able also to admonish one another."
18. Romans 16:16: "Greet one another with a holy kiss. All the churches of Christ greet you."
19. 1 Corinthians 6:7: "Actually, then, it is already a defeat for you, that you have lawsuits with one another. Why not rather be wronged? Why not rather be defrauded?"
20. 1 Corinthians 7:5: "Stop depriving one another, except by agreement for a time, so that you may devote yourselves to prayer, and come together again so that Satan will not tempt you because of your lack of self-control."

21. 1 Corinthians 11:33: "So then, my brethren, when you come together to eat, wait for one another."
22. 1 Corinthians 12:25: "So that there may be no division in the body, but that the members may have the same care for one another."
23. 1 Corinthians 16:20: "All the brethren greet you. Greet one another with a holy kiss."
24. 2 Corinthians 13:12: "Greet one another with a holy kiss."
25. Galatians 5:13: "For you were called to freedom, brethren; only do not turn your freedom into an opportunity for the flesh, but through love serve one another."
26. Galatians 5:15: "But if you bite and devour one another, take care that you are not consumed by one another."
27. Galatians 5:17: "For the flesh sets its desire against the Spirit, and the Spirit against the flesh; for these are in opposition to one another, so that you may not do the things that you please."
28. Galatians 5:26: "Let us not become boastful, challenging one another, envying one another."
29. Galatians 6:1: **[Bear One Another's Burdens]** "Brethren, even if anyone is caught in any trespass, you who are spiritual, restore such a one in a spirit of gentleness; each one looking to yourself, so that you too will not be tempted."
30. Galatians 6:2: "Bear one another's burdens, and thereby fulfill the law of Christ."
31. Galatians 6:4: "But each one must examine his own work, and then he will have reason for boasting in regard to himself alone, and not in regard to another."
32. Ephesians 4:2: "With all humility and gentleness, with patience, showing tolerance for one another in love."

33. Ephesians 4:25: "Therefore, laying aside falsehood, speak truth each one of you with his neighbor, for we are members of one another."
34. Ephesians 4:32: "Be kind to one another, tender-hearted, forgiving each other, just as God in Christ also has forgiven you."
35. Ephesians 5:19: "Speaking to one another in psalms and hymns and spiritual songs, singing and making melody with your heart to the Lord."
36. Ephesians 5:21: "And be subject to one another in the fear of Christ."
37. Philippians 2:3: "Do nothing from selfishness or empty conceit, but with humility of mind regard one another as more important than yourselves."
38. Colossians 3:9: "Do not lie to one another, since you laid aside the old self with its evil practices."
39. Colossians 3:13: "Bearing with one another, and forgiving each other, whoever has a complaint against anyone; just as the Lord forgave you, so also should you."
40. Colossians 3:16: "Let the word of Christ richly dwell within you, with all wisdom teaching and admonishing one another with psalms and hymns and spiritual songs, singing with thankfulness in your hearts to God."
41. 1 Thessalonians 3:12: "And may the Lord cause you to increase and abound in love for one another, and for all people, just as we also do for you."
42. 1 Thessalonians 4:9: "Now as to the love of the brethren, you have no need for anyone to write to you, for you yourselves are taught by God to love one another."
43. 1 Thessalonians 4:18: "Therefore comfort one another with these words."

44. 1 Thessalonians 5:11: "Therefore encourage one another and build up one another, just as you also are doing."

45. 1 Thessalonians 5:13: "And that you esteem them very highly in love because of their work. Live in peace with one another."

46. 1 Thessalonians 5:15: "See that no one repays another with evil for evil, but always seek after that which is good for one another and for all people."

47. 2 Thessalonians 1:3: "We ought always to give thanks to God for you, brethren, as is only fitting, because your faith is greatly enlarged, and the love of each one of you toward one another grows ever greater."

48. Titus 3:3: "For we also once were foolish ourselves, disobedient, deceived, enslaved to various lusts and pleasures, spending our life in malice and envy, hateful, hating one another."

49. Hebrews 3:13: "But encourage one another day after day, as long as it is still called 'Today,' so that none of you will be hardened by the deceitfulness of sin."

50. Hebrews 10:24: "And let us consider how to stimulate one another to love and good deeds."

51. Hebrews 10:25: "Not forsaking our own assembling together, as is the habit of some, but encouraging one another; and all the more as you see the day drawing near."

52. James 4:11: "Do not speak against one another, brethren. He who speaks against a brother or judges his brother, speaks against the law and judges the law; but if you judge the law, you are not a doer of the law but a judge of it."

53. James 5:9: "Do not complain, brethren, against one another, so that you yourselves may not be judged; behold, the Judge is standing right at the door."

54. James 5:16: "Therefore, confess your sins to one another, and pray for one another so that you may be healed. The effective prayer of a righteous man can accomplish much."

55. 1 Peter 1:22: "Since you have in obedience to the truth purified your souls for a sincere love of the brethren, fervently love one another from the heart."

56. 1 Peter 4:8: "Above all, keep fervent in your love for one another, because love covers a multitude of sins."

57. 1 Peter 4:9: "Be hospitable to one another without complaint."

58. 1 Peter 4:10: "As each one has received a special gift, employ it in serving one another as good stewards of the manifold grace of God."

59. 1 Peter 5:5: "You younger men, likewise, be subject to your elders; and all of you, clothe yourselves with humility toward one another, for God is opposed to the proud, but gives grace to the humble."

60. 1 Peter 5:14: "Greet one another with a kiss of love. Peace be to you all who are in Christ."

61. 1 John 1:7: "But if we walk in the Light as He Himself is in the Light, we have fellowship with one another, and the blood of Jesus His Son cleanses us from all sin."

62. 1 John 3:11: "For this is the message which you have heard from the beginning, that we should love one another."

63. 1 John 3:23: "This is His commandment, that we believe in the name of His Son Jesus Christ, and love one another, just as He commanded us."

64. 1 John 4:7: [God Is Love] "Beloved, let us love one another, for love is from God; and everyone who loves is born of God and knows God."

65. 1 John 4:11: "Beloved, if God so loved us, we also ought to love one another."
66. 1 John 4:12: "No one has seen God at any time; if we love one another, God abides in us, and His love is perfected in us."
67. 2 John 1:5: "Now I ask you, lady, not as though I were writing to you a new commandment, but the one which we have had from the beginning, that we love one another."

## PRECEPT FIVE:
### Unity Sets the Stage for Growth.

Why is unity so important to the health of your local church? Because you have been commissioned; sent out into the world as partners in ministry. Your local church is not about you; it's about the "other" person. It is about your becoming a servant, and not about being served. Growth is possible only when every ligament is operating in unity (Ephesians 4:6). This growth is "built up" by love (Ephesians 4:16). You have gifts that the Holy Spirit has given you to use in your local church. First Corinthians 7:7 says, "However, each man has his own gift from God, one in this manner, and another in that" (NASB). In 1 Corinthians 12:11, Paul says, "All these are the work of one and the same Spirit, and he distributes them to each one, just as he determines" (NIV). First Peter 4:10-11 says that we are challenged to manage these gifts by using them to serve someone else.

### Wisdom Point A
*Unity sets the stage for maturity.* I have stood in the ancient city of Ephesus twice this year, climbing over the ancient rocks of the theater, walking through the ruins of the Church of the Saint Virgin Mary, and buying fresh oranges

from a local stand. I like to walk through those ruins with my iPod, listening to worship music as I feed my spirit and lift up my prayers. It was in this ancient city that Paul wrote in Ephesians 4:13 to their church and said: "Until we reach unity in faith and in the knowledge of the Son of God and become mature, attaining to the whole measure of the fullness of Christ" (NIV). These are not only Christ's final words, but also it is our final goal (John 17:21). As we work for Christ, we obtain "oneness." This maturity comes about through becoming unified in Christ. We are brothers and sisters in Christ. But without unity, there can be no maturing in Christ.

### Wisdom Point B

*Unity is crucial for church growth.*

I was at lunch with a friend who has always had a great heart for evangelism. He became the evangelism minister at a local church and did so with great dreams. Once he started, he mobilized the congregation to reach out to the community and to the less fortunate like no one had ever seen before in that small local church. This church has been around for a long time. They have a wonderful heart for God. Yet, they are immature in how to handle conflict and relational problems that arise among each other. Just when new people began to attend the church and growth began to explode, the first weapon of the Enemy was division. People became critical of success and excellence. This church divided, and the hundreds of new people who had started to attend scattered like sheep without a shepherd. Wolves always spook the sheep.

Unity is possible, because we are first one in Christ (Ephesians 1:22-23). This "oneness" in Him "fulfills us" the Scripture says. It fills all things in every way. This unity in Christ enables us to "build up" the church as "one" as the place of the dwelling of the Holy Spirit (Ephesians

2:21-22). Acts 4:32 then explains that until He returns, our goal is to build the multitudes in the church into one heart and one soul. God let it be!

Unity must be maintained according to Ephesians 4:3. Here, we are told to "make every effort" and to "keep" doing this effort. To "make every effort" is to be especially conscientious in the discharge of this obligation. We are to be zealous, eager, and to pay a high price. Establishing unity is difficult, and we must work extra hard to maintain it. As we "keep" this mandate, we do so as guardians. We keep watch; we guard; and we preserve a state of "oneness" or harmony and one accord, as we "make this effort" and "keep" the "bond" according to this passage. Your church is a living organism, not a static system. We must be "bonded" to each other like shackled prisoners of hope. Through unified relationships and bringing various entities together, we "bond." Unity requires a long-term commitment from you and the rest of your congregation. It is a covenant of commitment to love unconditionally and a promise to mature together as "one." We all carry this responsibility to safeguard unity. We all hold the key of love to the foundation and protective gate of unity. Each of us places the framework of unity upon the foundation of love by engaging "one another." And when we faithfully maintain and keep these principles, we mature, grow, and reach out; oh, what a beautiful place to be—the local church thriving through unity.

**END NOTES**
Chapter Three
The Law of Unity: Part Two

[1] KJV Dictionary Definition: "Unity," *The King James Bible Page*, accessed January 1, 2013, www.av1611.com/kjbp/kjv-dictionary/unity.html.

CHAPTER FOUR

# THE LAW OF DISICIPLINE

 —— **The Knowledge Box** ——

**The Law of Discipline** is broadly defined as the confrontive and corrective measures taken by an individual, church leaders, or the congregation regarding a matter of sin in the life of a believer.

**The Precepts:**
1. All Discipline Flows From the Authority of God.
2. The God-given Biblical Rules for Church Discipline
3. The Bible Says Discipline Produces Wisdom; Rebellion to Authority Produces a Fool.

Correcting someone requires the precision of a sculptor, the steady hand of an artist, the eye of a surgeon, and the heart of a shepherd. In my book, *When Strong Men Wept*, I tell about my own journey as a young man who had to be corrected. And for that reason alone, this chapter is personal to me! I am a pastor, and I have had to administer discipline many times since my own correction. Neither seat is a comfortable place to sit—you will find pain in both places. Spiritual authority has abused me as well. I know the nightmare of being under the guillotine when a man drunk with power is holding the blade. However, correction from authority is still biblical. Church discipline is simply not a pleasant experience for any of us. What is church discipline, and how should it be carried out in the local church? Church *discipline* is broadly defined as "the confrontive and corrective measures taken by an individual, church leaders, or the congregation regarding a matter of sin in the life of a believer."[1] It is important for you to understand that discipline is a very important issue for church unity and growth. You need to realize that church discipline isn't about punishment; it's about training and restoring, and that makes all the difference in the world.

All church discipline must be done from the precept of love for the law of unity. Church discipline cannot be about insignificant issues, but only about divisive, moral, and doctrinal issues. There is a correct way to deal with sin in the church (Matthew 18; 2 Thessalonians 3:14-15). Church discipline is about a clear process of confrontation for correction and spiritual growth. It is a necessity to guard unity, doctrine, and righteous living. Galatians 6:1 warns those of us in spiritual authority to proceed with great caution "watching out for yourselves so you won't be tempted." Without church discipline, church government cannot be maintained, and thus chaos ensues. We cannot lose heart in church discipline at any time. Its purpose is simply to rescue those who are heading in the wrong direction. We are in the "reclaiming offenders" business, not in the retaliation business. Discipline is important for the fidelity of our beliefs. It protects the church from false teachers and immoral people who may damage the integrity of "OUR" principles. There are times when some people will have to be "put out" of the church to protect the larger body. There are clear rules for discipline in the Bible, and they must be instituted in a fair and orderly manner. Such discipline requires first-hand reports of serious offences, not petty differences over music or carpets. Correct information from an eyewitness (1 Timothy 5:19) is crucial so truth may emerge. Multiple, credible witnesses must come forward and state their case in an orderly fashion. Church discipline is a serious charge given to our leaders. Submitting to those decisions is just as serious (Romans 13:1-2).

## PRECEPT ONE:
### All Discipline Flows From the Authority of God.

When a person is disciplined, it suggests to us the presence of a secondary person or institution. The twenty-first-century believer must stay awake in this world and be aware of its present systems. We have discussed the fact that Scripture tells us in the last days "lawlessness" would appear (Matthew 24:12). *Lawlessness* is "being unrestrained by law; being contrary to the law; or being unruly." When society rebels against the law, they are rebelling against the lawgiver. God is our Lawgiver, and when we rebel against the laws of Scripture, we are rebelling against its Lawgiver. All authority belongs to a Sovereign God. Why?

> You alone are the Lord. You made the heavens, even the highest heavens, and all their starry host, the earth and all that is on it, the seas and all that is in

> them. You give life to everything, and the multitudes
> of heaven worship you (Nehemiah 9:6 NIV).

God has all authority, and He has clearly delegated this authority. When individuals believe that there is a God, then their actions will acknowledge Him through the way in which they yield to earthly authority. If you live in rebellion to the authority on this earth, you are a living mouthpiece that spreads its speech loud and clear that "there is no God." Jewish fathers set a wonderful example of this by the wearing of a yamaka (Jewish skull cap or *kippah* in Hebrew). It is a round symbol that fits upon the crown of a father's head. It is a symbol that the father of the house—the authority of the house—is he himself, first a man under the authority of God. I have often thought about the power of this Jewish tradition. One can only imagine how our Christian homes would be different if only our own children could see us every Friday night under the authority of God. It is this same issue of authority that can cause other people to yearn for the absence of God. Their agnosticism is a plea to live under no one's rules but their own. Thus, they are gods. So, rebelling against authority is a form of agnosticism.

There is a God, and He is the final arbitrator of all judgment. He is the head over everything. That is the reason God's authority flows down; there isn't a higher authority. He is the sovereign deliverer to every sure and right judgment. And He never makes a mistake in His judgments. Job 37:23 says, "The Almighty—we cannot reach Him—He is exalted in power! He will not oppress justice and abundant righteousness." Romans 2:2 says, "We know that God's judgment on those who do such things is based on truth." In Romans 2:5, Paul calls God's judgment "righteous judgment." The authority of God is a reflection of His character—perfect, righteous, and true (Psalm 145:17). He is just and right, which means His judgments are without error. The Bible says in Psalms 82:1 that "God judges . . . the gods." The Father has appointed a Day of Judgment (Acts 17:31), in which He will judge the world in righteousness by the man whom He hath ordained to judge the earth—Jesus Christ. John 5:27-30 says:

> He (Father) has granted Him the right to pass judgment, because He is the Son of Man. Do not be amazed at this, because a time is coming when all who are in the graves will hear His voice and come out—those who have done good things, to the resurrection of life, but those who have done wicked things, to the resurrection of judgment.

What I am saying is simple. All authority comes from the Supreme Authority. This Authority is perfect in all His declarations of justice. He never misses—ever! He then has delegated this authority downward. Each institution or person to whom He has delegated His authority must submit to Him and live with the sobering realization that he will stand before this Supreme Judge and give an account for his stewardship of this delegated authority (Hebrews 13:17). His divine commands came to man when the Holy Spirit carried His message into the hearts of men, and they wrote what the Holy Spirit was saying to them (2 Peter 1:21). Thus, the Holy Scripture is inspired, authorized, and reliable (2 Timothy 3:16). More than forty-six times the phrase—"it is written"—repeatedly asserts an authority for written Scripture. "Scripture says" is written seven times, and "according to Scripture" is written three times. This doesn't even take into account how Jesus Christ himself appealed 38 times (Luke 24:44-47) to the "Law and the prophets." The Scripture is not mere human opinion, but written authority from the One who has "all" authority (2 Thessalonians 3:6).

I recently stood in front of the grave of John the Revelator in Turkey. I am in awe of this man of God who was clever, dedicated, and focused to his mission of spreading the gospel. Even his words, some of the last words in the Bible, use stern and direct language to warn those who would try to change the words of God, and if they do so, they will be in danger of eternal judgment (Revelation 22:18-19). God is the ultimate authority, and His Word is the final authority.

## Wisdom Point A

*God the Father has delegated His authority to Jesus Christ.* In the Book of Matthew 28:18, Jesus Christ said: "All authority has been given to Me in heaven and on earth" (NKJV). Ephesians 1:20-23 says:

> He demonstrated this power in the Messiah by raising Him from the dead and seating Him at His right hand in the heavens—far above every ruler and authority, power and dominion, and every title given, not only in this age but also in the one to come. And He put everything under His feet and appointed Him as head over everything for the church, which is His body, the fullness of the One who fills all things in every way.

## Wisdom Point B

*The Scriptures are the written expression of the authority of God.* Please consider the following questions: Do you believe that God, the divine being, has all authority? Do you believe that His Scriptures are infallible? If you do, really do, then look at 2 Timothy 3:16-17 and what it says: "All Scripture is inspired by God and is profitable for teaching, for rebuking, for correcting, for training in righteousness, so that the man of God may be complete, equipped for every good work." If there is a divine authority and this "authority" has placed his laws in writing "to train in righteousness," then church discipline rests upon this divine authority, not a man. This divine authority begins with the word of this divine authority. In 2 Timothy 3:16, it tells us the role that Scripture plays in correction. It shows us that this divine Word is to be used for "rebuke"—a reproof of a person's personal life. False teachings or believing in false teachings is one such area mentioned. You can use it to "correct," restoring someone's life and doctrine by using it. It is used for "training" people to live righteous lives. Paul goes on to tell Timothy in Chapter 4, verses 2-3:

> Proclaim the message; persist in it whether convenient or not; rebuke, correct, and encourage with great patience and teaching. For the time will come when they will not tolerate sound doctrine, but according to their own desires, will multiply teachers for themselves because they have an itch to hear something new.

Paul writes this passage as if it is a military order to pastors. He tells Timothy "whether it is convenient or not." That's because it is never convenient to discipline. If someone enjoys confrontation and discipline, there is something gravely wrong with this individual. I believe there is great significance in the fact that Paul is instructing "pastors" about how to discipline. This is not the place for a prophet or someone who is judging harshly. There are places for prophetic people, but it's not in the presence of a sick lamb. There is great wisdom in Paul's words "correct and encourage with great patience and teaching." The purpose of discipline is to correct direction in a person's life. While discipline often brings pain into our lives, the outcome is worth the toil of sowing the seed of accountability. As the psalmist says, "Weeping may spend the night, but there is joy in the morning (Psalm 30:5).

### Wisdom Point C

*Our obedience to Scripture will eventually heal the pain of discipline.* Hebrews 12:11 tells us, "No discipline seems enjoyable at the time, but painful. Later on, however, it yields the fruit of peace and righteousness to those who have been trained by it." There is nothing fun about crying yourself to sleep, full of anxiety because of your stupid mistakes, while your mouth tastes the bitterness of the tears you created. It certainly is not enjoyable; rather, it is painful. However, the words "later on!" are beautiful words to us. Later on, after you have learned your lesson . . . Later on, after your new character has replaced the gossip from your old character . . . Later on, when you have taken your "mess" and made a "message" out of it . . . Later on, when that which almost killed you is being used to stop the death of other people in the same situation—it yields the fruit of righteousness. Then, the verse continues, "to those who have been trained by it" (Hebrews 12:11). This phrase is actually an ancient Greek phrase used by athletes who have been exercising for an important upcoming game. Discipline is hard work—for both sides. But thank God for sending His Son who endured His cross and took upon Himself our discipline! (Colossians 2:13-14; 1 Peter 3:18; 1 John 2:2). God the Father sent Jesus Christ to earth to die for the sin of humanity as the final sacrifice (Hebrews 10:1-18).

### Wisdom Point D

*God, "the ultimate authority," delegates His authority.* There is a divine authority, and He is God. He has given us the "Holy Scripture" that outlines His divine laws. He then delegates this spiritual authority to humans and institutions to steward His authority on earth. There are three institutions to which God has delegated His divine authority on earth: family, government, and the local church. Romans 13:1-5 tells us:

> Everyone must submit to the governing authorities, for there is no authority except from God, and those

that exist are instituted by God. So then, the one who resists the authority is opposing God's command, and those who oppose it will bring judgment on themselves. For rulers are not a terror to good conduct, but to bad. Do you want to be unafraid of the authority? Do what is good, and you will have its approval. For government is God's servant for your good. But if you do wrong, be afraid, because it does not carry the sword for no reason. For government is God's servant, an avenger that brings wrath on the one who does wrong. Therefore, you must submit, not only because of wrath, but also because of your conscience.

The Greek word for *authority* here is "delegated authority." A power delegated by the Sovereign God has given this authority to three primary institutions: the family, the authority of the state, and the local church. Be on guard, because this implies that these three institutions will one day give an account for their delegated responsibilities. Each of these three institutions received their authority from God.

### Wisdom Point E

*Jesus delegates His authority to the church leaders whom He calls.* A few weeks ago I was walking along in the old city of Ephesus in modern-day Turkey. As I walked passed the field of the gladiators, strolled down the marble road, and thought about the scrolls that were held in the library of Celcus, the thought hit me that I have just walked on the same road where young Timothy would have walked. Paul told Timothy in 1 Timothy 1:12, "I give thanks to Christ Jesus our Lord, who has strengthened me, because He considered me faithful, appointing me to the ministry." The call to ministry is a serious consideration. It is not the same as being a doctor or coal miner. It is a life's calling with many mountains and valleys. It certainly is not for the faint of heart. What is important for us to establish here is the seriousness for both the one who is called and those who are under the leadership of this call. We need to accept the sobering reality that God will hold all of us accountable for how we treat the leaders who are over us in the Lord. Those who are called must give an account for this call (Hebrews 13:17), and so will the ones who are to follow the leadership of godly people.

Paul, in Ephesians 4:11-13, tells us that Christ, the one who has the delegated authority, now delegates this authority further: "And He personally gave some to be apostles, some prophets, some evangelists, some pastors and teachers, for the training of the saints in the work of ministry, to build up the body of Christ." In Hebrews 13:17, it says, "Obey your leaders and submit to them for they keep watch over your souls as those who will give an account, so that they can do this with joy, and not with grief, for that would be unprofitable for you." Paul writes to the Corinthian church in 1 Corinthians 16:15-16 and says: "Brothers, you know the household of Stephanas: they are the firstfruits of Achaia and have devoted themselves to serving the saints. I urge you also to submit to such people, and to everyone who works and labors with them." Notice how anonymity cannot produce social order and peace in your local church.

### Wisdom Point F

*The body of Christ has been delegated authority through church leaders to lead and work in their gifts* (Matthew 10:1; 23:23; Mark 6:7; 13:34; Luke 9:1; Acts 20:28; 1 Corinthians 11:1; Philippians 3:17; 1 Thessalonians 5:12; 2 Thessalonians 3:7, 9; 1 Timothy 2:1-3; Titus 3:1). Finally, the leadership of the church is to delegate its authority to the body for ministry to be accomplished. Matthew 16:19 says, "I will give you the keys of the kingdom of heaven; whatever you bind on earth will be bound in heaven, and whatever you loose on earth will be loosed in heaven" (NKJV).

**Wisdom Point G**

*Be careful of anyone who questions authority without just* cause (1 Timothy 5:19). In the movie *12 Years a Slave,* one can see clearly that not everyone in power should have power. Furthermore, this movie clearly shows us that not everyone who professes Christ actually lives like Christ as they wield power. Submitting to the wrong person can be a horrible mistake.  If we simply live our lives by the thought that we are to submit to "spiritual authority," then I believe that our lives can quickly go astray. Hence, the reason for you to find **one** good, biblically believing, local church and plant yourself there "forever." Don't go to a church where you cannot walk in submission to its leaders. Remember too, there is not agreement until the point of disagreement arises. I am not saying that a member of the body cannot question spiritual authority, but what I am saying is that there are very clear rules on how, when, and with whom to do so.

Do you realize that Jesus Christ, Moses, Jeremiah, Stephen, all of the Apostles, and God himself have one leadership trait in common—they all have had their authority questioned by people who were nothing more than troublemakers. Even the devil recognizes spiritual authority (Mark 1:34; Luke 4:34; 9:1; 10:17; Acts 19:15; James 2:19). He may not submit to it either, but at least he recognizes its true presence. Many of us fail to recognize its true existence. Unity cannot be obtained or maintained without order. Order comes through a division of systems and leaders who lead them. If you question every call your music pastor makes, consistently judge each decision, without *biblical* merit, you are a troublemaker, and God will one day deal with you.

As a leader, Paul said in Philippians 2:2: "Make my joy complete" (NIV) by being at one with one another. There isn't an enemy big enough, strong enough, or wealthy enough to topple the church of Jesus Christ when it stands with its leaders charging forward. Most people whom I know in ministry are good and honest people. Our problem is not "clergy and adultery." It is deeper than "the piano player running off with the drummer." Our problem is a pandemic of immaturity.

> I will never forget the day a young man, whom I had sacrificially given my teen and college years to, brought me an underlined book. He had been a teenage alcoholic. Many times at the age of 18, I picked him up as a child; I bought him coffee, cleaned up his vomit, and laid him across a stone seat in the basement of a little Church of God. I really loved this young man. Now, years later I had gained the privilege of working with him. He had been released from prison, had stepped up to the plate of fatherhood and was a hard worker. I thought all was fine, until the moment I realized that I loved him much more than he ever loved or appreciated me. He and a few others had believed a lie told about me. "They" said I had stolen $45,000.00 from the church accounts and was using the church accounts to pay my debts. The truth is I gave away my raise and other raises to hire him during those early years when hiring additional staff. And, I would do it again. The truth is that I had not taken $45,000.00 from the church accounts; I had actually raised an additional $45,000.00 to pay back a debt that the church owed as an organization. The young man, having believed the lie with a grain of truth in it, took the side of my enemies and handed me an outlined book about the abuse of spiritual authority. If I had died that day, it would have been from a broken heart. I have kept that book as a reminder to me, and I have looked at it through the years. When I first received it, I was so hurt that not one page made any sense to me.
>
> Thank God, I had just been given an article from Oral Roberts that he wrote early in his ministry. One line stands out to me today: "Ask yourself first, when any critic attacks you, is there any truth in this?" As I look back on this devastating time in my life, I can

honestly say on this occasion "no." However, I now realize that I was building a staff, not out of love, but first from the standpoint of rules. We always legislate things we want to control. I knew that there were problems, but I could not see them. If I asked them, they replied, "Everything is fine." I had no solid proof of insubordination or the betrayal from two elders. But in my heart, I knew something was not right. Please consider this question: "How are your spiritual leaders supposed to change, correct, or defend anything if you don't FIRST go to them in love with a spirit of reconciliation and unity in your heart and kindly ask: "Is this true?" But, even when what we are wanting to control is good and right, the legislation and the letter of the law kill every time. You cannot legislate morality.

These people did not love their pastor. Now, they told *everybody* they did. But when times got tough, it was their pastor to whom they failed to show community. I was teaching on spiritual authority from John Bevere in hopes that the teaching would align the improper behavior. What a fool I was in that hour.

Behavioral problems in the church are not a discipline issue first; they are first an issue of the heart. Their hearts needed to be changed by loving their leaders. I know we all have heard a thousand stories about preachers who lie, cheat, steal, and commit adultery—and that is definitely wrong. But there are thousands more "members" who have done the same exact thing, and yet everyone is afraid to talk about it. Why? We are afraid someone is going to say, "You are abusing your authority." There is a real spiritual authority delegated by God the Father that flows through those who are called into ministry. Their job is not easy. And as the times grow darker, people are less faithful, and the love of many waxes cold, making it all that much more difficult to lead a local church. So, before you run off with a story about your church leadership, go to 1 Timothy 5:19 and begin your research. Then, adhere to the following rules for discipline in the Bible that are laid out here. You will be glad that you did!

## PRECEPT TWO:
### The God-given Biblical Rules for Church Discipline

Remember, discipline is not about punishment; it is about training and restoration. The New Testament lays out a clear pattern of spiritual authority. It is important to note that the internal pattern of discipline follows a pattern that God uses to "restore" and "correct" His own children. Hebrews 12:5-11 says:

> My son, do not take the Lord's discipline lightly or faint when you are reproved by Him, for the Lord disciplines the one He loves, and punishes every son He receives. Endure suffering as discipline: God is dealing with you as sons. . . . Furthermore, we had natural fathers discipline us, and we respected them. Shouldn't we submit even more to the Father of spirits and live? For they disciplined us for a short time based on what seemed good to them, but He does it for our benefit, so that we can share His holiness. No discipline seems enjoyable at the time, but painful. Later on, however, it yields the fruit of peace and righteousness to those who have been trained by it.

Did you read that passage? Church discipline begins when God himself, or godly church leaders deal with you and me as sons (and, yes, daughters!). If you are the one being corrected, here are some words of advice to you: Don't submit to discipline from a person who doesn't treat you like a father treats his son. It must be done out of love. I yearn to be a great father to my children. I really try hard at leading them spiritually. And, I absolutely hate to discipline them. I hate every moment of it. But as all parents know, if you love them, sometimes it's inevitable. If you don't love them, you don't care what kind of character or righteousness they will produce later in life—let them run wild. It also kills me to discipline anyone as a pastor, because I have been in the "other" chair. I have been in the chair when it was administered as punishment, and I have been in the chair as a father, for the purpose of future righteousness, and discipline. What a difference a little grace makes in your life when you need it. The key to discipline is, it first has to be administered by love with the Spirit of the heavenly Father (1 Corinthians 5:12-13).

## Wisdom Point A

> How you discipline is as important as what you are disciplining.

> I was sitting in front of a "fallen" minister one afternoon during a trial board in our denomination. I knew he was guilty, because you can't "kid" a "kidder." My sins were not his sins, but that doesn't matter. Nevertheless, I know the road that all fallen people take when they mess up—blame, hiding, and running. It broke my heart, because he kept his game face on throughout the entire process. He had a window to repent in a private session with me, where I had every intention of helping him by grace, accountability, and friendship. He didn't take the bait. So, he lost it all.

> Another time when I was confronting a fallen staff member, I went to great extremes to hide his sins. I was shocked when I realized that while I was taking his punches, figuratively placing my body over his, so he could get through this a little easier, he was secretly taking "punches" at me, lying about his sins, thus making me look like the "mean old pastor."

Neither of these situations ended well. But in both cases, the local church went about the administration of discipline so well that it produced great spiritual growth. When we follow biblical patterns for addressing issues, peace and protection can be assured every time. I have learned that when I lean on biblical precepts regarding church discipline, no matter how inconvenient (2 Timothy 4:2), great results always follow. When I lean on the wisdom of man to bring correction or alignment in the church, great folly ensues. It is also important to point out that in Hebrews 12:6, it suggests that those who allow instruction in their lives are sons, and the ones who cannot take correction are "not sons," but "illegitimate." These are strong words.

How we discipline, correct, and train is as important as what we are correcting or training toward. Discipline requires humility, patience, and gentleness in our own lives. We are to approach the broken and misguided with the love of a father and a firm understanding "watching out for yourself so you won't be tempted" (Galatians 6:1-2; 2 Timothy 2:24-25). This correction must be done without bias. And that's not easy for most people to do. One morning I was standing in a jail cell with an accused child rapist. I knew more of the story than what I was letting on when I visited him. He denied the entire event even though blood was literally on his hands. I don't have a lot of patience with those situations in life. But God spoke to me and warned me to let the earthly courts be the judge and for me to be the pastor.

As a pastor, you have to lead without bias. You have to love people regardless of their sins. If you never accept people where they are, you can never lead them to the place they could be one day. There is hope for everyone. It breaks my heart when people in my congregation get divorced from each other. As hard as I try not to choose sides, I almost always end up on the side of the one who has done the most repenting. Almost every time there seems to be those who fall and get up, and those who fall and run away further into the dark woods. They run as fast as they can away from God and away from teachings on righteousness. It is hard not to show a bias when one has clearly committed adultery, and one has clearly not committed adultery. It is very difficult not to show bias or be partial when one has abandoned the faith, turned to the value system of the world, and completely abandoned the person they once were. It's hard. But somehow, you and I have to learn how to muster up the courage to love people equally in discipline. Church discipline can be difficult; especially when we work so hard to follow the order laid out in Scripture, and at the end, find rejection from the one we asked to forgive us.

**Wisdom Point B**

*You are not a "speck inspector" or a "speck investigator."* Discipline is not about your perseverance in music or modest dress. The law of discipline is not about your opinion of a church law, denominational appointment, or color of pews; it's about a clear violation of Scriptures.

**Wisdom Point C**

*What causes are important enough to engage discipline?* How do you know what merits biblical discipline? First, when you encounter relational disruptions or divisive people (Matthew 18; Romans 16:17-18; Titus 3:9-11), it's time for church discipline. Second, when false teachings predominate over the fundamentals of faith, such as "the Virgin Birth," or the "deity of Christ," it's time for discipline (Romans 16:17-18; 1 Timothy 1:20; 2 Timothy 2:17-18). Third, when immorality is clearly present, confrontation in love is needed (1 Corinthians 5; 2 Thessalonians 3:10-15).

**Wisdom Point D**

*There is a three-step process for discipline.* I meet many good men and women who are pastors around the world. Most of them are loyal and highly committed to Christ.

Most of them, however, are burned out from immature believers in leading church positions. I am amazed at their faces when they hear me tell the story of church discipline at our church. We take it seriously, just like the apostle Paul told us to! In Matthew 18:15-17, Jesus Christ himself sets the laws of church discipline into motion. Most churches may confront wayward souls, but they don't have an emergency contingency plan if the "fire" is not put out. At CCC, we file a restraining order at the county courthouse against such people. In 14 years, we have had to do this only once. I feel strongly about Matthew 18 and its wisdom. Our elders and deacons are taught not to get involved in problematic relational issues until the third step of Matthew 18 arrives. Anyone who does so stands the real chance of being dismissed from authority at our church. Why? Because that is precisely the problem in most churches that keeps people immature. They skip stages one and two and go straight to stage three—and pastors let them do it!! Take a look at the wisdom in the process of these three stages which Jesus gave us.

**Step One:** *"You "Go" by Yourself" (Matthew 18:15).*
In the Bible, Jesus Christ teaches us that: "If your brother sins against you, go and rebuke him in private. If he listens to you, you have won your brother (Matthew 18:15). The one thing that stands out to me is the fact that Jesus says, "whether you are the "offender" or the "offended," YOU go." The other issue that stands out is that Jesus teaches that discipline must first begin in privacy. Every time I have watched a church or a group of Christians skip this stage, pandemonium bursts forth like the Fourth of July fireworks in New York Harbor. When we confront in private, we are giving dignity to the person being corrected. This process in step one, sets the tone for the overall purpose of reconciliation and restoration.

a.  When you "go," do so with love, grace, and mercy, remembering it could be you in that chair (Galatians 6:1).

b.  Separate the "sin" from the "sinner." We "ALL have sinned and fall short of the glory of God" (Romans 3:23). Good people, really good people, can make some very poor decisions.

c.  Do not go into the confrontation with preconceived judgments. Unless the sin was public and apparent to all, there is no sure way to know the truth at this point. Approach them with love, mercy, and grace. Listen and seek the facts first.

d.  If the person fails to respond to you, then warn him/her that another party will have to get involved, as you work through the process of Matthew 18:16. My experience with stage one has been a valuable one. Most of the time, they all will lie to you during this first initial confrontation. Nowhere does the Scripture give us direction on how long each stage should last, but mercy tells me as long as wisdom allows. People will not confess, if they think they are facing a guillotine.

> One night, I had to confront an elder who was caught up in pornography. I loved this person and truly believed in him. God knows that from the bottom of my heart my motive was simple—repentance, restoration, and reconciliation. He lied to me the first four times I inquired about his addiction. I had previous knowledge of his habits as he would keep a memory drive in his pocket full of pornographic pictures. After several conversations, I bluntly asked: "If you don't have a problem, what is the memory stick in your pocket for?" He broke and began to weep. I showed him mercy and told him that grace was available for the broken. He taught me a powerful lesson.

People are not going to confess anything to you if you act like their judge instead of their shepherd. The truth is, especially in discipline involving immorality, you need grace to make repentance possible in the first place.

Once you have exhausted all of your available resources to successfully accomplish step one, it is then time to move to step two.

**Step Two:** *"Go and Get ONE More Person"* (Matthew 18:16; 1 Timothy 5:19).

The second step in Matthew 18:16 says, "But if he won't listen, take one or two more with you, so that by the testimony of two or three witnesses every fact may be established." Mosaic Law required at least one additional witness in a court of law to convict another person (Numbers 35:30; Deuteronomy 19:15). Additional reasons for requiring another person was to guard against any misunderstanding of what was being attested to, as well as the seriousness of the situation. The underlying meaning could also be another safety mechanism to keep the issue from going public. It is my belief that the additional people (no more than two) are not to be elders of a local church. The involvement of elders sets the scene for stage three.

**Step Three:** *"Tell It to the Church"* (Matthew 18:17; 2 Thessalonians 3:14-15; 1 Timothy 5:20).

"If he pays no attention to them, tell the church. But if he doesn't pay attention even to the church, let him be like an unbeliever and a tax collector to you." This final stage has the same purpose as the other two stages: repentance and reconciliation. If the person in question rebels against the first two stages, then this final stage is to stop the rebellion and divisiveness by bringing it before the whole body (Matthew 18:17; 2 Thessalonians 3:14-15; 1 Timothy 5:20). Unfortunately, many times this stage sets an example of arrogant, independent, rebellious people who selfishly place their bitter reasoning ahead of the unity, safety, and peace of the local church. After the body denounces his behavior, if he is still not repentant, it is then time to set him out of the church. I know this is hard. I realize we don't live in this Mediterranean world any longer. However, this is not only a truth for the East; but it is also a truth for Protestants in the West as well. At CCC, we use this stage to bring in the elders of the church. When an elder gets involved, people know the seriousness of the offense. It is a clear message to the body that unity is of prime importance. In this final stage after the elders confront the issue one last time, we bring it before the body (2 Corinthians 2:6). Once we know that reconciliation is not possible, we formally file a restraining order against the person at our county court house.

Discipline is not about punishment. The purpose is not about embarrassing another human being, or humiliating someone publically. The goal of discipline is instruction in righteousness with the all-encompassing strategy of repentance, reconciliation, and restoration. If there is repentance, then the church must change its role with this individual. This demands from us acceptance and forgetting the past (2 Corinthians 2:7). After all, this was the goal of discipline from the start.

## PRECEPT THREE:
### The Bible Says Discipline Produces Wisdom; Rebellion to Authority Produces a Fool.

Discipline is necessary in life, and God knew that a person without it would never reach his/her potential. God's role in discipline is that of a Father. When God disciplines a human, it will eventually produce joy in his/her life (Job 5:17). The Scriptures call a man or woman who embraces discipline "blessed" (Psalm 94:12). We are told that a fool is identified because he despises wisdom and instruction (Proverbs 1:7). Such a person "errs" (Proverbs 10:17). While forsaking rebellion may require a grievous season, the one who does not forsake rebellion will meet death (Proverbs 15:10). This kind of person even despises his own soul (Proverbs 15:32). The proof of God's love is not a perfect day; the proof of God's love is correction (Revelation 3:19).

### Wisdom Point A
*Don't let the corrective discipline from authority make you despise or resent the rebuke of the Lord* (Proverbs 3:11-12). It's so easy to become bitter. A tough time handled the wrong way always produces bitter people. Guard your heart like a son that the father delights in (Proverbs 3:11-12).

### Wisdom Point B
*Listen to the correction of church leaders and grow.* The commands of the Lord are like a lamp that gives off a light from its teachings. When corrections and discipline are received, they produce a life that loves knowledge and discipline (Proverbs 6:23; 12:1). Such wisdom will bring honor to you again, because heeding to discipline shows prudence (Proverbs 15:5; 19:20).

Listening to authority and submitting to trusted leaders is never an easy road to travel. Often the road to repentance, reconciliation, and restoration is rocky, lonely, fearful, and full of vulnerability. It is my opinion that few Christians ever mature enough to reach this level of receiving and giving discipline. Spiritual authority is a creation of God the Father, delegated by His Son, and taught through His Spirit. It is hard work and requires great humility on the part of both parties. It is, however, possible to arrive at such a level of maturity. Satan's greatest weapon is divisiveness in the church. We need to pray that God will send us spiritually mature leaders who are bold enough to address problems the biblical way and lead with the specific procession of Matthew 18 in mind. What a weapon understanding church discipline and authority can be against our Enemy!

## END NOTES
Chapter Four
The Law of Discipline

[1] James Emery White, *You Can Experience . . . A Spiritual Life* (Nashville: Word Publishing, 1999), 201.

# THE LAW OF SUPPORT AND CARE

 —— **The Knowledge Box** ——

**The Law of Support and Care:**

*Support:* "To agree with, to show approval; to bear the weight; hold in position so as to keep from failing or sinking; to keep from weakening; to endure bravely."

*Care:* "Efforts made to do something, correct painstakingly; to be very watchful; give attention and oversight; be concerned or interested."

**The Precepts:**

1. Support and Care Begin With Heartfelt Compassion.
2. Support and Care Will Require the Discovery of Your Unique Strengths and Gifts.
3. Love and Compassion Begin in the Pew.

There are seven words that always make my day: "The church has been great to us." The concept of pastoral care is never regulated to any one person or office in the New Testament. Such support and care is to be carried out by a plethora of leaders who seek the welfare of the body. I visit many hospitals, but I love it when I hear that a deacon, an elder, or member has beaten me to the scene. As we approach this subject, it may seem like our subject is a gentle lamb; but beware, this lamb has teeth and it does bite. When this subject is approached in a wrong way, it wears out a pastor, it destroys pastoral homes, and it even builds bitterness in the body. It is a major cause of division and a killer of community. When this subject is approached with the wisdom of Scripture, it builds the church, encourages believers, builds unity like no other law, and matures the saints. The law of support and care is a powerful law that creates the conceptual foundation of community in a local church. How does the law of support and care actually work in the local church?

## PRECEPT ONE:
### Support and Care Begin With Heartfelt Compassion.

In 1 John 3:16-20, John says:

> This is how we have come to know love: He laid down His life for us. We should also lay down our lives for our brothers. If anyone has this world's goods and sees his brother in need but closes his eyes to his need—how can God's love reside in him? Little children, we must not love in word or speech, but with truth and action. This is how we will know we belong to the truth and will convince our conscience in His presence, even if our conscience condemns us, that God is greater than our conscience, and He knows all things.

Selfish people can never be great at compassion, because it takes too much emptying of oneself to reach outside your own needs. Selfish people cannot do that! Compassionate people are often humble people. Compassionate people are great servants of humanity. Jesus himself said: "I assure you: Whatever you did not do for one of the least of these, you did not do for Me either" (Matthew 25:45). Paul taught us in 1 Corinthians 12:26: "So if one member suffers, all the members suffer with it; if one member is honored, all the members rejoice with it." We are told to "Carry one another's burdens; in this way you will fulfill the law of Christ" (Galatians 6:1-3). What a powerful statement! Please consider the following questions: "In the midst of so many religious rules, how can a man find Christ?" or "How does a woman fulfill the law?" Romans 13:8, 10 tells us, "Do not owe anyone anything, except to love one another, for the one who loves another has fulfilled the law...Love does no wrong to a neighbor. Love, therefore, is the fulfillment of the law." Now we are told to "carry one another's burden" and this too fulfills the law. The Scripture says to us in John 15:13: "No one has greater love than this, that someone would lay down his life for his friends." When we love people out of compassion, we fulfill the law. This kind of love is important for receiving and giving grace. According to Ephesians 4:32, this kind of compassion forgives other people as well. Uncompassionate people are not only narcissistic, but they are also unforgiving. Never look for mercy from a narcissist. There is a reason why the theology of Philippians is rooted in Christ, the kenotic, humble leader. For-GIVE-n people GIVE. Support and care is defined by "love and forgiveness." Isn't that the gospel in a nutshell?

## Wisdom Point A

*When love motivates support and care, bridges are built.* Have you ever heard someone say, "They don't have a heart." They are usually implying that the person in question doesn't care, which essentially means "they don't love and care for me." Small acts of kindness will open doors previously shut. That's because supporting someone in need melts the most hardened of criminals. It really is, in every way, the mystical presence of Christ. For example, my father-in-law prays, "Lord let us be your hands and feet." Oh, how true! It's an old cliché, but it's true: "People don't care how much you know, until they know how much you care." It is, after all, the story of the Cross itself (Philippians 2:6-11). But as in all of God's laws, there are protective boundaries and instructions for implementation. In Ephesians 6:6-8, it says:

> Not only while being watched, and in order to please
> them, but as slaves of Christ, doing the will of God
> from the heart. Render service with enthusiasm, as to
> the Lord and not to men and women, knowing that
> whatever good we do, we will receive the same again
> from the Lord, whether we are slaves or free (NRSV).

The word "heart" is actually the word for "soul." We serve our fellowman from the source of our ultimate allegiance—Jesus Christ. We support and care for "one another," because we gladly serve as "slaves for Christ."

In Colossians 3:23-24, it teaches us another valuable principle: "Whatever you do, do it enthusiastically, as something done for the Lord and not for men, knowing that you will receive the reward of an inheritance from the Lord. You serve the Lord Christ." Jesus told His disciples, "And whoever wants to be first among you must be a slave to all" (Mark 10:44). In John 21:16, Jesus asked Peter "a second time, 'Simon, son of John, do you love Me?' He said to Him, 'Yes, Lord, You know that I love you.' He said to him, 'Shepherd My sheep.'" We provide support and care for other brothers and sisters because we love Him.

This love spills over into every relationship in which we engage. This kind of love requires a sacrificial love.

Support and care cannot happen in your local church without the use of spiritual gifts. It is important to realize that those gifts are an issue of grace, while love is a fruit of the Spirit and is proof of a branch with a divine relationship, firmly connected into the vine (John 15:1-8). There is nothing more dangerous than a busy church working without love. Paul said in 1 Corinthians 12:31: "And I will show you an even better way." That better way is love. Love is a commitment to act. It is a verb. This love cooperates and finds meaning in you, using your spiritual gifts to support and care for others. Karl Holl explains: "Grace creates an inner affection, a feeling of gratitude which must find expression and for which the highest is not too much to do."[1]

Support and care for you the believer must operate out of love; for it is the proof that you value the worth of man and believe that he has been created in His image. I have often thought about how many times Paul equates serving with the subject of partiality. When we truly believe that we are supporting and caring for someone who has been created in the image of God, we are assuming a basic understanding of equality. It was Kierkegaard who said, "Your neighbor is every man, for on the basis of distinction, he is not your neighbor, nor on the basis of likeness to you as being different from other men. He is your neighbor on the basis of equality with you before God: but this equality absolutely every man has, and he has it absolutely."[2]

You will have to look hard for an agnostic or atheist who spends his time feeding the poor or helping other people. But for the church, it is a natural response. It bubbles up naturally out of the ground of a restored heart. It flows through the veins of self-sacrifice. It streams constantly out of the river of gratitude. Yes, to love in this way requires the presence of a slave. Support and care are the qualities of a slave in the first century. We serve one another when we support them. We honor one another when we care for them. To do compassion correctly requires great humility.

## Wisdom Point B

*Someone needs your strength.* Support and care require that the strong bear the weakness of those who have no strength. Romans 15:1-3 says to us, "Now we who are strong have an obligation to bear the weakness of those without strength, and not to please ourselves. Each one of us must please his neighbor for his good, to build him up. For even the Messiah did not please Himself." Support and care is not about pleasing ourselves. What the church needs now are strong, healthy, mature, Christians—from the pulpit to the pew and out the door. We need them to accomplish the call of evangelizing the world. We need them, because one man cannot meet the needs of one congregation. We need them, because "strength" is needed to serve, and when everyone is "weak," it overburdens the strong. It is time to grow up in the house of God. Growing up requires leaving the childhood tendencies that think you are the only one in the world. It demands sharing, and it requires giving, not receiving all the time. It requires self-sacrifice. The more servants, the "stronger" the people of your church will be. The more "weak ones," the less effective your church will be. You know a person is headed into maturity when he begins to serve in his "gifts."

You have been equipped with a very special set of giftings. Only you can communicate your road to maturity. Only you can tell the story of perseverance in your life. You didn't do it alone, but you can tell the story better than anyone else. People need to hear your story. They need other people to heal. People need you.

In recent years, there have been major developments in a new form of philosophy called positive psychology.

What I find mesmerizing is the fact that one of the seven habits of happy people within the positive psychology movement is the habit of "strength and virtue." Those people who discover their unique strengths and use them for a purpose greater than themselves are considered to be the happiest people on earth. It reminds me of the words of Matthew 10:39, "Anyone finding his life will lose it, and anyone losing his life because of Me will find it." Total surrender to Him and His work on earth is the way to total fulfillment. Corné Bekker says it most efficiently:

> The values of kenosis (emptying yourself out for others) allow the leader to transcend narrow selfhood, to locate the 'other' in the mutuality of love, and to truly enter into the world of the follower where the leader becomes the servant of the 'other.' This is the state of mutual acceptance, vulnerability and receptivity.[3]

How can you guard deep community in your local church? Does God really want to use "you" to support and care for other believers? Yes and here's how. The law of support and care finds its way into the hearts of the Body when individual members of the Body discover and are employed in the use of their "gifts."

### Wisdom Point C

*There are times when the support and care will require an economical ethic to community.* Please note that I am not suggesting a socialist gospel. As 1 John 3:17 tells us, we have a moral obligation as Christians to use our resources to help other brothers and sisters in times of trouble. Every Christmas, Covenant Community Church lavishly gives to a large number of families in the tri-state area. What is such a blessing to me is how the "Body" uses their resources to bless other people in the name of Christ. One little girl took her toys, washed them up, and sold them on eBay so another child could have a Christmas. One man received an unexpected bonus at work and gave it to buy the remaining "untaken angels." Another family purchased furniture for a single mother who was getting her life back together. Look at what a unified, giving church can do if they pool their resources.

I know that much fraud exists in this world, especially, if you help people who are down on their luck. My friend Jake is the assistant director at People for Care and Learning, a global aid organization. They do benevolence in the name of Christ better than anyone I know. He has taught me so much about helping people, especially orphans. What is amazing to me is how much fraud there is in this global business. Unfortunately, many times this fraud is in the name of Christ.

Knowing which individual to give to is as important as knowing how to give. Salvation is rooted in giving (John 3:16). As believers, we are to share our resources with other believers in need. But, I believe wisdom necessitates the conduit of the local church. One, it gives the body of Christ collective identity. Two, it serves as a protective mechanism against fraud. Three, it provides order and gives dignity to those being helped, because the leaders of your church will know about the many needs of your local church better than you do. This is what makes the church great.

Knowing how and to whom to give helps provide integrity in overall giving. It helps to ensure, to a greater standard, the proper assimilation of resources. But the greatest reason is the message it sends to the world as the collective body of Christ. It has been one of the defining hallmarks of Christianity since its inception. As early as the writing of the *Didache* (a first-century manual to the local church on administrative issues), we were admonished to share with our brothers and take care of one another. The great theologian Tertullian said that even the pagan world knows how much we care for each other because they say, "See, how they love one another."[4] Julian the Apostate, an enemy of early Christianity admitted, "The godless Galileans fed not only their poor, but ours also."[5] Yet the most powerful ancient quote comes from Aristides in 125 A.D.

> They walk in all humility and kindness, and false-hood is not found among them, and they love one another. They despise not the widow, and grieve not the orphan. He that hast distributed liberally to him that hath not. If they see a stranger, they bring him under their roof, and rejoice over him as if he were their own brother: for they call themselves brethren, not after the flesh, but after the Spirit of God; but when one of their poor passes away from the world, and any of them see him, he provides for his burial according to his ability; and if they hear that any of their number is imprisoned or oppressed for the name of their Messiah, all of them provide for his needs. . . ."And if there is among them a man that is needy and poor, and they have not an abundance of necessaries, they fast two or three days that they may supply the needy with their necessary food."[6]

By the time of 250 A.D., the church was tending to over 1,500 widows in Rome alone. They took care of the orphans, the sick, the disabled, buried the dead, cared for slaves and prisoners, and helped find work for those in need. "Early Christianity distinguished itself from its competitors in a variety of ways, but no distinction stands out more clearly than its corporate consciousness and co-hesiveness. Pagans as well as Christians discerned the difference."[7]

This kind of collective giving is what makes people interested in Christianity. It has for over 2,000 years. First John 3:17-19 says,

> If anyone has this world's goods and sees his broth-er in need but closes his eyes to his need—how can

> God's love reside in him? Little children, we must
> not love in word or speech, but with truth and action.
> This is how we will know we belong to the truth and
> will convince our conscience in His presence.

It is a call for the body to unify its resources in His name.
Community, at times, requires benevolence. This is clear
in the famous passage of Acts 2:42 where we see the sacrificial giving among the members of the body of Christ.
Community requires supporting and caring for each other
in tangible ways. We need each other. T.S. Eliot posed a
powerful question when he asked: "What life have you
if you have not life together? There is no life that is not
in community, and no community not lived in praise of
God."[8] Paul Hanson, expounding on his words, remarked:
"He thereby pointed to a truth verified both by social sci-
entists and by our own practical experience: we receive
life, we foster life, and we pass life on within the context of
fellow humans."[9]

## PRECEPT TWO:
### Support and Care Will Require the
### Discovery of Your Unique Strengths and Gifts.

Every believer has a role to play in the local church,
and that would include you as well. Not everyone sings,
preaches, or plays the lead part in the Easter production;
however, it takes all kinds of people to make your local
church an effective place.

> Recently, I took a tour through the ancient city of
> Corinth. It was astonishing to see where Paul stood
> before the Bema Seat, or the pieces of brass and pot-
> tery that made this city so famous. But, when I stood
> in their ancient museum and personally witnessed
> the "sacrifices" that the ancient Corinthian people
> would bring in hopes that the Greek god Asklepios

(or Asclepius) would heal them; I didn't truly understand the many metaphors Paul used to describe the "body of Christ." In this museum, there were dozens of terra cotta images molded into human genitals, hands, feet, eyes, arms, legs, fingers, etc. Do you remember what Paul said to the Corinthians in 1 Corinthians 12:21? Paul said: "So the eye cannot say to the hand, 'I don't need you!' or again, the head can't say to the feet, 'I don't need you!' But even more, those parts of the body that seem to be weaker are necessary." When Paul uttered those words, every Corinthian knew exactly what he was talking about. Their whole life was built around the daily sacrifices to Asklepios where they would make terra-cotta images of whatever body part was ill and in need of healing, then offer it to the god in hopes of divine healing.

The gifts that God has given you were meant to heal and encourage someone who is sick and tired. They were given to you to wait on the sick, feed the poor, and comfort those who need mercy. You have been given a gift to give away. Every one of you has a special gift, given by the Holy Spirit to be used to help support and care for the body of Christ. "Based on the gift they have received, everyone should use it to serve others, as good managers of the varied grace of God" (1 Peter 4:10). It is sad to see how many believers expect constant care, but they never give any of their own time for the "common good" of other believers.

## Wisdom Point A

*Someone in the Body or the world may be suffering because you haven't discovered who you are in Christ.* Where would the world be today had the Christian scientist Johannes Kepler not discovered his call to science in the name of Christ? Millions of people would still be dying of diphtheria had Louis Pasteur not known his gifting. What if Walt Disney would have lived his life as a recluse? Can you imagine a world without a Billy Graham? It is an unbelievable thought that he could have chosen to do something else with his life! What if the world had never heard Vestal Goodman sing, or watched Pete Rose play baseball, or listen to Bill Hybels speak? What a sad, sad world we would be living in. I have said many times that the piece of land with the most poems, the largest amount of beautiful music, the place where you will find the greatest ideas never spoken, the most unimaginable art never painted, and the best preachers never heard is in your local graveyard. Don't die with that talent in your hand. Let the Holy Spirit use you to support and care for the world via the conduit of the gift of God in you.

Throughout the years, I have encountered many people who were "hurt" because no one called, baked a dish, or came by, and I agree that those things "should" have happened. But the greater question is not "Why didn't you?" but "Why did the body not know?" Where have you been? Do you really expect a church to get to know you when you arrive fifteen minutes late and leave before the altar call begins? How do you expect people to know your intimate needs when you never join a small group, volunteer for a project, or attend another service through the week? It is almost impossible. At CCC, we were caught off guard with the tremendous growth we had in the beginning. It was a blessing, as well as a huge responsibility. Today, we have evolved into a spiritual leadership structure. We believe much like what is found in the New Testament—we have pastoral ministries, elders, and deacons. All our people are divided into a deacon system. It is the only way a church our size can provide the needed and necessary biblical care for our people. Yet, it still demands involvement on the member's part. This involvement dictates the necessity of the individual knowing his/her spiritual gifts. The needs of any size congregation can be overwhelming. But when the members are activated for support and care

THE LAW OF SUPPORT AND CARE

through the enablement of their discovery of their personal strengths and gifts, something magical happens. People's needs are met. People feel supported. They sense the care of the body of believers. It's only when we sit back and expect "the preacher" to do it, because "it's his job" that the local church looks like a failure. This is not the plan of God. And NOWHERE in Scripture can you find otherwise. However, if people are placed into service, for the maturity of the Body, and the common good of the "brethren," watch out! And here's why!

**Wisdom Point B:**

*You must know your gift to support and care effectively.* Have you ever watched "American Idol" or "The Voice" when they are dealing with people who can't sing? It's sad when someone thinks that he/she is a wonderful singer, but is clueless that his/her "gift" is actually making the dogs howl! Yet, there is one thing sadder than someone who thinks he can sing and can't; it is someone being able to sing with a wonderful God-given voice and refusing to sing. There is nothing sadder than an artist who won't paint, a singer who won't sing, or a preacher who won't preach. So many people do not know who they are; therefore, they can't be a blessing of support and care to anyone. Knowing your gift is crucial; not knowing your gift is downright dangerous. When you know who you are, you won't let people abuse you as something you are not. Everything ever created has a God-given purpose, and that purpose comes out of the source from which it came. When God wanted a bird, He spoke to the air; when He wanted a fish, He spoke to the waters; and when He wanted a plant, He spoke to the dirt; but when He had you on His mind, He spoke to Himself. Your potential comes out of the source of God himself. This God has given you spiritual abilities that the Bible called spiritual gifts. It's a crucial, intellectual subject in which all believers need to be educated to fully support and care for those around them.

## Wisdom Point C

*Don't be ignorant of your spiritual gifts.* What is a spiritual gift? Paul expressed his deep desire that we "not be ignorant" regarding spiritual gifts (1 Corinthians 12:1). First Timothy 4:14 admonishes all of us, "Do not neglect the gift that is in you." First Peter 4:10 warns us that we all will be held accountable for our stewardship of these gifts. God's will is for us to bear much fruit. John 15:8 says, "By this my Father is glorified, that you bear much fruit; so you will be My disciples" (NKJV). John tells us that "they" would know that you are My disciples because of our love for one another. Now, John says that the Father's proof of our discipleship is the fruit we bear. Your gift can be some of the fruit God has been looking for in your life.

Gifts are not natural talents; they are the source of joy in the Christian life. There are no ungifted believers—period—especially not you! Gifts are plural, not singular. You can have more than one, but no one person can have them all at the same time. In Romans 12:3-8; 1 Corinthians 12:8-10, 28-30; Ephesians 4:11, we see the many different kinds of gifts that can be distributed throughout the Body. There are many free tests online that can help you discover your gifting. I encourage you to know who you are, so you can be a blessing to someone else. As Robert Morris said, "There is only one thing you can possibly give God that would constitute an extravagant gift—yourself."[10]

If we are going to build a strong community, we have to have a spiritually healthy community. To be spiritually healthy, a congregation must mature to the point that each member knows his/her "gift." This will require maturity. Knowing your gifts is a big step in the right direction. The apostle Paul taught us in 1 Corinthians 12:11 that the "Spirit" appoints each individual in the local church with a "gift" of the Spirit. These gifts are to manifest themselves (12:7; 14:12) through the individual for the common good of all. The fascinating information here is what is not spoken.

God created all of us. He knows that it is better to give than receive. Furthermore, in His infinite wisdom, He also knows that He created us with a specific purpose. Recent research has provided us a wealth of information from positive psychology. One of these seven traits of a happy, optimistic person is to understand one's calling and use it for the good of another person. So when God created the concept of gifting the believers in the local church, He did so knowing full well that it would produce happy, joyful people. This happiness has a source, and that source is the freedom we now walk in, thanks to grace. According to Greek sentence structure, these gifts come "through" not "by" the Holy Spirit, and they are directly a gift as a result of the grace of God (1 Corinthians 12:11). "They are its concrete expression."[11] You don't earn or deserve the "gift" that God gives you, because it is given by grace. As Dr. Gilbert Bilezikian says, "Ministry is a responsibility for all."[12] God has equipped you with a special gift of the Spirit. It's your job to discover these gifts. And it's actually the job of the leaders in your local church "to equip the saints for ministry." The pastors in your local church have a mission, and it does not necessarily require attending the funeral of your cat. Paul says in Ephesians 4: "And He personally gave some to be apostles, some prophets, some evangelists, some pastors and teachers, for the training of the saints in the work of ministry, to build up the body of Christ" (vv. 11-12). "Gifts" were God's idea for you. Paul says in Ephesians 4:7-8: "Now grace was given to each one of us according to the measure of the Messiah's gift. For it says: When He ascended on high, He took prisoners into captivity; He gave gifts to people." In other words, He rescued you from hell and now desires your participation in helping keep other people from the same demise.

The reason why we want to use our gifts for support and care is quite simple. We are a spiritual product of someone else's sacrifice in ministry. If they had not obeyed the call to operate within their gifts, we quite possibly might not have ever met Christ. As my friend Mitchell Tolle says, "Somebody has touched your clay!"

## Wisdom Point D

*Don't underestimate the importance of your gifts.* Unfortunately, many will emphasize only the miraculous or dynamic gifts mentioned in Romans 12:3-9; 1 Corinthians 12:1-31; Ephesians 4:2-12; and 1 Peter 4:10-11. But this is not the way it should be at all. The "power gifts" are not more important than the "vocal gifts" or the "service gifts." Paul, in 1 Corinthians 12:21, makes the equality of the brethren abundantly clear. "Ignorance about spiritual gifts is a major reason for church dysfunction, but it is not the only one. Often sinful comparisons are allowed to create hierarchies of glamor, visibility, and status among ministries...some believers are reluctant to contribute their service because of its apparent insignificance" (12:14-20).[13]

The law of support and care enables you to be the Christian that Christ intended for you to be all along! Don't deprive the Kingdom of your powerful potential. When you don't work in your gifting, you become a detriment to your local church. The Holy Spirit has given you a gift that is unique to you. This doesn't mean that you are the ONLY one who can play drums. No, He has given you more than one gift, but not all the gifts reside in you. There is this need for "the other" here. You need the other body members to function in your gift properly. They need you to do the same. It is no wonder that too many local churches are obsolete, antiquated, and dysfunctional when the most basic understanding of unity is the wisdom regarding how to operate in your spiritual gifts. In the early days of CCC, I was constantly being asked, what seemed to me at the time like the dumbest question I had ever heard, "You mean you WANT me to work in my gifts?" It took me some time to catch on, but I finally did. Many of them were being held back from working in their gifts. This happens frequently when pastors become insecure, deacons become power hungry, or a member remains immature and intimidated by the gifts of others. The apostle Paul gives the best defense of why you need to get involved in your local church—people need your support and care via your spiritual gifts.

> And He personally gave some to be apostles, some prophets, some evangelists, some pastors and teachers, for the training of the saints in the work of ministry, to build up the body of Christ, until we all reach unity in the faith and in the knowledge of God's Son, growing into a mature man with a stature measured by Christ fullness. Then we will no longer be little children, tossed by the waves and blown around by every wind of teaching, by human cunning with cleverness in the techniques of deceit. But speaking the truth in love, let us grow in every way into Him who is the head—Christ. From Him the whole body, fitted and knit together by every supporting ligament, promotes growth of the body for building up itself in love by the proper working of each individual part (Ephesians 4:11-16).

What a powerful passage about church growth, health, and unity! The law of support and care is essential, because it operates through the gifts of each individual member of your local church. This process builds the body of Christ and causes it to grow into maturity. It also enables the church to become a strong congregation, highly committed to one another. They no longer "float" from church to church. They have grown up through operating in their gifts and are content in their calling. As they serve each other through their giftings, a deep love takes place. This love happened by the "proper working of each individual part." Marx was right: "Religion is the opiate of the masses. Religious institutions dull people to their responsibilities as disciples of Jesus. Wake up!"[14]

## PRECEPT THREE:
### Love and Compassion Begins in the Pew

I love evangelism. To me, it's every Christian's mandate and the central balance in every local church next to discipleship itself. So, I understand how easy it is to forget some very important underlying principles, like this one: Biblical outreach begins in the church, not outside of its walls. In the law of unity, we spent a great amount of time discussing the biblical concept of "one another." It is central to all the laws of community. In the law of support and care, it is a crucial piece as well. It is not only a crucial piece for us today, but also, it was so crucially effective in the first century that Emperor Julian, who hated Christianity, wrote this: "Nothing has contributed to the progress of the superstition of these Christians as their charity to strangers, the impious Galileans provide not only for their own poor but for ours as well."[15] Support and care flow out of love and compassion. John 15:13 tells us, "No one has greater love than this, that someone would lay down his life for his friends." The famous passage in Matthew 25:35-40 contains a word that many of us miss. It's the story where Jesus says that when we do acts of kindness to the least important people, that we are actually doing these acts of kindness to Him. It's the word "brother" in verse 40 that we miss. Feeding the poor in Africa is important. Serving the homeless in Austin is a crucial piece of strategy for the local church. But according to Jesus himself, when we give food, a cup of cold water, shelter, clothing, medicine, or care, it should start with our "brothers and sisters." This is how the world will know you belong to Christ.

### Wisdom Point A

*It takes a sacrificial love to support and care for a person.* "Love never surrenders a part of self while reserving the essential self: it surrenders the essential.[16] There is one truth that every parent and pastor realizes, you can't be great at your job if you are selfish. Children have a way of wearing down this vice within parents. I will deny myself immediately to gratify and meet the needs of my children. As a pastor, you place yourself last many times, because deep within your heart, every pastor is a spiritual parent. As workers in the kingdom of God, you too must take up your cross and follow Him daily (Luke 9:23.) You too, must lay down your life for your friends, even the friends who may not always appreciate it.

> The great John Hedgepeth taught me this valuable lesson many years ago. He pastors the 4,100 member Northwood Temple Church in Fayetteville, North Carolina. He is one of the most sacrificial leaders I know. He has given his life for his flock, tirelessly tending to his sheep. That is a rare trait in ministry today. When I was young, I worked for him as a youth pastor. There were so many times that he would humble himself in situations (where I knew he was not in the wrong) just to save a sheep. I didn't understand that deep love and compassion then, but I do now.

Compassion is important for support and care because it is rooted in love. You can't have compassion for something you don't love. Ilia Delio said:

> Jesus, the image of the Father, reflects all of the Father's love to us, especially in the cross, where love is poured out for the healing of the world. What this means on a deeper level is that compassion is part of God's humility. Compassion is not an admirable trait that God acquired once He decided to have a creation. No, compassion is God's love that so extends itself to the other without asking for anything in return, that it may be one with the other in all things. The compassion of God is the Father stretching forth in love to the Son so that the Father is completely one in love with the Son.[17]

Therefore, we stretch forth to the "other" to complete-ly love. I know you probably know the famous John 3:16 passage. But, do you know the 1 John 3:16 passage? "This is how we have come to know love: He laid down His life for us. We should also lay down our lives for our broth-ers." Romans 12:1 tells us, "Therefore, brothers, by the mercies of God, I urge you to present your bodies as a living sacrifice, holy and pleasing to God; this is your spir-itual worship." God is calling you to lay down your life so you can, in the end, save it. God is calling you to offer your body as a living sacrifice. Jesus gave Himself as a live and living sacrifice. Can you imagine with me, what your local church could look like if we were to truly lay down our lives for "one another?"

In Philippians 2:3-4, we understand through this kenotic passage to, "Do nothing out of rivalry or conceit, but in humility consider others as more important than yourselves. Everyone should look out not only for his own interests, but also for the interests of others." Let's build a great community in your local church by laying down our lives in service to Christ. You and I should remember that it was the grace of God that purchased our freedom, and that in our poverty we are now rich (2 Corinthians 8:9). It isn't really about divesting yourself of all your resources, but it is about sharing your "abundance" and "prosperity" with those in need (2 Corinthians 8:14; 1 Corinthians 16:2).

This abundance of grace causes our hearts to overflow in gratitude to others, because we have been given abundance while in a former state of poverty. Second Corinthians 9:7 instructs us to give freely, never under compulsion but out of a great heart, because "God loves a cheerful giver."

### Wisdom Point B

*Support and care loves a person like family.* The sense of family abounds in both the Old and New Testament with plentiful metaphors of familial affection. The young pastor

Timothy was told by the seasoned teacher Paul: "But If I should be delayed, I have written so that you would know how people ought to act in God's household, which is the church of the living God" (1 Timothy 3:15). The metaphor of family evolves naturally in the Scriptures with God being called our "Father" and members being the "sons" and "daughters" (2 Corinthians 6:14-18), living in "the household of faith" (Galatians 6:10; Ephesians 2:19). We are then called "The children of God" (1 John 3:1-24). When someone joins your local church, they should be joining a family, and you should be gaining a "brother" or "sister."

Acts 2:42 explains this concept very well. There was this sense of fraternity; many of them had paid a high price for joining this "Christian family," and in doing so, they often lost their jobs and families. In this ancient world where no Medicare existed and where retirement was a familial issue, many early believers were left with no one to take care of them. A bishop in the third century wrote, "This has been our custom from the beginning, to do good in manifold ways to all Christians, and to send contributions to the many churches in every city, in some places relieving the poverty of the needy, and ministering to the Christians in the mines."[18] As I travel to the original places in which the New Testament times took place, more and more I realize how much early believers **needed** one another just to make it in life. To these early believers, this was *agape* in its truest form. "Love was not a noble feeling, but very concrete assistance, especially for fellow believers. In the tradition of Matthew 5:43-48, *agape* can occasionally include people outside the church. But the mainstream of New Testament language reserves *agape* for conduct within the communities."[19] What began as an individual conversion now morphs into interdependence, because the liberty they have all found now leads them naturally into service.

This new family, as Acts 2:44 tells us, "had all things in common." In other words, they shared their resources when needed with other members. Many churches want fellowship and intimate friendship with a deep community, but they miss the structure by which these things are obtained in a local church:

1. *"They devoted themselves"* (1 Corinthians 16:15): This Greek phrase means that they "adhered with strength." It meant that you were remaining and continuing steadfast with someone. You can't expect a unified, loving community when people get a "spiritual divorce" every six months. You can't support or care, neither can you be supported or cared for, if church leaders cannot find you or don't know which church you are going to attend this week. Church leaders as well need to know that you are devoted and strongly adhering to one local church, so they can know who to help with the resources they distribute. At CCC, we receive at least 10-15 calls a day from people wanting us to pay their light or gas bill or give them money to go see their dying mother in Milwaukee. We biblically have learned to ask this question first: "Where do you attend church?" Most will say some unknown church down the road where they don't even know the pastor's name! But our answer is simple. Your needs as a believer are to be considered first through the resources of your own congregation. Being devoted helps your church leaders to know who is committed, and thus should be biblically considered for support and care. Being devoted steadfastly to someone such as a great Bible-believing church will aid your maturity, because you can find a place to work in your gifts. So, take a look at what they devoted themselves toward.

2. *Teaching:* The Word of God is our instruction manual and is the divine set of orders for the church and all of its workings (2 Timothy 3:16). The early church members devoted themselves to understanding the teachings of the church. The instructions in the Bible are not multiple choices; they are not for your selectiveness or rearrangements; but they are for you and me to obey (Deuteronomy 6:4-9). And when we do, we have a promise of life and life more abundantly (John 10:10).

3. *Fellowship:* This word actually meant they devoted themselves to a close relationship with each other. It was a fraternal love, a brotherly love, and a giving kind of love for one another. They served one another's needs. It was more than a meal; it was a high commitment to one another. Second Corinthians 6:14 says, "Do not be mismatched with unbelievers. For what partnership is there between righteousness and lawlessness? Or what fellowship does light have with darkness?" This verse isn't instructing us to not reach out relationally with the unsaved; indeed, we must do these things. But, it is telling us to watch whom we call an "ally"; don't yoke with an alien spirit. It comes from the understanding of a yoke of oxen tied together. Yet, here it suggests that instead of two oxen of the same species, it is two different kinds of species trying to pull together. These are animals of a different nature. It means being yoked with someone entirely different from you. A person who doesn't know Christ cannot share in your maturity as a believer—iron sharpens iron.

4. *Breaking bread and prayer:* They spent so much time around each other that they often found themselves eating with one another in what was originally called a love feast. However, here, this is probably

referring to the devotion they had to assembling themselves together for worship and service to one another. They would "break bread" through Communion and pray. They devoted themselves to the assembling of the saints (Hebrews 10:25).

In the law of support and care, we must never forget our responsibilities to love, build bridges, use our strengths for the weak, mobilize our resources, and discover our spiritual gifts as we operate in service through sacrificial love. This kind of environment where support and care are fueled by sacrificial love births a family atmosphere. We are, after all, our brother's keeper (Genesis 4:9).

## END NOTES

### Chapter Five
### The Law of Support and Care

[1] Karl Holl, *The Distinctive Elements in Christianity* (Edinburg: Clark, 1937).

[2] Soren Kierkegaard, *Works of Love* (New York: Harper, 1963), 72.

[3] "The Philippians Hymn (2:5-11)," *As an Early Mimetic Christological Model of Christian Leadership in Roman Philippi:* "Inner Reflections on Leadership," Corné Bekker, January 27, 2010; August 1, 2006, www.innerresourcesforleaders.blogspot.com/.

[4] "The Tertullian Project," December 10, 1999; December 26, 2013, www.tertullian.org/quotes.htm.

[5] Edward J. Chinnock, *A Few Notes on Julian and a Translation of His Public Letters* (London: David Nott, 1901), 75-78.

[6] Justin Martyr, *Apology of Justin Martyr*, eds. Rev. Alexander Roberts, James Donaldson, and A. Cleveland Coxe (Tartow, Ohio: Suzeteo Enterprises, 2012), 42-43.

[7] E. Glenn Hinson, *The Early Church: Origins of the Dawn of the Middle Ages* (Nashville: Abingdon Press, 1996), 170.

[8] Paul D. Hanson, *The People Called: The Growth of Community in the Bible* (San Francisco: Harper and Row Publishers, 1986), 1.

[9] Hanson, *The People Called*, p. 1.

[10] John Kie Vining, *Servant Church: Drooling and Dreaming of the Milk and Honey of Church Relevance* (Cleveland, Tenn.: Derek Press, 2008), 227.

[11] Robert J. Banks, *Paul's Idea of Community: The Early House Churches in Their Cultural Setting* (Peabody, Mass.: Hendrickson Publishing, 2009), 92.

[12] Gilbert Bilezikian, *Reclaiming the Local Church as Community of Oneness* (Grand Rapids: Zondervan Publishing, 1997), 69.

[13] Bilezikian, *Reclaiming the Local Church*, p. 81.

[14] Alan Hirsch and Dave Furgerson, *On the Verge: A Journey Into the Apostolic Future of the Church* (Grand Rapids: Zondervan, 2011), 55.

[15] "Sustainable Traditions: Empire and Love," December 24, 2013; January 01, 2013, www.sustainabletraditions. com/tag/Julian-the-apostate/.

[16] Francois Varillon, *The Humility and Suffering of God* (New York: Alba House, 1905), 44, 46.

[17] Ilia Delio, O.S.F., *The Humility of God: A Franciscan Perspective* (Cincinnati: St. Anthony Messenger Press, 2005), 811.

[18] Gerhard Lohfink, *Jesus and Community* (Philadelphia: Fortress Press, 1934), 156.

[19] Lohfink, *Jesus and Community*, 156.

# THE LAW OF JUDGING

## The Knowledge Box

**The Law of Judging:** The act of judging is the act or process of the mind in comparing its ideas, to find their agreement or disagreement, and to ascertain truth; or the process of examining facts and arguments, to ascertain propriety and justice; or the process of examining the relations between one proposition and another.

**The Precepts:**
1. "Judge Not" Is Greatly Misunderstood.
2. Who Am I to Judge?
3. What Am I to Judge?
4. How Am I to Judge?

Nothing breaks my heart like critical people in the church. I feel for them and the person at the other end of their wrath. In order to judge someone, you have to deny your own culpability and assume that you stand completely correct on each matter. Judging is tricky business in a world full of fallen people. Ask any member of the public for a verse from the Bible, and they will most likely be able to quote "Judge not" (Matthew 7:1 NKJV). It is most certainly the favorite verse for lukewarm believers who love to quote this verse in defense of their lack of obedience to God. Using this verse doesn't remove anyone's responsibility to obey. "The real underlying definition of 'judging' is a person's hatred for spiritual truth, reproof, and correction."[1] These things are elements of judging. I realized years ago why the average person does not want the true God to exist. If there is no "God," then we are left to judge ourselves; therefore, we become "gods." But if there is a God, we shall stand before Him and give an account of the life we have lived. So the "bad news" is, there is a God; the good news is, His judgments are always a hundred percent accurate. However, this chapter is not about the doctrine of divine judgment, neither is it about the fact that we will all stand before the judgment seat of Christ (2 Corinthians 5:10). This chapter is about how to handle critical people who judge other people in the church and then bring divisiveness to the body of Christ.

## PRECEPT ONE:
### "Judge Not" Is Greatly Misunderstood.

When you take a good theological look at Matthew 7:1-5, you might be surprised at what you find. It is one of the most misquoted verses in the entire Bible. As we discussed earlier, those who often fall short ethically love to use it in their defense; when in actuality, it isn't even alluding to the covering over of poor behavior. The Bible actually uses the word "judge" over 162 times. Judgment is actually a way in which God brings about repentance so we do not suffer in the final judgment (1 Corinthians 11:32). This passage is not saying that we should forbid critical thinking; rather, it is saying that God is the only one who has a right to condemn or avenge. We, on the other hand, have a mandate to critically evaluate and analyze people and situations in the church within the boundaries of the Word of God. John 7:24 tells us to "Judge with right judgment" (NRSV). James 4:12 reminds us, "There is only one Lawgiver and Judge, the One who is able to save and to destroy; but who are you who judge your neighbor?" (NASB). But we are reminded in the Book of Romans 2:1-3, not to judge people when we are guilty of the same offense. What Matthew 7:1 is about is the hypocrite and his/her inability to judge someone. It is a call to hold our tongues from being critical of other people.

## Wisdom Point A

*Don't be hypocritical in your judging.*

I stood there in the dark room completely shocked at his pretentiousness. How he felt "right" in passing judgment on this elderly volunteer was sobering. She had taken four boxes of Christmas candies left over from the yearly present drive for children in our area. He, on the other hand, had been released from prison after serving several years for a first-degree murder charge of a 4-year-old baby girl. The tears rolled down the worn face of this aged volunteer. She meant no harm; after all, the presents had all been delivered and every child had left satisfied. She was on a fixed income and was propelled into poverty when her husband of 50 years died of a sudden heart attack. Left alone with no children nearby, she made the best of life that she could. He, on the other hand, was from a wealthy family. The kind where money can often purchase the justice needed. He demanded that she be removed from the church as a thief. He brutally rallied his coconspirators to avow for "righteousness." Somehow, he had forgotten the more than four boxes of candy canes, Christmas candy canes at that, for which he was exonerated many years ago. Yes, he was guilty, not out of a lack of reason, but of sound judgment. One night his temper got the best of him as he shook his girlfriend's 4-year-old baby girl. He shook and shook, never allowing a moment of sanity to guide his horrible behavior. The little girl hung in his arms like a ragdoll. Unknown to him, she died from a retinal hemorrhage caused from his habitual shaking. Now, somehow, he felt "justified" in serving judgment on a candy-cane case when he himself was released on a technicality of justice from murder. Ironically, the one who was released on a technicality of justice wanted to serve justice on a technicality. The irony of life would be funny had it not been so grievous.

Why is it so easy to forget the fact that we too have been forgiven?

Matthew 7:1 says, "Judge not, that you be not judged" (NKJV). This misquoted verse too often serves as a protective fortress for the unrighteous pretender. Jesus is not forbidding judging; He is forbidding the hypocritical to judge and the harshness of judging anyone unkindly. Judging has disastrous consequences. So, here is a motivation not to judge someone else—realize that however you judge someone, you will be judged by the same standards (v. 2). The very act of judging establishes a set of criteria to which the one judging must answer. This passage condemns not the gavel of insight, or the justice of evaluation, but the brutality of the hangman who does not seek justice, but the thrill of criticism. It is condemning the disposition of a person to look unfavorably on the character and actions of another. It is the essence of the violation of the law of love. It is unkind criticism. It is the kind of judgment that no human being can live up to. The Greek word here for "judge" is the one with the most exclusive intent toward judging other human beings. Jesus is calling to the courtyard of life the guilt of the one who judges harshly, hypocritically, and without love. Even God's judgment is restorative in nature (Romans 2:2). Matthew 12:36-37 reminds all of us that on the Day of Judgment they will give an account for every careless word they speak; "for by your words you will be justified, and by your words you will be condemned" (NKJV). Jesus is saying "don't pass judgment on people," and "don't decide if other people are guilty." It is a call to end sharp, unjust criticism.

## Wisdom Point B

*To slander your brother, you must assume that you are the "Judge."* The enemies of God nicknamed James "Camel Knees," because he was known as a man of prayer. This half-brother of Jesus stood like a beacon of light in a dark world full of chaos. He spoke in a "matter-of-fact" style, and I guess that is why I love him so much. He said in James 4:11-12:

> Do not speak evil against one another, brethren. He who speaks against a brother or judges his brother, speaks against the law and judges the law; but if you judge the law, you are not a doer of the law but a judge of it. There is only one Lawgiver and Judge, the One who is able to save and to destroy; but who are you to judge your neighbor?" (NASB).

His argument here is against the sinfulness of judging someone with critical speech.

Slander was considered a vice in the ancient world. Here, this passage suggests that slandering is taking place behind the back of the believer by another believer. Unbelievable, but it happens in the local church somewhere every day. It is an act of condemnation among people who

125

do not live under condemnation (Romans 8:1). A slandering "brother" or "sister" in Christ will find a "brother" who is lacking and whom they feel is worthy of rejection. Slandering believers are presumptuous. They must assume a superiority to speak harshly against another person. The word James uses for slander is actually the same Greek word for devil. James is comparing the actions of a slandering "brother" to the actions of Satan himself. When you slander a person, you are actually trying to inflame others against the person being criticized. They are harsh words about the absent. It is a living contradiction of the law of support and care. There must be unity in the body of Christ.

The psalmist said of God, "I will destroy anyone who secretly slanders his neighbor, I cannot tolerate anyone with haughty eyes or an arrogant heart" (Psalm 101:5). Why do we think that God winks at slander and lowers the gavel on murder? In ancient Judaism, they were considered to be one and the same. In Judaism, there are four great sins that correspond with four great virtues. One of the great virtues was making peace between one another. The great sins were idolatry, incest, murder, and slander. According to ancient rabbis, "the last of which is as bad as all the other three put together (Jerusalem Talmud, Peah 1:1 (15d).[2]

What people fail to realize is when you slander another person, you criticize and judge him harshly, without love; and according to Matthew 7, you are slandering the law of God. Behind this law is a lawgiver. And as a slanderer, you have placed yourself in a superior position to God himself. Ancient Rabbis often called *slander* the "third tongue," because it slays three people: "the speaker, the listener, and the one spoken about. Not only do speech violations cause death (Proverbs 18:21), but they also deprive a person of a place in the world to come."[3] Yes, you read it correctly. God places judging critically in the same bracket as idolatry, incest, and murder! Unity in the local church is once again paramount on the mind of God. He has clearly given us laws that dictate even the smallest critical judgments against one another. It takes only one small spark to burn down a forest.

## Precept Two:
### Who Am I to Judge?

Matthew 7:1 forbids judgmentalism, but not moral discernment. The Bible, as we have learned, does not tell us to never judge a person. This is a misunderstanding of the masses. We are not to be judgmental, harsh, critical, or unloving. John 7:24 says, "Stop judging according to outward appearances; rather, judge accordingly to righteous judgment." First Corinthians 2:15 tells us, "The spiritual man judges all things, but is himself to be judged by no one" (RSV). We also read in 1 Corinthians 6:1-6, that "Do you not know that the saints will judge the world?" (RSV). First Corinthians 5:12-13 gives us further insight into judging situations properly when it says: "For what have I to do with judging outsiders? Is it not those inside the church whom you are to judge? God judges those outside. 'Drive out the wicked person from among you'" (RSV). In dealing with church matters, the apostle Paul said this: "Let him who has done this be removed from among you . . . I have already pronounced judgment . . . on the man who has done such a thing" (RSV). It should be clear to you now that there is a stark difference between judging someone with slander, harshness, or a critical spirit, which is the true meaning of "Judge not," and in judging a person's life or situation with moral discernment.

### Wisdom Point A
*Biblical judging requires critical thinking.* There is a fine line between judging someone critically and judging

someone's actions with critical thinking. In John 7:24, we are told to "Stop judging according to outward appearances; rather judge according to righteous judgment." Here, *to judge* means "to separate, to distinguish, to discriminate between good and evil; to choose the good, to judge as to form or give an opinion after separating and considering the particulars of a case; to judge in one's mind as to what is right, proper, and expedient; to determine." In this passage, Jesus' opponents had been judging critically, not with critical thinking. The accuser of Jesus judged (as Matthew 7:1 warned) with "harshness" and a critical spirit based on appearances, not the facts. John 7:24 says that we shouldn't judge by appearances, but on facts, with the truth. The Greek language comes with tenses that give us a certainty with timing and direction. Here, the tenses in this passage tell us to stop the act in the process. This is followed by the implication of urgency. Judging someone wrongly is a serious offence in Scripture. The motives behind your judgment are just as serious. Isaiah 11:3 says, "His delight will be in the fear of the Lord. He will not judge by what He sees with his eyes, He will not execute justice by what He hears with His ears." Notice the capital "He's" in the verse. God neither judges by His eyes nor by His ears; He judges rightly by moral discernment in the context of one's obedience to faith. He judges by facts, not opinions derived from outward forms. The Bible does NOT say for us to never judge. It does tell us, however, to judge compassionately and with moral discernment.

### Wisdom Point B

*What am I not to judge?* There should be two things very clear to you by now: One, the world thinks all judging is wrong and this misquoted scripture—Matthew 7:1-5—is really about judging people unfairly, with a slanderous, bitter criticism. Two, Christians are to judge—they are to distinguish between good and evil. They are to form an opinion after separating and considering the particular case; thus determining what is right and what is wrong based on the context of obedience to the faith. So, where are the boundaries? Dr. Joseph Millmouth has written a wonderful strategic outline as to how biblical judgment should not and should be issued in the local church.[4]

1. *We are not to judge people based on our personal convictions or preferences* (nonmoral). Romans 14:1-23 gives us these parameters.

> When I was young, there was a group of people near where I lived who swore to me that wearing shorts would send me immediately to hell. I did not spend the majority of my young years in a local church. These same people told my mother that she too would end up in hell if she continued to wear blue jeans—pants were reserved for men only. Even as a child, I did not understand this reasoning—how a piece of clothing could be responsible for such eternal devastation. I know hundreds of people who do not attend church because of such teachings which have caused them to feel like living a Christian life is impossible.

Paul says clearly that we must not make judgments from personal preferences. The local church should be a diverse place with every stratum of society coexisting in one place. Romans 14:1-23 gives us some additional wisdom on how we are to interact in our lives together:

a. The weak brother is important (Romans 14:1). While I may have no problem with a particular social issue like shorts or eating meat, I must respect my weaker brother's position. His faith is obviously affected by certain kinds of conduct. I must withhold my liberty to protect his weaker conscience.

    b. We must accept him without attempting to settle such disputable matters, and we should avoid starting an argument (Romans 14:1). Our opinions and personal convictions to or not to is never the main point. The main point is always to encourage and strengthen the other brother's faith.

    c. We must respect the other person's conscious decision to accept or refrain from certain issues. Spiritual maturity is living life with ambiguity; i.e., understanding deep within that you can be wrong and that your convictions may be different from another believer's, and then being ok with that assessment.

    d. Tolerance is crucial to the unity of a local church: We have to maintain a correct attitude with one another. The one who eats meat cannot despise the one who doesn't eat meat. Those who don't eat meat cannot pass judgment on the one who consciously decides to eat meat. There are some questionable moral issues about which Scripture does not give enough clarity; therefore, we need to be quiet where God has chosen not to reveal His will.

    e. There is a tendency of the strong believer to look down on the weaker believer. This is a subtle form of pride and arrogance that often masquerades as pity. We cannot regard the "other" brother or sister as inferior simply because we hold different personal convictions. The weaker brother is often the biblical tyrant and thus guilty of the same offence, because he holds that the strong are sinners.

2. *We are not to judge people by outward appearances* (John 7:24; James 2:1-4). All Christians do not look alike. We serve a God of diversity and creativity.

There is nothing at all bland about our God. It can cause great harm in God's diverse ecosystem when we demand that all Christians dress the same way, or like the same kinds of music, or enjoy the same kinds of tastes. Such Christianity does not embrace freedom, but legalism. We are to stay away from superficial judgments that could hurt members of our body of believers.

3. *We should withhold critical judgment of another's Christian service to God* (1 Corinthians 4:1-5). A critical attitude can kill a passion for service. We are to encourage one another and build up the body (Hebrews 10:24-25). Do you know that even your pastor needs encouraging? The elders need encouraging; they don't need your critical judgment based on superficial conclusions based on what someone saw or heard. They need you to be mature, using critical thinking as you judge matters.

4. *We are not to let our mouths run wild as we express our opinions about other brothers and sisters* (Exodus 23:1; 1 Corinthians 5:3-5; 1 Timothy 5:19; Titus 3:1-2; James 3:2; 1 Peter 2:1). The tail of a scorpion doesn't have the poison that some Christians' tongues possess. Some of the greatest workers of the church are now missing in action because they became a causality of friendly fire. Their gifts have stopped; and their hearts have dried up like water puddles on a hot summer afternoon, because a friend wounded them whom they thought truly cared about them. I am not making excuses for their abandonment, for none will be sufficient on Judgment Day. What I am doing is making my point clear—be careful with your words of judgment. Make sure they are seasoned with love, stirred with sweeteners, mellowed by time, and melted by reason.

## PRECEPT THREE:
### What Am I to Judge?

Knowing what to judge is as important as knowing what not to judge! As committed believers, what are the boundaries for judging in love? In what areas do Christians make judgment?

A. *Christians are to judge relational disputes between the members of the body of Christ.* In 1 Corinthians 6:1-8, it gives light to this subject very well.

> Does any one of you, when he has a case against his neighbor, dare to go to the law before the unrighteous, and not before the saints? Or do you not know that the saints will judge the world? If the world is judged by you, are you not competent to constitute the smallest law courts? Do you not know that we will judge angels? How much more matters of this life? So if you have law courts dealing with matters of this life, do you appoint them as judges who are of no account in the church? I say this to your shame. Is it so, that there is not among you one wise man who will be able to decide between his brethren, but brother goes to law with brother, and that before unbelievers? (NASB).

Well, so much for not judging, when Paul himself explains to us that judging properly is actually an element of spiritual maturity and the future of every believer! Paul is so adamant about believers being judged by other righteous members of the body that he begins this Greek sentence with the equivalency of "How dare you!" He suggests to us that it takes a lot of "gall" to take another believer to a secular court when such issues should be handled inside the local church or ecclesiastical body! The issues of the church are to never spill over into the secular world! We are to be sober and diligent to make sure our house is in order. This will require mature leaders, as well as submitted and seasoned members. The world cannot judge by biblical values.

B. *The body of Christ, through the local church, is to judge unrepentant members:* According to 1 Corinthians 5:3-5, certain unrepented sins need to be addressed within the public forum of the local church. First Corinthian 5:9 says, "I wrote to you in my letter not to associate with sexually immoral persons—not at all meaning the immoral of . . . this world. But now I am writing to you not to associate with anyone who bears the name of brother" (NRSV). Such a statement would assume a judgment has been made on a member of the body. In the law of discipline, we laid out the process of Matthew 18:15-20. As a member of a local church, never forget that the goal is never punishment, but restoration (Galatians 6:1-5). Such judging of a believer is to lead to restoration; however, if the brother is unrepentant, then fellowship is to be refused until repentance is evident to the body (1 Corinthians 5:11-13; 1 Thessalonians 1:8; 3:6; Revelation 2:20-24).

C. *We are to judge the doctrine of teachers in our local church by God's Word* (Matthew 7:15-20; Acts 17:10-11; Romans 2:20-24; 16:17-18; 1 Corinthians 14:29; Colossians 2:8; 2 Timothy 4:3-4; Titus 1:10-16; 3:10; Hebrews 13:7; 2 Peter 2:1-22; 1 John 4:1; 2 John 1:10-11; Revelation 2:20-24). In Romans 16:17, Paul says, "Now I urge you, brothers, to watch out for those who cause dissensions and obstacles contrary to the doctrine you have learned. Avoid them, for such people do not serve our Lord Christ but their own appetites. They deceive the hearts of the unsuspecting with smooth talk and flattering words." The apostle Paul begins this passage with a very strong

Greek word, which in essence says very strongly, "I want you to pay close attention." "Paul places strong stress on unity and regards the dissensions as contrary to the teaching you have learned."[5] He instructs the local church of Rome to judge false teachers by the following:

1. **Watch** out for them: You have to watch the behavior to judge a false teacher. The best predictor of future behavior is past behavior. Do they live by their own words?

2. They will **cause** dissensions and pitfalls. They are "marked" by doctrinal divisions and moral offenses. The word "offense" is the Greek word for "deathtrap." Paul is saying that this subject is so important to judge correctly, that if we fail to identify false teachers, their poison has the power to take life away from the believer. It's a word that designates what is fatal.

3. They **teach** something different. The word used here is "contrary," meaning something nearby, or immediate vicinity. There is often only a hair's difference between the truth and a lie. You judge a false teacher by his/her false teachings. One way to begin is to compare it with what you have been taught by other good teachers whose behavior confirms their doctrines.

4. **Avoid** them. You are to judge them by marking them (Philippians 3:17). We are to look out for false teachers. Keep watch by judging doctrine by knowing the truth.

5. They are **selfish**: We can judge the presence of a false teacher by the character trait of selfishness. The Greek word is "own belly." They live for their own self-interest, not being the kenotic shepherd of Philippians 2:6-11. Their final aim is a luxurious life.

6. **Smooth** talkers: They use good words to represent themselves. They manipulate you by their good language.
7. Full of **flattery:** You judge the presence of false teachers by their ability to flatter someone for their own purposes.
8. **Motives** are to deceive. They know the right way but purposefully lead others in a different direction.
9. Their **hearts.** This suggests that false teachers go after innocent people who may be morally pure, but deficient of prudence.

D. *We are to judge the character of potential leadership.* The fivefold ministry of ministers, elders, deacons, and church leadership are to judge potential leaders against the specified characteristics mentioned in Scriptures (Luke 10:40; Romans 16:1-2; Acts 6:1-7; Philippians 1:1; 1 Timothy 3:1-13; Titus 1:5-9). The Bible is clear in setting forth leadership qualities for potential leaders.

E. *We are to judge the behavior of unruly members in the local church* (Matthew 18:15-17; 23:23; 1 Corinthians 5; 2 Corinthians 2:4-11; 7:5-13; Galatians 2:1-14; 1 Thessalonians 5:14; 2 Thessalonians 3:6-15; 1 Timothy 1:18-20; 5:20; Titus 3:10-11). We must judge correctly, basing our conclusion on facts gathered and the arbitrator of all final truth—God's Word. The action of discipline is actually preceded by the law of judgment. We must first come to a rational, fact-gathering conclusion before discipline is instituted. I have a rule at CCC, and it has cost me over the years. I don't move on words; I move and take action only upon the reception of facts that can be proven. So much damage has been done in the house of God because someone took action solely based on the words of another person, while ignoring the

potential truth reported elsewhere. God has giv-
en us His Word to know what is right and what is
wrong. This is not decided by feelings or personal preferences, but only upon the perfect Word of
God.

F. *We are to judge ourselves* (2 Corinthians 13:5-7; Galatians 6:4; 1 Peter 4:17). The Scripture tells us that
"For the time has come for judgment to begin with
God's household; and if it begins with us, what will
the outcome be for those who disobey the gospel of
God?" (1 Peter 4:17). I tell my congregation all the
time, "I am not going to go around pointing my finger at anybody. I have all I can take care of by keeping myself straight." In 2 Corinthians 13:5, Paul
says: "Test yourselves to see if you are in the faith.
Examine yourselves." Paul is telling the church at
Corinth that they should examine themselves, not
cross-examine him! Such personal evaluations are
important for our own faith development. First Corinthians 11:31 tells us, "If we were properly evalu-
ating ourselves, we would not be judged, but when
we are judged, we are disciplined by the Lord, so
that we may not be condemned with the world."
In other words, it is far better for us to judge ourselves than to have to be judged by God; endure
His loving discipline, or far worse, be judged by
the world. Lamentations 3:40 says, "Let us search
out and examine our ways, and turn back to the
Lord." The passage is challenging us to "test our
way of life." It is so easy to drift from God when we
do not stay sober, awake, and diligent at all times
(1 Corinthians 15:34; 1 Thessalonians 5:6; 1 Timothy
3:2; Titus 2:12; 1 Peter 5:8). While there is a roaming
lion seeking whom he may devour (1 Peter 5:8), we
have a prize ahead of us in the high calling of Jesus Christ; therefore, we run this race set before us

(1 Corinthians 9:24; Hebrews 12:1) in hopes of hearing Him say one day, "Well done, good and faithful slave" (Matthew 25:21).

## Precept Four:
### How Am I to Judge?

There is a reason why Paul told Timothy that those who labor in full-time ministry are worth double honor. It is often hard and difficult work to walk people through the different stages and journey of life. Nothing is as difficult as having to bring correction in a loving way to a person who has matured enough to know that it is needed and part of the job of a pastor. Here are some guidelines to help you!

1. Matthew 7:2-4 reminds us to **be very careful** how we judge matters. As you now know, this passage is not admonishing us to never judge, but to judge rightly; because we will be judged by how we judge others.

2. John 7:24 warns us to **not judge by appearances** because they too can be deceiving. We need spiritual discernment and facts woven through the truth of the Word of God to judge righteously.

3. Romans 2:1-3 challenges us to **never judge people of sins we ourselves are committing.** In doing so, we are actually condemning ourselves. The Bible says here "we are without excuse"(Romans 2:1). This is a legal term and implies we are without a defense. It has the underlying meaning of hypocritical involvement. The deeper theological meaning here may be referring to the fact that we all will stand before the judgment seat of Christ in our true character.

4. Galatians 6:1 speaks of judging with the **heart of a shepherd**. It says, "Brothers, if someone is caught in any wrongdoing, you who are spiritual should restore such a person with a gentle spirit, watching out for yourselves so you won't be tempted. Carry one another's burdens; in this way you will fulfill the law of Christ."

5. Exodus 23:1 gives us great guidance by reminding us to **avoid saying what is untrue.** I have a friend who lived a horrible life before her conversion. She is always saying, "My life is already bad enough without adding anything else to it." When you are dealing with failure in your life, the last thing you need is to have to deal with lies and untruths when what you have done is sufficiently evil enough.

6. Ephesians 4:29 tells us to **avoid saying what is unnecessary** (see also Proverbs 13:3). Again, the role of judging is to bring discipline; the role of discipline is to correct wrong direction, so tomorrow you can live in a higher standard of righteousness. All these measures are never to be about punishment; it's always about correction. I am not saying that there are never consequences to our choices. But when a leader leads with punishment, I find that to be a dangerous sign. True biblical leaders are shepherds, leading in "gentleness" (Galatians 6:1) for the sole purpose of restoring a lost sheep back to the safety of the sheepfold. Saying what is unnecessary can be like pouring salt into an open wound. When you are judging a matter for the restoration of a believer, the issue is repentance, not the vileness of the issue. The details of the horrible sin are not the issue, but true repentance and restoration of the believer. I realize that in many cases where repentance has been refused, a fact-finding committee is often assembled, and that is correct

and right, in hopes that it might lead to true repentance.

7. Proverbs 18:8 instructs us to **never be unkind** in our judgment (see also Proverbs 13:3; 15:1; 15:4; 2 Corinthians 5:18; Ephesians 4:15; James 1:19; 3:10). The sting of gossip or slander is like coming upon the scene of a horrible car wreck, finding the person pleading for help on the side of the road, and ignoring their pleas while you check your voicemail messages. When you could have been a help to someone in dire need, you tended to yourself, adding "insult to injury."

Judgment is a harsh word, so that is why the Scriptures guide us as believers to approach the subject with great caution, love, and in the fear of God, knowing full well that in the matters in which we judge, we too will be judged. It is important to note that all of us were facing judgment once upon a time in a not so distant past. We were as guilty as anyone could possibly have ever been considered guilty (Romans 3:23). Yet, in our guilt, God the Father, the Supreme Judge (Psalm 50:8; Hebrews 12:23; 1 Peter 1:17), sent His arbitrator to our final court hearing (1 Timothy 2:5). The verdict was certainly guilty and with no hope of parole (Romans 5:12). We were sentenced to "life" in prison (Ephesians 2:3; Romans 6:23). But the arbitrator whom God the Father sent became our "scape goat" (Leviticus 16:21-22; John 1:29). He became so involved with our judgment that He decided to petition the courts for our freedom (Romans 5:8). He voluntarily approached the Judgment Seat and asked for the Supreme Judge to allow a "substitution" in this case (John 3:16; Romans 3:24; 5:8; 1 Corinthians 6:20; 7:23). He took our place, bore our sorrows, and took upon Him the punishment meant for you and me (Isaiah 53: 5). The gavel came down on an old rugged hill called Mount Calvary. According to the Old Testament, blood was the only atonement for sin. So on the day of our trial, blood was spilled (Hebrews 9:22). He became our sacrificial lamb, because He who knew no sin became sin (2 Corinthians 5:21). He paid the price for our attorney's fees, and all court costs. We were fully exonerated while in a guilty state; we were set free from sin and death (John 8:32; 2 Corinthians 3:17; Galatians 5:1, 13-14; 1 Peter 2:16). Keep that in mind the next time you have to judge someone else. It might just be helpful to their case as well (Luke 7:36-50).

# END NOTES

## Chapter Six
## The Law of Judging

[1] "The Doctrine of Divine Judgment," Jake Gardner, accessed December 26, 2013; December 1, 2013, www.thedoctrineofdivinejudgment.com.

[2] Rabbi Elliot N. Dorff, *Tikkun Olam: Repairing the Broken World* (Woodstock, Vermont: Jewish Lights Publishing, 2007), 70.

[3] Dorff, *Tikkun Olam: Repairing the Broken World*, pp. 69-70.

[4] "Can or Should Christians Judge One Another?" bibleteacher.org, www.bibleteacher.org/Judging.htm.

[5] Leon Morris, *The Pillar New Testament Commentary: The Epistle to the Romans,* ed. D.A. Carson (Grand Rapids: William B. Eerdmans, 1988).

## CHAPTER SEVEN

# THE LAW OF HUMILITY

## The Knowledge Box

**The Law of Humility:** Grounded in the character of God; low in heart; a sign of genuine religion; a prerequisite for honor; a prominent Christian grace: "the noble choice to forgo your status, deploy your resources, or use your influence for the good of others before yourself."

**The Precepts:**
1. Humility Is the Essential Trait for All Church Leadership.
2. Humility Is Most Vividly Expressed in the Cross of Christ
3. Humility Is Required for Authentic Use of Your "Gifts."
4. Humility Can Be Faked by Immature Believers.
5. Humility Is the Virtue to Safeguard All Elements of Unity.

Awe—the virtue of all virtues—is the one virtue from which all other godly virtues flow. Nietzsche looked at it as "the great lie of the weak that cunningly transforms cowardice into an apparent virtue."[1] Freud described it as a masochistic guilt complex and Adler as the feeling of inferiority. Shakespeare lamented pessimistically, "Is there any genuine room in this world for 'such' a person?"[2] To the Greeks, it was the exaltation of freedom and the despising of subjection. In Homer's *Iliad*, Zeus robs a man of half of his self-worth when he brings him close to the day of servitude, while the Princess Andromache was required to be "humble" when she became a slave.[3] The Greek aristocratic culture saw the worth of a man as being determined by his parentage, and thus they despised the lowly state.

God's humility has always made the flesh of men uneasy. However, there have been those who have taken on the leadership spirit of Christ and gained the proper understanding of a leader's effectiveness, if such a leader leads from the orthodoxy of Christology. Humility is vital. Jonathan Edwards called it "distinguishing"; Kant said it was "the proper perspective of oneself."[4] Andrew Murray defined it as "the place of entire dependence upon God." Saint Thomas of Aquinas, a thirteenth–century philosopher, said it is "the byproduct of the virtue of temperance."[5] Issac the Syrian said, "Without it . . . our works, our virtues, and all of our asceticism are in vain." St. Benedict said there were twelve degrees for properly understanding how to live out a humble life. Everett L. Worthington Jr. describes it as the "quiet virtue."[6] Ilia Delio, a Franciscan sister, saw it as a form of love when she wrote: "Whenever we speak about love, we are speaking about relationships. . . . Incarnation we might say is God bending low to embrace the world in love."[7] She believes that humility is not a quality of God but the essence of God's love. Andrew

Murray would concur, because he believed that "there is no love without humility."[8]

God is calling charismatic leadership within His church to the issue of loving the very people they profess to lead. Love will change how one leads. And such love is rooted in humility, not as one of many virtues, but the virtue from which all other virtues spring. Humility is a tough pill to swallow for many leaders in the Charismatic Movement. It is even harder to define for my Evangelical believers and almost impossible for the secularist. However, John Dickson hits the mark with his definition of humility in his book, *Humilitas: A Lost Key to Life, Love, and Leadership*, where he defines humility as, "The noble choice to forgo your status, deploy your resources or use your influence for the good of others before yourself."[9]

What is humility and what do the Scriptures actually teach local church leadership about the proper application of leading with humility? First-century believers understood the word "humility" as the height of offensive language. In plain English, the word *humility* to a Greek culture was on the same playing field as a line of expletives. The word humility comes from the Latin word *humilis*, which translates as "humble, low, or from the earth."[10] The Greek and Hellenistic worlds used the word *humility* only in a negative sense. It "resonates with the state of being lowly, servile, mean, and insignificant."[11] To the Greek culture, the word *humility* was used to describe "a notable figure in prison, someone with the lack of spirit or human dignity, and a servant associated with ungodliness."[12] Even Alexander the Great tried to introduce the concept of "falling prostrate before rulers and failed when he was met with extreme Greek resistance."[13] It is amazing that Christ used the word *humility* frequently to describe Himself or the requirements for those leaders who would truly decide to follow Him, even if this meant to follow

Him inside a culture that saw such humility as a negative attribute to one's character. And, He said it knowingly to a world of Hellenistic Jews! However, this same term when applied biblically carries a positive, not a pejorative, intonation. The word *humility,* or its relation, occurs 34 times in the New Testament.

## PRECEPT ONE:
### Humility Is the Essential Trait for All Church Leadership

In churches all across America, people are too often voted in by a popular vote rather than submitted by the leaders and confirmed by the body. Too often in the American church, we fail to choose our leaders in biblical ways as we set up church boards modeled after Henry Ford rather than the precepts in God's Word. Yet, there is one nonnegotiable characteristic of all church leaders. Whether you are an usher, an elder, a deacon, a teacher, a preacher, an apostle, or worker in the altars with your gift of mercy, you are the most effective when you lead with humility. It is indispensable as a worker for Christ and such an absolute truth that even Jim Collins, the Stanford University business analyst in his best-selling book, *Good to Great,* listed eleven qualities with five levels, with five being the highest level. The one key factor reaching a level five was an attitude of humility.

> We were surprised, shocked really, to discover the type of leadership required for turning a good company into a great one. Compared to high-profile leaders with big personalities who make headlines and become celebrities, the good-to-great leaders seem to have come from Mars. Self-effacing, quiet, reserved even shy—these leaders are a paradoxical blend of personal humility and professional will. They are more like Lincoln and Socrates than Patton or Caesar.[13]

Humility is crucial for the success of a local church.

## Wisdom Point A

*The sign of a truly great leader is humility.* Truly great leaders are not tyrants. They lead with the "other" firmly in their mind. While the media may spotlight the narcissistic, selfish, and bombastic, history tells a different kind of story. John Dickson rightly believes that to be humble requires an act from a certain height. "True humility assumes the dignity or strength of the one possessing the virtue, which is why it should not be confused with having low self-esteem or being a doormat for others. In fact, I would go so far as to say that it is impossible to be humble in the real sense without a healthy sense of your own worth and abilities."[15] You find, as Paul said, "Strength is made perfect in weakness" (2 Corinthians 12:9 NKJV). Dickson goes on to point out how humility is an indispensable quality of a leader because of its power to persuade. He says humility actually enhances persuasiveness because it is such a compelling character trait. What a true statement, especially in a world where predominantly everyone you are leading is a volunteer! Leadership is fundamentally a relational issue, and so much more within the community of faith!

## Wisdom Point B

*Only leaders who embrace humility can transcend from selfhood and reach the "other."* Dr. Corné Bekker says, "The values of kenosis (humility that empties itself out for another) allows the leader to transcend narrow selfhood, to locate the 'other' in the mutuality of love, and to truly enter into the world of the follower where the leader becomes the servant of the 'other.' This is the state of mutual acceptance, vulnerability and receptivity."[16] Yves Raguin believes that humility places us in the posture of receptivity. Bekker goes on to say, "When leaders, having practiced kenosis, are able to enter the world of their followers and take the posture of their servants, relationships of mutual trust and healing are formed that in time removes the social and power distance between them in mutual liberation and transformation."[17] To make your local church the best it can be, your leaders must transcend into the lives of people. To do this requires humility. It builds relationships where pride destroys them. It encourages where pride discourages. Humility is the "grease" for every "spoke in the wheel" of ministry.

### Wisdom Point C

*Compassion is a product of humility.* What is it that causes a leader to "reach out," thus denying himself to help someone he often doesn't know personally? It is compassion. Dr. Ilia Delio says:

> Jesus, the image of the Father, reflects all of the Father's love to us, especially in the cross, where love is poured out for the healing of the world. What this means on a deeper level is that compassion is part of God's humility. Compassion is not an admirable trait that God acquired once he decided to have a creation. No, compassion is God's love that so extends itself to the other without asking for anything in return, that it may be one with the other in all things. Compassion is the Father stretching forth in love.[18]

*Compassion,* for Delio, is God's ability to "get inside the skin" of someone else in order to respond to their needs and provide care. She continues:

> The truly loving person breathes in the pain of the world and breathes out compassion. The compassionate person identifies with the suffering of others in such a way that she or he makes a space within their heart, a womb of mercy, to allow suffering persons inside and to embrace them with arms of love.[19]

THE LAW OF HUMILITY

As leaders, we must be willing to suffer with those we lead so that Christ's love may heal their wounds. It is like the salt metaphor in the Bible. Unless salt touches the meat, it has no hope of preserving it (Matthew 5:13-16). The local church needs leaders who are compassionate; thus, we need humble leaders who are compassionate leaders.

## PRECEPT TWO:
### Humility Is Most Vividly Expressed in Leadership Through the Idea of the Cross of Christ.

There are many theologians who believe that Philippians 2:6-11 was not written by the apostle Paul but by the very members of the first-century church as a leadership hymn, moments after the crucifixion of Jesus Christ. It is one of the oldest hymns in the New Testament, making it is one of the oldest passages inside the New Testament. Paul borrowed this well-known language. What is often unfortunate is the fact that the first- century church may well have known this, but the twenty-first-century church has lost its meaning in translation over the years. This Philippian Hymn is also called "The Kenotic Hymn." The word *kenosis* means to "empty out." So the deeper meaning of this passage is the implication that Christ, as our example of leadership, took His power and emptied Himself out for others, rather than use His power to be served Himself. He was kenotic, meaning He emptied Himself out as a leader. It is important to first do a small amount of research on the Book of Philippians, so you can more fully understand this passage.

### Philippi: The Culture of Status
The leadership of ancient Philippi would have awakened every morning to an optimal view, for the sea was on one side and three mountains were on the other. It was a

commanding presence as it stood upon the rocky slopes of a steep hill on Mount Pangaeum. The Macedonian city was named after Philip II, the father of Alexander the Great. Today, the city is referred to as Filibedjik. Antiquity knew her as "The Springs,"[20] and as Christians, we know her as the firstfruits of European Christianity. Her religious landscape was eclectic with the gods of Bendis, Isis, Jupiter, and Mars. There was no Jewish synagogue since "there were fewer than ten Jewish men in the city; this was the minimum requirement to establish a synagogue."[21] Her fame spread when the assassins of Julius Caesar fell upon her soil. Her official language was Latin. She was a cultural phenomenon, strategically placed along the Ignatian Way. Philippi stood as the chief city of four Roman districts. The city received the "highest possible status for a Roman provincial municipality, the *ius Italicum*, which meant that it was governed by Roman law."[22] Philippi, in all her glory, was enamored with her status as she carried a distinct civic pride regarding titles and privileges. Hellerman suggests Philippi was enamored by a social upward mobility: "Epigraphic testimonials to the social status of individuals abound in and around Philippi to a degree unparalleled elsewhere in the empire. Those who enjoyed positions of honor had an incessant desire to proclaim publicly their status in the form of inscriptions erected throughout the colony."[23] She held the second most powerful place in the ancient world next to Rome herself. The leaders of the city bore the titles of Roman power.

> Members of the community (in Philippi) came from the upper-echelons of the social ranking order, that the community experienced substantial inner and outer communal and religious conflicts, and that some of the communal conflict arose from an apparent values conflict between the Christian call for humble service and the Philippians culture value of pursuing public social honor.[24]

It is interesting that Acts alludes to the extremity that the Philippian people placed upon status and rank. In Acts 16:20, we notice the use of "captain," meaning a "very high political importance and the official vocabulary of the Hellenistic government."[25] Luke, the author of Acts, used the dignified title for magistrates in Acts 16:20, 22.

### It Was a City With a Heart for Arrogance

The people of Philippi were encompassed by a world of social status, more so than any other place within the empire of Rome. "Those who enjoyed positions of honor had an incessant desire to proclaim publicly their status in the form of inscriptions erected throughout the colony."[26] Roman citizens were quite sensitive toward the marks of inequality. Tacitus called such lower classes "citizens of repute." Aelius argued for the self-preservation of his own social elite system when he said, "Those who think that they should be superior should calculate that if they willingly destroy their inferiors, they injure their own source of pride."[27] In the *Iliad*, the honor of Odysseus was bound up with the restoration of his material possessions. Achilles' honor was dependent, not upon his character, but on the gifts that were given to him. It was Plato who first expounded to the Greek culture the meaning of honor and its relationship to ethical natures. He called it "inward honor" and referred to it as a moral element.[28]

The Philippian Hymn is found in 2:6-11. It gives us the model for the role of humility in leadership. Christ is the supreme model as He led with tremendous humility through the cross. It is no mistake that this kenotic hymn was placed in a letter to the city of Philippi, nor is it a mistake that Christ was the model of humility, for in Him we see the value of humility for leadership.

## Wisdom Point A

*The humility of Christ governs the ego (Philippians 2:5).*
This passage reads: "Make your own attitude that of Christ
Jesus." The original Greek word for *attitude* is "mind." The
word humility was originally an agricultural word known
eventually as "humus" meaning dirt, soil, or earth. The
word *Adam* comes from the Hebrew word meaning "soil
or earth." Humility, after all, is the acknowledgment of
one's insufficiency. All church leaders lead better when
they remember where they came from! The word "mind"
means to think deeper by means of our minds and our
emotions. It implies the feeling of an inward disposition.
It is actually a verb in the Greek language and implies the
use of an action by using the head and the heart. It gives
us great insight into how Jesus thought about each of
us—He led with humility with us on His mind and heart.
Great leaders lead with their followers on their hearts and
minds.

In Philippians 2:6, it reads: "Who, existing in the form
of God, did not consider equality with God something to
be used for His own advantage." If the God of the universe humbled Himself from His previous position to
serve humanity, then what else would we need as believers to believe that we too are to humble ourselves as we
lead His people? If the One who created all things walks
in humility, how should the "one" He created walk? We
should walk in humility, not exploiting our leadership positions, but using our authority for use only when it benefits the other. When we lead in the local church with an
ego, we are assuming the wrong form. The words used in
chapter 2, verse 6, do not mean "shape," but the outward
expression of the inward nature. The power of this verse
is in the absence of exploitation of His position. It's the
absence of ego. The humility of Christ governs our egos,
because it gives us the necessary form to emulate. Those
local church leaders who lead with egos have often lost

their biblical form and too often exploit their positions. When we lead as Christ, our humility governs our success and deepens our relationship with others, because we are approachable. Pride makes us unapproachable. Humility is power under constraint.

## Wisdom Point B

*The humility of Christ teaches us that the call to power is a call to serve.* In Philippians 2:7, it says: "Instead He emptied Himself by assuming the form of a slave." The word *empty* is the Greek word *kenosis* and means that Christ emptied Himself out or poured Himself out like a drink offering (2 Timothy 4:6-7). In the Greek culture, emptying out oneself as a god was absolutely unheard of; this just didn't happen. If you were a Greek god, the people were expected to "empty themselves" out for you! You yielded to its power; the power did not yield to you, and certainly not for your benefit. Yet, Christ did exactly this within this first-century culture. The underlying issue here is the self-restraint of power. Christ had all power (Matthew 28:18), and He restrained this power and used it for the benefit of the other. Kenotic power is not found in the emptying of power, but in the restraint of power, never using it to exploit other people. "We can say that the height of God's all powerfulness in creation is shown in the powerlessness of God's love on the cross. . . . It is no wonder that the cross of Jesus Christ stands as the symbol of God's omnipotence, for it is indeed, God's power to love unconditionally."[29] God's power is rooted in the love of God. This love gives out, it serves, it never seeks its own, it isn't prideful (1 Corinthians 13); it is full of compassion for the other person.

Christ's humility teaches us to restrain power and use it only for the benefit of another person. It is never to be exploited for our own benefit. This kind of humility leads the local church with passion and love for people, because the power of God is guided by love. True love never surrenders only part of itself while holding the essentials for itself; true love gives (John 3:16). It gives the power it has for the protection of the ones who are most vulnerable. God's humility is a form of power that is restrained for service.

## PRECEPT THREE:
### Humility Is Required for the Authentic Use of Your "Gifts."

Saint Basil once wrote, "If God supplies you with some gift, beg him that he might teach you how this gift can help you progress in humility . . . or else beg him to remove the gift from you so that it might not become the cause of your downfall."[30] Paul's admonishments about the gifts are preceded by, "For the grace given to me, I tell everyone among you not to think of himself more highly than he should think" (Romans 12:3). John Piper believes that Paul is not just saying use your spiritual gifts, but use them with humility. The use of spiritual gifts requires humility, because someone is always on the receiving end of their use.

### Wisdom Point A
*We are responsible for the humble stewardship of our "gifts."* Have you ever noticed that prideful people are often hiding disabilities? Their bravado increases in hopes that you would not see the cracks in their armor. As we mentioned in Romans 12:3, the apostle Paul brings up the issue of humility before he introduces the importance of working in the spiritual gifts. Saint Basil (A.D. 330–379) again gives wisdom here. He said, "Tell me why you should be proud? What do you possess that you have not received? But you have received it, why are you boasting as if you have not received it?" Basil understood that our gifts are given by grace. It you sing, you sing only by the grace of

God; if you speak, you speak only by the grace of God. If you usher, teach, lead youth, perform the work of an elder or deacon, you do so only by the grace of God. You are a slave—a steward of the manifold graces of God (Matthew 25:20-22; 1 Corinthians 4:2; 7:22; Galatians 1:15; Titus 1:7-9). The treasure is not ours, but given to us as a charge to do well (Matthew 5:16; Ephesians 2:8-10; Galatians 5:16; Titus 2:14; Hebrews 13:16). A leader who understands stewardship recognizes the value of humility, because stewardship itself implies "selflessness." When we work in our gifts with humility, we are not denying our gifts; we are expressing thankfulness for the grace of God. Douglas Hall wrote, "Stewardship describes a Christian within a world they do not own and do not control, but in one in which they act responsibly."[31] Galatians 4:2 suggests to us that we are entrusted with the gifts of God as slaves. So whatever gift you have in the local church please listen carefully. It's not about you. Slaves have no rights. You don't have a right to sing next Sunday anymore than a greeter has the right to greet at the same door every week. You have a right to work in your gifts in the humility of Christ. That would mean working where there is a need, not necessarily where there is a spotlight. Humility helps all of us to place our gifts in their proper perspectives, because those gifts are about blessing the body with service as a servant. The words of Psuedo-Macarius (Fourth-Fifth centuries) are most appropriate here:

> If one sees a puffed up person by arrogance and pride because he has received grace and even if he should perform signs and should raise the dead, if he, nevertheless, does not hold his soul as abject and humble and does not consider himself poor in spirit and an object of abhorrence, he is duped by the devil and is ignorant. Granted he has performed signs but he is not to be trusted. For signs of a Christian is this, that one is pleasing to God so as to hide oneself from human eyes.

> And even if a person should possess the complete treasures of the King, he should hide them and say repeatedly: "The treasure is not mine but another has given it to me as a charge. I am a beggar and when it so pleases, he can claim it from me".... This is the very sign of a Christian, namely, the very humility.[32]

## Wisdom Point B

*Humility brings gratitude to the gifts and talents in others.* The humble heart is always grateful to God. The humble heart trusts God in knowing that the Holy Spirit makes no mistakes in their distributions (1 Corinthians 14:1.) Real humility is needed in your local church, because it keeps people from being jealous of the gifts of other believers. Humility is actually having a real sense of your own talents and abilities; it isn't a call to curb your strengths. To be humble in this arrogant world takes a lot of self-confidence. It takes even more confidence to acknowledge and celebrate the gifts of someone else. As John 3:27 tells us, "No one can receive a single thing unless it's given to him from heaven." Honoring the gifts of others safeguards unity by the mighty power of the humility of Christ.

## PRECEPT FOUR:
### Humility Can Be Faked by Immature Believers.

> Under the old Blue Bridge in Nashville, Tennessee, where the destitute used to live, a homeless man chased me with a knife. In the winter of 2006, on my way to bury an elderly lady who died of cancer, I flipped my truck 15 feet in the air while it rolled five times across the snow and ice. On a retreat with teenagers from Northwood Temple Church, I fell out of a canoe into freezing water and almost died from hypothermia and shock. One Thanksgiving weekend, I returned home from Lee University to find our house in disarray from a robbery—while unknown to me, the culprits were hiding in my parents' bedroom.

We all have lived through dangerous points in our lives, but never a more dangerous one than when we find ourselves around people who hide their pride through what Paul called "false humility" (Colossians 2:18).

## Wisdom Point A

*False humility is spiritual botulism to unity.* False humility attacks our central nervous system in the body of Christ. It stuns our movement and takes our breath away. The body becomes numb when false humility enters into it because the preciousness of trust and community are rendered immovable. It is the most acute of all toxins in the body of Christ. The phrase "false humility" is used only twice in Scriptures (NKJV). Both times are actually recorded in Colossians 2:18, 23 and are surrounded by four verses on legalism. Paul tells the Colossian church that such pompous leaders could actually end up disqualifying them from the cause of Christ! It's dangerous because it is the faking of a submitted life in Christ. How do you spot such diseases in the local church?

## Wisdom Point B

### Twenty-One Ways to Identify False Humility

1. *An act of humility:* That is exactly what it is—an act. So end the play and stop the production by asking these people to really serve. The person who struggles with false humility knows how to act as a servant, but can't really serve. You can't fake joyfully serving others.

2. *Give people small tasks to fulfill.* If they are not faithful with the little things, then pride is masking their real motives. Pride wants the big jobs; pride loves the spotlight; and pride hates the insignificant and the unpopular.

3. *Try to teach people something important.* At the end of the day, humility is known by a person's ability to be taught. Humility is teachability.

4. *Watch for people who use their power for their own benefit.* Humility will always use power to benefit the other person. False humility will use power to set up leadership structures, which at the end of the day will serve only them and their leadership positions.

5. *Give a person a gift.* I learned a long time ago that it took more humility to receive a complement or a gift than it did to reject one. False humility will bristle at being on the receiving end of a gift. Individuals like the power of giving, not the vulnerability of neediness.

6. *Give a person a book.* I will never forget the day I realized that giving a book to someone was a special art. I love to read, so giving me a book is like giving a kid a candy bar. But never give an insecure leader a book, because he/she will resent it and feel like you had an ulterior motive. This type of person is not secure enough to learn in front of you or through your giving.

7. *A leader with false humility likes to look humble.* So, ask this individual to follow a lesser-known leader. Great leaders are even better followers. Placing a leader with false humility in a lesser position of authority will force his inner character out into the light. When the only time you can lead is when you are "the leader," then you are not a leader.

8. *The individual with false humility serves you with a subtle ulterior motive.* This person may work hard; he/she may praise you; and this person will certainly tell you how much he/she loves and appreciates you. Don't trust it. These people are waiting for their shot of success through the pathway of your hard work and successful relationships. You are bait to them. And you will recognize them by how they leave your presence.

9. *Leaders with false humility will start ignoring you when you lose or change positional authority.* False humility only loves you when you are in charge.

10. *People with false humility are never grateful.* They truly believe that you have added nothing of value to their lives and that the climb to success was accomplished by no one but them.

11. *A leader with false humility longs for positional authority positions.*

12. *Leaders with false humility never honor long-term relationships.* They honor relationships as long as they are receiving.

13. *People with false humility get angry when they fear embarrassment.* If you hurt their pride, you will stir their anger.

14. *Image is more important to an individual with false humility than character.* Image is character without substance.

15. *A leader with false humility is never actually vulnerable.*

16. *You can buy the silence or vote of a leader with false humility.*

17. *Leaders with false humility will never defend you when you find yourself left alone with the Enemy.* They silently wait for your weakness to be exposed and then humbly respond in pseudo love when in the privacy of your presence.

18. *Leaders with false humility will always answer a question based on what is politically correct for them.*

19. *People with false humility hide from controversial issues by being silent for fear of being disliked or losing political favor.*

20. *A leader with false humility will hide until your weak moment.* Then, he/she will "humbly" lead.

21. *People with false humility use the appearance of humility to hide from the spotlight.* They fear the exposure of light that might one day shine on their true dark deeds.

Humility is our greatest asset as we move the kingdom of God forward. People with false humility will never serve the kingdom of God, because their hearts have failed the kenotic test of Philippians 2:6-11. Our Great God has sent His Son as a humble servant to all of us. This alone should stand as the model for all of us as we engage people through our leadership in the local church.

# END NOTES

## Chapter Seven
## The Law of Humility

[1] André Louf, *The Way of Humility* (Kalamazoo, Mich.: Cistercian Publications, 2007), 4.

[2] Jeanine Grenberg, *Kant and the Ethics of Humility: A Story of Dependence, Corruption, and Virtue* (New York: Cambridge University Press, 2005), 137.

[3] Gerhard Kittel, Geoffrey William Bromiley, and Gerhard Friedrich, *Theological Dictionary of the New Testament*, Logos Software (Grand Rapids: Eerdmans, n.d.), 1.

[4] Grenberg, *Kant and the Ethics of Humility*, p.137.

[5] Louf, *The Way of Humility*, p. 7.

[6] Everett L. Worthington, *Humility: The Quiet Virtue* (Philadelphia: Templeton Foundation Press, 2007), 14.

[7] Ilia Delio, O.S.F. *The Humility of God: A Franciscan Perspective* (Cincinnati: St. Anthony Messenger Press, 2005), 30.

[8] Andrew Murray, *Humility* (Radford, Va.: Wilder Publications, 2008), 29.

[9] John Dickson, *Humilitias: A Lost Key to Life, Love, and Leadership* (Grand Rapids: Zondervan, 2001), 24.

[10] "Humility," *Wikipedia, The Free Dictionary*, n.a., 2008, http://en.wikipedia.org/wiki/humility/(accessed October 28, 2008).

[11]Louf, *The Way of Humility*, viii.

[12] Gerhrd Kittel, Geoffrey William Bromiley, and Gerhard Friedrich, *Theological Dictionary of the New Testament*, Logos Software (Grand Rapids: Eerdmans, n.d.), 1.

[13] Kittel, et.al. *Theological Dictionary of the New Testament*, p. 1.

[14] Jim Collins, *Good to Great: Why Some Companies Make the Leap . . . and Others Don't* (New York: HarperCollins, 2001), 13.

[15] Dickson, *Humilitias: A Lost Key to Life, Love, and Leadership*, pp. 24-25.

[16] "The Philippians Hymn (2:5-11) As an Early Mimetic Christological Model of Christian Leadership in Roman Philippi," *Inner Reflections on Leadership*, Corné Bekker, January 27, 2010, August 1, 2006, www.innerresourcesfor-leaders.blogspot.com/.

[17] "The Philippians Hymn (2:5-11), www.innerres-ourcesforleaders.blogspot.com/.

[18] Delio, *The Humility of God*, p. 81.

[19] Delio, *The Humility of God*, p. 92.

[20] Walter A. Elwell, ed., *The Baker Encyclopedia of the Bible*, (Grand Rapids: Baker House Books, 1988), 1,675.

[21] Craig Evans, ed., *The Bible Knowledge Background Commentary: Acts-Philemon* (Colorado Springs, Colo.: Cook Communications, 2004), 574.

22 Evans, *The Bible Knowledge Background Commentary: Acts-Philemon*, p. 574.

23 J.H. Hellerman, *The Humiliation of Christ in the Social World of Roman Philippi: Part One* (Bibliotheca Sacra, 2003), 328.

24 "The Philippians Hymn (2:5-11), www.innerres-ourcesforleaders.blogspot.com/.

25 Kittel, et.al., *Theological Dictionary of the New Testament*, p. 1.

26 Joseph Hellerman, *Reconstructing Honor in Roman Christi as Curus Pudorum: Society for New Testament Studies Monograph Series* (New York: Cambridge University Press, 2005), 328.

27 Hellerman, *Reconstructing Honor in Roman Christi as Curus Pudorum*, p. 328.

28 Walter A. Elwell and Phillip W. Comfort, eds., *The Tyndale Bible Dictionary* (Wheaton, Ill.: Tyndale Publishing, 2001), 611.

29 Ilia Delio, *Franciscan Prayer* (Cincinnati, Ohio: St. Anthony Messenger Press, 2004), 42-43.

30 Louf, *The Way of Humility*, p. 18.

31 Douglas Hall, *The Steward: A Biblical Symbol Comes of Age* (Grand Rapids: William B. Eerdmans Publishing, 1990.

32 Louf, *The Way of Humility*, p. 36.

# THE LAW OF LEADERSHIP: PART ONE

 —— **The Knowledge Box** ——

**The Law of Leadership:** It gives an organization its vision and ability to translate that vision into a godly reality. It is the art of getting things accomplished through people. It is influence in thinking, behavior, and development. It is a kind of influence that provides purpose, direction, motivation, and character. It is motivated by love and care when initiated by believers.

**The Precepts:**
1. Leaders in the Local Church Are Ambassadors for Jesus Christ.
2. The Demands of Community Require an Order to Leadership.

Leadership on any level in a local church is often difficult work if it's done correctly. Whether you are leading a disgruntled Board of Elders, trying to convince an alcoholic grandmother into attending rehab, launching a new ministry to the poor, or working with an adulterous man, it all requires this one, seemingly small, often unconscious trait—influence. I often find myself thinking about secular leadership where one has another's financial future in his/her hands. However, when leading in a nonprofit organization, there are no financial incentives. You can't reward with promotions or extra vacation time. It's more difficult than that, because your only power to lead is found through your character and ability to influence people. No one has the antiquated luxury of positional authority anymore. I like the old proverb that says, "If you think you're leading and no one is following you, then you're only taking a walk!" How true!

Leadership has been studied for hundreds of years. Mill manufacturers in the South first started studying it as a science in the days when people would swear that leaders were born with certain traits. Men like Frederick Winslow Taylor emerged by defining the science of management. Max Weber, Fred Fiedler, Kurt Lewin, and R.M. Stogdill contributed an immense amount of thought to the subject of leadership. Today, people pay thousands of dollars to be trained for leadership positions. Some still believe leaders are born; however, I could not disagree more. I believe leaders are made. What makes a great leader? Fire, testings, temptations, troubles, and trials all contribute to making a leader. In 1 Peter 1:6-7, it says, "You rejoice in this, though now for a short time you have to struggle in various trials so that the genuineness of your faith—more valuable than gold, which perishes though refined by fire—may result in praise, glory, and honor at the revelation of Jesus Christ." First Corinthians 11:19 says, "There must indeed, be factions among you, so that those who are approved may be recognized among you." When you look at the great leaders in the Bible, you don't find the lap of comfort; what you find are men and women who paid the price for great leadership:

- Abraham and his faith to build a nation (Genesis 18:18);
- Moses and his journey in growing and leading a vast organization with multitudes of people (Deut. 1:15);
- David's passion to place God first (2 Samuel 6:14; Acts 13:22);
- The prophets had boldness to speak truth to the powerful (2 Kings 1:16);
- The disciples had leadership abilities in organizing the infant movement (Acts 6:2; 17:6).

These all show us the roles of biblical leaders. Our local churches need leaders of character and men and women who are sold out to God. The local church needs men and women who will follow, commit, and uphold church leadership; after all, we are ambassadors for a King.

## PRECEPT ONE:
### Leaders in the Local Church
### Are Ambassadors for Jesus Christ.

In biblical times, when they called you an ambassador, you were thought to be functioning as a representative of a ruler's authority. The word was used to speak of the emperor's legates and of the leaders of his embassies between towns. "It was universally accepted that an ambassador, whatever his message and however delicate or risky his mission, would be treated with respect and dignity, accorded appropriate hospitality, and guaranteed a safe exit. To disregard or insult the envoy was to disregard or insult the sender."[1] In this world of antiquity, to be an ambassador implied three things:

1. You had been commissioned for a special assignment.
2. You were the official representative of the sender.
3. You had the right to exercise the authority of the sender.

Ambassadors do not act on their own authority, but under the commission of a great authority who sent them. In ancient times, they were sent out from the king as envoys to foreign countries as a sign of friendship and goodwill in hopes of establishing healthy relationships. These ambassadors often pleaded the cases for the various locations in which they journeyed to the king on behalf of the relationship they would make. The leaders in your local church are ambassadors for Jesus Christ. They have been given delegated authority to lead in the special assignment of their calling. They are the official representative of Jesus Christ on earth and have the right to exercise His authority on earth (Matthew 28:18.)

**Wisdom Point A**

*To scorn an ambassador or to mistreat him is to scorn and mistreat the government that sent him.* In ancient Rome, an ambassador held the responsibility of bringing others into the family of the Roman Empire. Paul, by his use of this word, is implying that leaders in God's house are actually ambassadors who speak for the King, thus inviting others to join His royal family. To reject their plea is to reject the plea for the King of kings Himself.

To mistreat the local leaders in your church is to mistreat Christ. It just doesn't get any plainer than that! So many people love to mention how "God will hold that pastor accountable!" Yes, He will. However, He will also hold church members accountable for how they treated their pastors, elders, deacons, and church leaders. Were you a burden to lead, or were you a blessing? God knows, and as Hebrews 13:17 says, "Obey your leaders and submit to them, for they keep watch over your souls as those who will give an account, so that they can do this with joy and not with grief, for that would be unprofitable for you." The word *obey* actually means "to be moved by kind words." The thought of your Christian leaders should move you to think kind and warm thoughts of them. The word *submit* means to "yield, cease to fight, or to surrender." You are not in God's will when you fight every issue your leaders bring up. I knew of one church that fired their pastor for wanting to have a say in the individual they were going to hire as a youth pastor. The Bible tells us that our leaders "watch over our souls." This means they are attentive to spiritual things and that this calling is a sobering reality because they will directly give an account before God as to their watchfulness.

### Wisdom Point B

*To send him away is to break off relations with the government and the ruler he represents.* Too often there is abuse within spiritual authority; however, this fact does not negate the greater realities that spiritual authority does exist. It not only exists, but it is also directly connected to the authority of Christ. Protestants have a really tough time with this one. But our Catholic friends grasp this idea better. In the Bible, ambassadors could not be independent. They could not speak in their own name or communicate their own ideas. What they did, however, was bring the presence of the one they were representing. Second Corinthians 5:20 says, "We are ambassadors for Christ, certain that God is appealing through us, we plead on Christ's behalf." The grave danger of rejecting an ambassador is equal to rejecting the one who sent him. The ambassador of God has been sent to reconcile humanity to the love of God. If we reject His ambassadors, then the appeal to be reconciled is null and void. Romans 10:14-15 says, "But how can they call on Him they have not believed in? And how can they believe without hearing about Him? And how can they hear without a preacher? And how can they preach unless they are sent?" The Greek word for preacher is actually "herald" and has the implicit notion that this herald carries the message for a higher authority. This is the way God saves. Romans 10:17 says, "So faith comes from what is heard, and what is heard comes through the message about Christ." Therefore, the message of Christ is impossible without divine communication. Preachers spring forth first by divine command. They have been sent by God. Isaiah 52:7 reminds us, "How beautiful on the mountains are the feet of the herald, who proclaims peace, who brings news of good things, who proclaims salvation, who says to Zion, 'Your God reigns!'" An offense to a man or woman of God is an offense to God himself. They are messengers of His sovereignty and have been accredited to act on behalf of His name. This concept of priests being messengers of God is a concept rooted firmly in Hebraic culture. First Chronicles 16:22 says, "Do not touch My anointed ones or harm My prophets." God uses the possessive pronoun "My" in describing His ministers. He has consecrated His peculiar people to be ministers of reconciliation (2 Corinthians 5:18-20). When we reject the pastors (Ephesians 4:11-13) whom God sent, we are rejecting His messengers and the voice of reconciliation. It is not a personal offense to the pastor or church leader; it is strictly an offense to sovereignty.

### Wisdom Point C

*The role of the priesthood is ancient and blessed.* God wants to bless you and your local church. But how does this blessing come to us? Ancient Judaism records from Hilel in Avos 1:12: "Be among the disciples of Aaron the Kohen, who was a lover of peace and a pursuer of peace, who was a lover of people and drew them close to the Torah."[2] To a Jewish man, the blessings on his family were to be pronounced by a Kohanim—a priest. You may be asking, "Aren't we all now made holy (Hebrews 10:10) and priests (1 Peter 2:5) for God in the New Testament?" The answer is yes and no, because there is still a separation between the body and the priesthood.

In ancient Israel, "Korach, one of the nation's most distinguished citizens, amassed a significant following and they sought to repudiate the designation of Aaron as the sole Kohen Gadol. (Aaron was the first High Priest: Kohen Gadol.) Since every Jew had heard God's voice at Sinai, they argued, all the people are holy."[3] So why should Aaron, the Levitical priesthood be considered "Kohen Gadol," the high priest with the function of unifying Israel as one nation when all of Israel heard God's voice? Korach and his rebels wanted all of Israel to assume the role as the voice of God to unify the people, not just Aaron. Logically, it made sense to the Jews in the Old Testament, and it may seem even more logical to assume this position in the New Testament since 1 Peter 2:5, 9 says:

> You yourselves, as living stones, are being built into a spiritual house for a holy priesthood to offer spiritual sacrifices acceptable to God through Jesus Christ. . . . But you are a chosen race, a royal priesthood, a holy nation, a people for His possession, so that you may proclaim the praises of the One who called you out of darkness into His marvelous light.

Just as Aaron was a symbol of unity and reconciliation for Israel, pastors and ministers today should be symbols of unity and reconciliation. No religious law can be sufficient if the church is destroyed by strife. Here is what Rabbi Nosson Scherman says about the role of the priest as unifier to both God and man.

> Aaron strove to institute peace among Israel, the peace that exists when man is at harmony with himself, because he is living according to the tenets of

> harmony with his fellows, because he is happy at
> their good fortune and they assist him in achieving
> his. By pursuing peace, Aaron unified Israel. He saw
> unity as a means, not an end, however. The Mishnah
> (Avos 1:12) describes Aaron as a lover and pursuer
> of peace and a lover of people, but it does not stop
> there—the Mishnah concludes by making clear the
> underlying motive of his activities, and he drew (the
> people) close to the Torah…By his personal example
> as well as by his preaching, he established the prin-
> ciple that man's noblest goal is to serve God as He
> commanded and that man's most satisfying success
> is to take a step toward that goal.[4]

Pastors, like the Levitical priesthood are not called to perform rituals they are called with the primary responsibility of reconciliation of people to God. Ministers seek to connect those who are far from God and like any great shepherd they seek the happiness and well-being of those whom they lead. This kind of sacrificial leadership and heart for unifying God and man is what brought the Shekinah upon him. So, this priest of God carried with him the presence of God and the collective presence of the people whom he was leading (Israel). He, the priest was to consecrate himself, as were the people, thus each one's holiness was to reinforce the other. I told my congregation last Sunday, "My character, or lack thereof, affects you, and your character, or lack thereof, affects me." When we live poor moral lives, it really does have an effect on the rest of the body. The Old Testament priest represented God and the people, and it was his office that led and kept the unity of Spirit.

This priesthood, like the ambassador, did not act on his own behalf. "They are representatives of the people even to the point where their vestments are paid for by communal funds, in order to demonstrate…that they act for all of Israel."[5] It was the mission of unity and reconciliation that created this role of priest. A healthy church acts in many ways as a healthy Jewish community, because they believed.

> True peace is the presence of harmony, when every man fulfills his proper function and every resource is utilized properly...Aaron chose to eradicate strife and sin by elevating the combatants and refining sinners. That path is the best, but sometimes it is inadequate, as in the situation Phineas faced, a frightful situation in which the only way to exercise love and create peace was to remove the source of strife.[6]

Spiritual authority is here to establish order so that peace might reign, and this is and always will be, the essence of the priesthood—the blessing of peace between God and man and man with himself. The ancient rabbis believed that Aaron loved peace and pursued it by love. The Zohar teaches that a "Kohen (priest) who does not love his congregation should not ascend the platform to utter the blessings."[7] Here is where we find the New Testament concept of a loving shepherd (John 10:11.) The priesthood operates out of love for the people of God on behalf of God himself.

### General Office of Believers

It is important to note that all believers carry the responsibility of the priesthood in the New Testament. Tim Keller, in his book *Center Church*, does a great job of pointing this out. He acknowledges that the Bible refers to every believer as a prophet, priest, and king: A prophet, because believers are called to bring truth to the people around them; a priest because believers are to serve sympathetically; and a king because we are all supposed to call others into love that is accountable. Each of the members of the body has been given a "gift" for ministry. Keller believes that this is so because God wants the service to Christ to arise out of the grassroots of a local church. I believe Keller is correct that the Body has a special place through "general offices" in the local church. Keller does make a note of a "special office" created by the same Holy Spirit.

> The very same Spirit who generates the spontaneous, explosive ministry and growth is also the giver of the gifts of apostle, prophet, and pastor/ teacher (Ephesians 4:11), as well as of governance (Romans 12:8). To be exercised, these gifts must be publically recognized by the congregation, which requires some kind of organization. There is no way to exercising the gift of governing (Romans 12:8) unless we have an institutional structure—elections, bylaws, ordination, and standards for accreditation. No one can govern without some level of agreement by the whole church about what powers are given to the governors and how these powers are given to the governors and how these powers are legitimately exercised. So the growth and flourishing of spontaneous ministry depends on some institutional elements being in place.[8]

To Keller, this office represents the way Jesus Christ has ordered His church by the Spirit's wooing. He makes a fantastic point when he states: "Jesus commissions the leaders of the church by assigning them gifts, and so when we select our church leaders, we are simply recognizing the calling and gifts of the Lord."[9] This means that it is the Holy Spirit who calls men and women into this office. We all know that there are people who do not feel called into full-time ministry, but they do teach and should evangelize. However, a growing church demands structure and order to facilitate new converts and manage the body in such gifts. There are people with the gift of mercy who will lead large outreaches of mercy that require a fully committed life, not just a service as a body member. To say that God himself has called men and women into the priesthood and they hold His delegated authority as His ambassadors is not to diminish the office of the believers or the importance of their gifts. No man is an island unto himself. The body has need of a head, and the head has need of a body. What is essential here for you and me to realize is that both these functions, the general office (gifts) and the "special office," are both called by the same Spirit. Healthy local churches have a clear order of spiritual authority that serves in their calling out of deep love with a strong mission for reconciling man to God. This same healthy church is full of members who know who they are in Christ and understand their personal "gifts of the Holy Spirit." This unique balance is what grows a church according to Ephesians 2:21: "The whole building being put together by Him, grows into a holy sanctuary in the Lord." Understanding these "special offices" created by the Holy Spirit is crucial for the success of establishing a healthy, unified, and evangelistic church.

## PRECEPT TWO:
### The Demands of Community Require a System of Order, Which Establishes Leadership.

Even the fathers of leadership science knew that the more people you have to lead, the more workers you might need. Early leadership theorists often began with the

Scripture account in Exodus 18:25 where Jethro tells Moses that the load he is carrying is too much for one person. His father-in-law teaches him a principle of leadership that has defined management for ages by dividing up the workload under leaders of 10, 50, 100, and 1000. Unfortunately, the ignoring of this verse has been the silver bullet to finish off every preacher who died on the battlefield. As I travel the globe, too often I find exhausted godly men and women who are trying to do everything themselves. And too many times they are forced to do so from an antiquated expectation of what it means to be a pastor. I have a real heart for pastors and the people they lead to be healthy, because we are never going to fulfill the Great Commission until we build healthy churches to hold them! That has been God's plan for over 2,000 years, and I strongly suspect He isn't going to change His mind anytime soon (Matthew 16:8)!

**Wisdom Point A**

*There are distinct offices for spiritual leadership.* One man or woman was never meant to be the church or to build the church. As a matter of fact, God in His infinite wisdom preordained the building of His church and said: "I will build My church, and the forces of Hades will not overpower it" (Matthew 16:18). Notice the personal pronoun "My" once again. This possessive phrase strictly implies ownership; He calls the "church" His. I find it further interesting that Jesus Christ never once looked at the twelve disciples and said: "You are My church." He reserved the title "church" for the body of believers, specifically those called out to a special meeting. This wonderful invention of Christ would require specific order and that order has been laid out in the Church Epistles. Our problem today is the culture that we have developed via the Catholic Church, Protestant Reformation, and the Great Awakening, which created an ecclesiastical body that eventually forsook the involvement of laity. And because we have lost this original order, we have lost the effectiveness of the original local church.

In the Book of Ephesians 1:23 and Colossians 1:18, it tells us that Christ is the head of the Body. Second Timothy 3:15-17 instructs the church that we are all subject to the Scriptures as our rule of discipline and life. No one has independent authority apart from Christ and His Word. Jesus delegated this power to the Apostles (Matthew 28:18; Ephesians 5:23). Jesus started the multiplication of disciples as leaders in Luke 10:1-24 when He sent out the Seventy. After His ascension in Acts 1:15-26, we find that the responsibility for the continual development of order and leadership appointments began to fall on the Apostles. Their first organizational action was to replace Judas. We find in Acts 6:1-4, that their second known action was the creation of leaders for practical ministry. The Apostles were commissioned by Jesus to preach the Word, teach, and make disciples (Matthew 28:18; Mark 1:4; Luke 3:3; Acts 2:1-20; 8:35; 1 Corinthians 2:12-13; 7:17; 14:37-38; Ephesians 2:20; 2 Thessalonians 3:14; 2 Timothy 4:2). The Apostles were being burdened down by the practical ministry tasks before them—the needs of widows, and feeding the poor, etc. So, the Apostles distinguished between the ministry of the Word and waiting on tables. Acts 6:1-5 says:

> In those days, as the number of the disciples was multiplying, there arose a complaint by the Hellenistic Jews against the Hebraic Jews that their widows were being over looked in the daily distribution. Then the Twelve summoned the whole company of the disciples and said, "It would not be right for us to give up preaching about God to wait on tables. Therefore, brothers, select from among you seven men of good reputation, full of the Spirit and wisdom, who we can appoint to this duty. But we will devout ourselves to prayer and to the preaching ministry. The proposal pleased the whole company.

While we can notice a distinction between the gifts of the priesthood and laity, what we cannot find is any attempt to separate the two from service together. What is so important for the growth and success of your local church is the order of ministry found in the Word of God. In Matthew 26:5 and Acts 5:26, we see a clear distinction between the rulers and priests of Israel from the people of Israel. In Hebrews 5:3, we find a distinction between the high priest and the priest. However, in Hebrews 4:16; 9:10, we can also find very clearly in the Scriptures that every believer now has access to God. Here is what is truly important for your church. While there are differences and distinctions between the priesthood (Ephesians 4:11) and laity, there are to be no attempts to separate them. They need each other and are codependent upon each other's giftings.

In Acts chapters 7 and 8, we see where two disciples/deacons, Stephen and Philip, both preached and taught the Word of God. When the church expanded into Asia and Europe, such a mission called for greater organization. We see in Acts 14:23, the first mention of New Testament Christianity's reference to "Elders." The Bible actually gives a local church a bit of leeway in establishing elders and deacons. We know for sure they were appointed by apostolic authority (see Acts 20:28; Titus 1:5-9; 1 Thessalonians 5:12; Hebrews 13:7). Later, Paul tells the young pastor Timothy of the Ephesian church the defining characteristics of such elders or bishops. We know that these elders were the shepherds over the "flock of God" (1 Peter 5:2). The Pauline characteristics in 1 Timothy 3:1-7 and Titus 1:5-9, continue the theological understanding of the sacredness of a "calling" and the "laying on of hands" by ordaining (Acts 6:6; 13:2, 3; 1 Timothy 4:14; 5:22). It is interesting to note that the Apostles called themselves elders (1 Peter 5:1; 2 John 1; 3 John 1). Throughout time, the title "Bishop" began to refer to those men who were over cities and regions. Originally, before the growth of the local church, this title referred to elders (Acts 20:17, 28; Titus 1:5-7).

> Recently, I was standing in the ancient city of Smyrna in Turkey, which is today called Izmir. I strolled through the ancient agora and thought about the persecutions that took place in this city. One such martyrdom was the "Bishop" of Smyrna called Polycarp. Polycarp was a disciple of John the apostle. Saint Jerome wrote that John as the "Bishop" of Smyrna had ordained Polycarp.

There are countless stories within the first century where men were commissioned as "Bishops" over regions due to the unbelievable growth of the local church (Acts 17:6). The efficiency of this fledging organization is a marvel still today. The order that growth established is possible today as is the growth that came from this order long ago. Paul instructs the church in 1 Thessalonians 5:12-13: "Now we ask you, brothers, to give recognition to those who labor among you and lead you in the Lord and admonish you, and to regard them very highly in love because of their work." Leadership in a local church is a necessity as is the involvement of laity. Together they have the power to grow a sapling into a mighty oak tree.

### Wisdom Point B

*Jesus Christ personally created offices for spiritual leadership to lead the local church.* The Holy Spirit has given each saint a spiritual gift to use for the edification of the local church (Romans 12:6-8; 1 Corinthians 12:4-21; Ephesians 4:7-13). There is a difference between operating in a spiritual gift and operating in a spiritual office of leadership. The Holy Spirit gives the first, whereas, Jesus Christ himself gives the later. The Book of Ephesians says that Jesus Christ personally gave specific gifts of leadership to administer the church, for the organization of their giftings, and for the maturity of the body. I believe that the functions of the offices mentioned in Ephesians 4:11 still operate within the twenty-first-century church, albeit under different names or in different fashions, but nevertheless, still operate to mature the believers. No one is better at helping us understand this modern day-dilemma than Alan Hirsh and Tim Catchim. Their book, *The Permanent Revolution: Apostolic Imagination and Practice in the 21st Century*, is a must-have for your bookshelf. They like to call it a Theo-genetic code and practically imply that it's a silver bullet against the enemy of the church. Theologically, I wonder if they are not correct in their assumptions. The problem is, as Upton Sinclair once said: "It is difficult to get a man to understand something when his salary depends upon his not understanding it."[10] Hence, the previous history lesson! In Ephesians 4:11, it gives us the details of Jesus Christ's gift of leadership offices for the development of the saints in the New Testament church. There certainly were offices in the first-century church, but I cannot find where they were dismantled or even hints in the Scripture where they would have ceased.

In Ephesians 4:11-12, it says, "And He personally gave some to be apostles, some prophets, some evangelists, some pastors and teachers, for the training of the saints in the work of ministry, to build up the body of Christ." The first point we should make is that it was Jesus Christ who "personally" gave, not just the office, but the men and women for the office. He created the office, and He called the officers. Here, unlike the gifts in 1 Corinthians 12, the gifts are the individuals themselves. And this is what I want to focus on as we look at New Testament leadership. The point here is not to argue whether these gifts are used today, and I believe that they are, but to argue that a separate office existed that was distinct from the body. This was clearly pointed out in the New Testament.

Paul is pointing to their use as leaders who equip the body for ministry. He specifically writes that such offices were given by Jesus Christ as a gift to the body. He mentions apostles, which extended the work of Christ, brought order, and established Christianity in new places, much like modern-day church planters or networks of churches who build the gospel effectively into regions. An *apostle* builds movements and develops churchwide health. Ironically, the apostle was often called an ambassador. Barnabas was also called an apostle (Acts 14:4, 14), as were others (Romans 16:7; 2 Corinthians 8:23; Philippians 2:25). The *prophet* was the one who saw eternity and received special revelation. They, as Hirsh and Catchim said, were "guardians of faithfulness." The prophet calls the people of God to live faithfully and to abandon the values of this world. They speak truth strongly and boldly. Paul tells us in Ephesians 2:20 that God's household is "built on the foundation of the apostles and prophets, with Christ Jesus himself as the cornerstone." Prophets are passionate speakers for righteousness and sense deeply the drawing of God's Spirit. They are not afraid to confront wrong living. They hate the status quo and anyone who functions as a guard on its wall. We need their prophetic urgency.

The *evangelist* fulfilled a role that was itinerant and stationary. Today's model of the evangelist, I believe, is often misguided (2 Corinthians 8:18; 2 Timothy 4:5). They recruit body members to reach out to the community. They publically share the gospel in a variety of ways. They are bold apologists as they proclaim the gospel presence to the lost. Philip was considered a deacon and an evangelist (Acts 21:8; 8:4-12). They invite, they call forth, and they proclaim the reunion of man and the gospel.

Paul wrote next, "some pastors and teachers." In the Greek, these two words are connected only by one article, which implies a very close connection with each other. There are some theologians who argue that these two offices are one in the same. However, in the Word, we can clearly see that while all pastors are teachers, not all teachers are pastors, because Paul tells Timothy that all "bishops" must be able to teach (1 Timothy 3:2). The word *pastor* is used in the New Testament only here in Ephesians 4:11. The word *shepherd* is used multiple times (John 21:16; Acts 20:28; 1 Peter 5:2). The function of the pastor can be the same as an elder or bishop (Acts 14:23; 20:17, 28; Philippians 1:1; 1 Timothy 4:14; 5:17, 19). These pastors exercise the gift of leadership through nurturing and caring for the "flock of God" (Acts 20:28-29; 1 Peter 5:2-3). They managed the church (Romans 12:8; 1 Thessalonians

5:12). And, they were to be regarded with love for "their work" (1 Thessalonians 5:12). They model after the "Good Shepherd" (Matthew 18:12-14; Luke 15:3-7; John 10:11-18; Hebrews 13:20; 1 Peter 2:25; 5:4). Shepherd/pastors lead the congregation into maturity. They lead the local church into spiritual maturity and the community into reconciliation to Christ. Pastors provide primary leadership for the local church (1 Timothy 3:1-5; Titus 1:5-9). They protect congregations (1 Peter 2:25; 5:1-4). They are to minister, preach, care for, instruct and equip the believers. They are to be mature believers (Acts 14:23).

The concept of *teacher* is closely connected to the concept of pastor. They give expositions and application to Scripture (Acts 15:35; 18:11, 25; Romans 2:20, 21; Colossians 3:16; Hebrews 5:12). They explain the Word of God (1 Corinthians 4:17; Romans 16:17; 2 Thessalonians 2:15; 2 Timothy 2:2; 3:10). They actually carry an authoritative function in the local church (2 Timothy 1:13-14; 2:1-2; 1 Timothy 3:2; 5:17; Titus 2:2). Their roles were to be duplicated, and every teacher was encouraged to equip other teachers (1 Timothy 4:13, 16; 2 Timothy 2:2). All teachers were encouraged to live what they taught (Ephesians 4:20-21). This is crucial to the growth of the local church, because you can't obey what you do not know. Their wisdom brings understanding to the body. It can be an office or a spiritual gift, because teaching is a normal part of church life (Romans 12:7; Colossians 3:16; 2 Timothy 2:24). When this role functions as a gift, it can help the pastor train saints to do the work of ministry (Ephesians 4:8-11).

It is abundantly clear that God has always set men to represent His interest on this earth. From the early priesthood of the Levitical rights to the New Testament emergence of office gifts personally given by Jesus Christ for the maturity of the saints, we see a path of distinctive leadership—leadership different from the leadership of the body and its spiritual gifts, yet never separated.

# End Notes

## Chapter 8
## The Law of Leadership: Part One

[1] Murray J. Harris, *The Second Epistle to the Corinthians: A Commentary on the Greek Text* (Grand Rapids: William B. Eerdmans Publishing Company, 2005).

[2] Rabbis Nosson Scherman and Meir Zlotowitz, eds., *Bircas Kohanim: The Priestly Blessing: Background, Translations, and Commentary Anthologized From Talmudic, Midrashic, and Rabbinic Sources* (New York: Mesorah Publications, 1991), 13.

[3] Rabbis Scherman and Zlotowitz, eds., 15.

[4] Ibid., 16.

[5] Ibid., 22.

[6] Ibid., 23.

[7] Ibid., 24.

[8] Tim Keller, *Center Church: Doing Balanced, Gospel-Centered Ministry in Your City* (Grand Rapids: Zondervan, 2012), 346.

[9] Keller, *Center Church*, 346.

[10] Alan Hirsch and Tim Catchim, *The Permanent Revolution: Apostolic Imagination and Practice for the 21st-Century Church* (San Francisco: Jossey-Bass, 2012), 3.

## CHAPTER NINE

# The Law of Leadership: Part Two

 —— **The Knowledge Box** ——

**The Law of Leadership:** It gives an organization its vision and ability to translate that vision into a godly reality. It is the art of getting things accomplished through people. It is influence in thinking, behavior, and development. It is a kind of influence that provides purpose, direction, motivation, and character. It is motivated by love and care when initiated by believers.

**The Precepts:**

3. Two Main Roles of Oversight Inside the Daily Administration of the New Testament Church: Elders and Deacons
4. Ethical Requirements for Elders in the Local Church
5. Ethical Requirements for Deacons in the Local Church

 ————————————

NOTE: In this chapter, only the precepts will be noted. The Wisdom Points are given as alphabetized letters.

Leadership is an art that takes practice and precision. Great leadership does not happen by sheer accident, it is often developed in the fires of living and in the shadows of great failures. Leadership requires a ferocious emotional fortitude that quitters never seem to master in the game of life—the "stick-to-it" mentality that says: "I may die, but it won't be from being shot in the back while running away from the battlefield!" Real leaders have a quite solitude, a simple faith, a tough skin, and a tender heart toward the things of God.

You have been entrusted as the body to confirm church leadership that will be called upon to make tough decisions and spend sleepless nights so that the church may never know an "inkling" that the situation ever happened. Godly leaders will often lead quietly through troubled times so not to stir up fear within the body. Good shepherds never spook the sheep they love. They may speak as "one" after times of long days and weeks of deliberations. They will do difficult work that is often the most unseen, and yes, unappreciated task of managing the community of the local church. So, whom you confirm is more important than what office you are confirming. The right leader can make the most colossal task look like child's play. The right leader creates a smooth flow to the church and of managing the community.

Leadership today is often thought of as being disconnected from character and wisdom. The worst leader can make the most menial tasks look like impassable snow-covered mountains. They have a gift of looking at the rolling hills of Western Kentucky and convincing the masses that Pikes Peak in the Colorado Rockies is directly in front of them. They complicate the simple things in life when they engage a mission without seasoned wisdom. A city mayor is caught on camera smoking crack, and days later on television, he is trying to explain to his followers why such an incident does not affect his ability to lead on a day-to-day basis. A senator is caught taking a bribe, while using tax payers' money to pay his prostitute. He says, "I made a bad decision, but it doesn't affect my ability to lead." A congressman exposes his private parts via a text to a woman who is not his wife. He gets caught, and then repeats his own offence. A year later, he has the hubris to run for mayor where he says, "My private life has no bearing on my public office of leadership."

All these incidents do affect one's followers, because leadership is a gift of wisdom. Proverbs 14:8, 33 tells us that wisdom comes when things are understood and the reasons are clearly comprehended. A wise person can pass on wisdom. How can a fool pass on that which he does not truly comprehend? Wisdom benefits all people. Again, whom you confirm is as important as what office you are confirming. You can teach administration, train in relational etiquette, and sharpen intellect, but character has to be developed through long trials and a seemingly never-ending journey of faith (Romans 5:4).

## PRECEPT THREE:
### Two Main Roles of Oversight Inside the Daily Administration of the New Testament Church: Elders and Deacons

**First Peter 5:1-2 says:**

> Therefore, as a fellow elder and witness to the sufferings of the Messiah and also a participant in the glory about to be revealed, I exhort the elders among you: Shepherd God's flock among you, not overseeing out of compulsion but freely, according to God's will.

**Philippians 1:1 says:** "To all the saints in Christ Jesus who are in Philippi, including the overseers and deacons."

**James 3:1:** "Not many should become teachers, my brothers, knowing that we will receive a stricter judgment."

Two main passages give us our ethical requirements for elders (1 Timothy 3:1-13; Titus 1:5-9) and only one for deacons (1 Timothy 3:8-13). The words elder/bishop/pastor are used interchangeably in the New Testament. In 1 Timothy 3:1-7 and Acts 20:28, the word is used to refer to the office of a bishop. This office began inside the local church, and after the church exploded, new believers increased, demographics expanded, and this role was elevated to the oversight of regions and countries. The word *bishop* means "overseer." In Titus 1:6-9, this word means pastor or shepherd. Here again the same word is describing the same people. Finally, in these scriptures—Titus 1:5, 7 and 1 Peter 5:1-2—the word is used for the office of elders. As we discussed earlier, the ministerial offices are appointed by Christ. It is then the responsibility of the church to appoint the elders—one of the fivefold ministries in the church (Ephesians 4:11). I believe then that the body confirms and is asked to pray for discernment and confirmation (Acts 6:2, 5).

The ministerial function of deacons comes from a word which means to be a servant. While "elders" have the responsibility of oversight, deacons have the responsibility of aiding those who have the oversight of the local church with physical and logistical needs of the church. They do so to aid the elders/bishops/pastors in concentrating on their primary calling (Acts 6:1-6). The apostles desired to "devote [themselves] to prayer and to the preaching ministry" (Acts 6:4). Deacons serve the practical ministry within the local church. Their job is crucial for many reasons. Their office functions in a healthy way—they safeguard the communal life of the church, as well as the spiritual vitality of the fivefold ministry. There would be many more pastors on the field today had the church been mature enough to assume its role in helping its leaders carry the immense burden of congregational care. They too have clear ethical responsibilities laid out in the Scriptures      (1 Timothy 3:8-13). Whether it is an elder/bishop/pastor or a deacon, the first discerning issue for the church body is to discern the call of God upon their lives.

*Discerning the call of God is important to every believer.* Those more mature believers in your local church will see the call of God on your life. The Holy Spirit will make it visible to those who know you and to those who are over you in the Lord. Trust their discernment and listen to what they see birthing in your life. Saying yes to the call of God on your life is a serious thing; many fail at saying yes.

It is often a sad double feature when one looks at those who struggle with God's call on their lives. On the one hand, I have watched college-degreed men fail to find a job in a plentiful job market, and end up selling shoes, because they refused to submit to the call of God. On the other hand, I have seen some say yes, who, quite frankly, were not mature enough to have said yes, and in the end, made a wreck of not only their lives but of several others as well. Saying yes to the call is a serious proposition to ponder. This call may come to you in the desert like it did to Moses, or in a tabernacle like it did to the child Samuel, or on the road to Damascus like it did to Paul (Exodus 3:1-12; 1 Samuel 3:1-18; Acts 9:17). Such a calling often comes with a fire inside like it did with Jeremiah when he said it was "like a burning fire shut up in my bones" (Jeremiah 20:9 NKJV). Paul said, "And woe to me if I do not preach the gospel" (1 Corinthians 9:16). To be called to preach is to be called directly by God, because preaching is never something that a man decides to do. Although all men are called by God to minister, not all men and women are called by God into full-time ministry.

Paul said to Timothy that when one desires to be a pastor, "He desires a good work" (1 Timothy 3:1 NKJV). All believers are called to be saints and witnesses (Romans 1:7), but not all are called to be apostles (1 Corinthians 12:29). This calling, as we have spoken about in Ephesians 4:11, comes from the will of God. Jesus, in Matthew 4:20, called Peter and Andrew to leave their boats (livelihood) and come and follow Him. You can see that Jesus demanded that some clearly break away from their previous professions to leave it all and follow Him. What you need to know to support your local church is that God has laid out rather clear rules for the appointment of His offices. This office builds on the offices of the fivefold ministry mentioned in Ephesians 4:11 with the biblical concept of elders.

## PRECEPT FOUR:
### Ethical Requirements for Elders in the Local Church

How do we know who is ready to be a leader in our local church? Is it wealth? Popularity? Longevity? Intellect? We will explore the role of the overseer in the local church, specifically the ethical responsibility of the elder/bishop/pastor. (*In this law, we will note only the precepts and assume that each accented point will be understood as a wisdom point.*) These are all the same word in the Greek language. As we have discussed, an elder can be a full-time minister or a supporting leader in the local church. Quite a bit of leeway is given in Scripture for churches today as they establish biblical order. One reason is because the word for bishop/elder/pastor is often used interchangeably in the Bible. In Acts 20:17, 28 and Titus 1:5, 7, we can clearly see that these terms appear in the New Testament as positions, if not fully interchangeable. The good news is that the same God who gave us instructions on the establishment of the Old Testament priesthood has also clearly sent us a prescription as to what is required of these priestly functions in the New Testament. In 1 Timothy 3:1-7; Titus 1:5-9; 1 Peter 5:1-4, we find such a list of qualifications. While it is true that many pastors understand these prescriptions, often because of an uninformed laity, decisions are made regarding spiritual leadership with no biblical authority guiding them. Too often, popular votes and boards are set up in the church much like Apple or IBM, and the truth is, God's house is not Apple or IBM. The rules are not the same. Boards do not guide the local church. Henry Ford may have been a great man, but the house of God is not an assembly line, and it does not require governmental structures influenced by the postindustrial revolution. His house operates on a different set of rules. We don't elect; He chooses, and we discern His choices. A witness of the Holy Spirit within the body then confirms those choices. After their call has been established, how do we discern the character of biblical leaders? These characteristics start in 1 Timothy 3:1-7:

> This saying is trustworthy: "If anyone aspires to be an overseer, he desires a noble work." An overseer, therefore, must be above reproach, the husband of one wife, self-controlled, sensible, respectable, hospitable, an able teacher, not addicted to wine, not a bully but gentle, not quarrelsome, not greedy—one who manages his own household competently, having his children under control with all dignity. (If anyone does not know how to manage his own household, how will he take care of God's church?) He must not be a new convert, or he might become conceited and fall into the condemnation of the Devil. Furthermore, he must have a good reputation among outsiders, so that he does not fall into disgrace and the Devil's trap.

A. **1 Timothy 3:1:** "This saying is trustworthy: "If anyone aspires to be an overseer, he desires a noble work." The first phrase is simply expressing the fact that the preceding statement can be trusted. It is important to realize that desiring or even accepting the office of a bishop was a call to danger and great sacrifice in the first century. The word *aspire* means to "stretch oneself out." It implies that someone is grasping for the office. It is a Greek word that carries with it a strong desire to reach a goal. Remember, to do so in the first century was to place your life and your family in great danger. Christianity was not a legal religion, and that meant many of the original leaders were first volunteers, and second they were not accepted by society with any respect or reverence. And this was a culture built on respect, shame, and honor! It is important to note that the Scripture is telling us that it is better for a person to "want" to volunteer for this office than it is for a church body to "ask" someone to fill this office. The desire is often a confirmation of the call.

When Paul says "he desires a noble work," he is not referring to the honor of the position, because there was no honor to this position in the beginning. He is saying that the work is an honor, not the position.

B. **1 Timothy 3:2:** "An overseer, therefore must be above reproach, the husband of one wife, self-controlled, sensible, respectable, hospitable, an able teacher."

1. **"Therefore"**: The simple word translated from the Greek into English as "therefore" could be read as "behooving" the overseer to be above reproach. This implies that the office of overseer naturally has a certain required nature, which is natural for its fulfillment.

2. **"Above Reproach"**: This doesn't mean select a human being without sin. It means that we must select a person whom the congregation sees as

"blameless" which means "without fault." It means that people cannot give grounded replies to their accusations. This is a great place to make a very important point. Your leaders will have lies told on them. They will be falsely accused. They will be hated. These are not signs of poor leadership, but rather godly leadership. Matthew 5: 11-12 reminds us:

> You are blessed when they insult and persecute you and falsely say every kind of evil against you because of Me. Be glad and rejoice, because your reward is great in heaven. For that is how they persecuted the prophets who were before you.

3. **"The husband of one wife":** The injunction here is written with Greek words aimed at immorality, polygamy, and concubines—all of which were present among the Jewish population in the first century. The words for "man" and "wife" are gender specific, but the emphasis here is on the fidelity of marriage.

4. **"Self-Controlled":** The next two words are used to address the issues of drunkenness in the Eastern world. This word was used to speak of temperance in the use of alcohol. Here, it is referring not just to the use of wisdom concerning wine, but being sober in the clear sense of being clearheaded in one's mind and thoughts. It suggests that our leaders should be clearheaded in order to "watch" out for the congregation lest the Enemy should arrive unexpectedly. They are to be free from rash actions. They are not flighty or unstable. Elders are solid and unmovable, and it is their character and longevity that gives their voice weight and power. It takes a sober man to be vigilant. A drunken man is

unaware of his dangers, but a sober man is keenly aware of his surroundings. These are leaders who are trustworthy and balanced in their judgments.

5. **"Sensible"**: *Sensible* means to be disciplined in one's freedoms. Leaders are to be self-restrained in all passions. These leaders are "discrete," which is the actual Greek word used in this sentence. They are temperate and self-controlled. One should look for these important attributes, because leaders who lack self-control cannot lead. These kinds of leaders live by commitment, not by feelings. They are fully committed, no matter what day or season. Anyone can lead in the shade of fall, but to lead in the dead of winter, the toil of spring, or the heat of summer takes a sensible leader.

6. **"Respectable"**: The original word here is actually the Greek word for decorum. This is not only referring to the virtue of dress and demeanor, but also to the inner life of a leader. What a leader expresses outwardly is often an utterance of what is inside. Plato used this word to refer to a citizen who quietly fulfills his duties as an earthly citizen—one whose earthly life is in order. It comes from the English word "cosmetics." It is referring to the kinds of leaders who have inward holiness and beauty that permeates the outward exterior.

Notice that the first two words express a leader's inward disposition, while the last one combines with the first and causes an outward disposition of leadership. To lead sensibly does not mean that people will not disagree with your position. It does mean, however, that as a leader you live your life with such inward and outward convictions that those who do disagree with you must leave the argument, respecting your character as a leader.

7. **"Hospitable":** This word means that one is friendly to strangers. It implies that an elder should be a "people person." The word implies friendship, and to be kind to others. Lest you think this characteristic of leadership is a lightweight issue, look at 3 John 9, 10 and notice how harshly John criticizes Diotrephes who showed poor hospitality. In the first century, the early church leaders were deeply dependent upon this gift as they spread the gospel to new cities. There were no buildings, and there was a lot of social pressure not to belong to this Jewish sect. To take in a stranger required a warm heart. Leaders who desire the office of bishop/elder/pastor must have a warm heart for those who are strangers to Christianity and to those who find their way into our houses of worship looking for God. Church leaders must remain closely connected to the maintenance of external relationships.

8. **"An able teacher":** Teaching is a charisma from God; that is to say, it is a gift given by grace. It is linked in Ephesians 4:11 with the office of pastoring and singled out in 1 Corinthians 12:28. All pastors must teach, but not all teachers are pastors. It implies that our church leaders should have a good grasp on the Word of God in order to be able to teach it to others. The role of elders is not to supervise the pastor with a watchful eye lest he embezzle the resources of the local church; but the role of elder is to protect the doctrinal fidelity of the local church to make sure its mission aligns with its doctrine. In other words, our orthodoxy influences our orthopraxy. The phrase here simply means that our church leaders should know God's Word, because they will be called on to teach it to those who do not. This is actually a warning for the modern-day American church that places leaders in church positions because of wealth,

popularity, or influence. What qualifies an elder is his grasp of God's Word not his grasp of the stock market.

C. **1 Timothy 3:3:** "Not addicted to wine, not a bully but gentle, nor quarrelsome, not greedy."

We have been told by Paul what church leaders are to be; now we are being told clearly what they are not to be.

1. **"Not Addicted to Wine."** I spent a great deal of my life working with alcoholics and drug-addicted individuals, both professionally and pastorally. You can believe me when I say that there is nothing worse than a "mean" drunk. Many times an individual's personality when intoxicated is the exact opposite of the person's personality when sober. A mean drunk lashes out at people, is rude, and is oblivious to how his or her behavior affects those nearby. "Not addicted" means that leaders don't linger long behind their wine. This passage implies addiction. Our leaders should not act like drunks who brawl and indulge in violent conduct toward others. A drunk loves to quarrel with people, and a quarreling drunk usually ends up striking out at someone.

2. **"Not a bully":** It's a shame to hear stories of how church leaders came to blows over arguments about hymnals or a projector on the wall. Church leaders are normal people just like you. However, quiet-tempered people who carry a chip on their shoulders are not ready to be your leaders either—no matter how popular they are in the community. These kinds of people are always ready with their fists. I still remember my first experience with an elder like this.

> I was a youth pastor in a large church with a bunch of juvenile delinquents whom I truly loved. One of these fatherless kids popped off to an elder in a parking lot one night. The red-faced elder nearly came to blows with this kid who could not have found the Book of Matthew if his life had depended on it. I remember thinking at the time how ironic it was to hear an elder get so angry and curse so profusely at a child. He blew his top way too quickly. The point isn't about getting angry, but about browbeating and threatening violence, which this elder did to this wayward teen.

We need elders who prefer to use their minds for reasoning rather than their fists for settling disputes. True leaders never use their unbridled tongues to wound the conscience of others. Godly leaders are not greedy and do nothing to dishonor their character.

3. **"But gentle."** Real leaders are longsuffering in their relationships to troublemakers. They are yielding and kind; they do not have a quarrelsome character. True leaders have sweet reasonableness. They are often tolerant and shower others with clemency. Choose a leader full of kindness and who is gracious.

4. **"Not quarrelsome."** A hotheaded leader is a live example of someone who lacks inward control. It is our outward traits that give evidence of our inward control. True leaders in your church should not be contentious or disposed to fighting. This verse is plainly telling us to choose leaders who do not love to quarrel and fight with people. Wise men shun all needless strife. Wiser men choose their battles carefully . . . very carefully. When a person loves strife and conflict, he is a

spiritually sick individual. You were not created for such behavior. Good leaders are full of wisdom, and James 4:1 reminds us that wars and fighting among us only come from a great war that is going on within us.

5. **"Not greedy":** This passage is not a defense to keep your pastoral staff in poverty. The Bible clearly says otherwise (Acts 18:3; 1 Corinthians 9:14; 7-13; Philippians 4:10; 14-18; 1 Thessalonians 2:9; 2 Thessalonians 3:6-10; 1 Timothy 5:17). However, there must be some reason why Paul uses this phrase six times in the Pastoral Epistles. We know that he told the young pastor Timothy, "The love of money is a root of all kinds of evil, and by craving it, some have wandered away from the faith and pierced themselves with many pains." The culture of Ephesus, as were the Jewish and non-Jewish communities, was well aware of this phrase. One old phrase said: "The love of money is the mother-city of all evil." The key for Christians is the word "root." We are firmly told that love first belongs to God (Luke 10:27). To love money before loving God is to say, "I love myself more than I love God." It is a form of self-love. A root is an expression of how something grows. We grow away from God when we get greedy for money, when we love it more than we love God. The love of money causes us to covet the wrong objects in this world. It's not really about money; it's about misplaced love. Leaders must guard their hearts, because loving money more than God is the root from which we are led away from our first love.

D. **1 Timothy 3:4:** "One who manages his own household competently, having his children under control with all dignity." (If anyone does not know how to manage his own household, how will he take care of God's church?)

I have often responded to people who ask me "why preachers' kids are so mean?" by saying, "Because they play with the deacons' children all day." It's tough to be in ministry; it's even tougher when you are the child of a minister. Your job is to love your pastor's kids as if they were your own, defending them, protecting them, and keeping them safe in the fold. I have lost count of the numerous children of preachers who have left the faith simply because of what working in the family did to damage their image of God.

I sat recently with a PK who was showing her years of hard living. Her father was a bishop over a certain state for a denomination. When I was told of her arrival for lunch, I imagined a person who may have become "bent out of shape" over dad's antiquated belief system. But instead, I met a woman still in love with her daddy and soon realized over dinner conversation that it was the church she hated, not her father. She had watched him take one too many unfair sucker punches.

I sat another time with a pastor's two boys who somehow continued to serve God. They each wept while they reminisced of the early days of ministry. Their parsonage had no heat and no working stove. The boys were young and hungry like all teenage boys at that age. They had no money to purchase groceries, only faith to pray for some—and pray they did! To their surprise, an elderly saint was awakened by God early one morning and told to go and buy "that pastor down the road" some groceries. On the doorstep that morning were steaks to replace the bologna, and fresh vegetables to replace the discounted cans of peas. The pastor's wife, in her excitement to finally cook her family a decent meal, suddenly remembered that she had no stove. Being new to the area, she called up the church clerk who lived only a few doors down the street to ask if she could use her stove for just a little while. To her heartbreak, the clerk exclaimed with a tenacious voice, "No!" Thank God, the heartbreak that day never made its way into the bitter soup that poisons pastor's children. Adam and Eve had a bad kid. They sinned, but they also learned to fear God and live for Him. You can't say that Cain's home was dysfunctional. So, yes, an elder's child is to be disciplined and under control. But, they are not perfect; they are not without mistakes. We all learn the same way—through our mistakes.

This passage is not about presenting the perfect child or marriage for the congregation to emulate. Paul makes a connection about management when he says that management for a bishop starts in his own home first. If he is accomplished in his home with managing his children, he can be trusted to manage the household of God. Leaders are called to minister at home first. How many of us actually take this passage as seriously as we should? Few of us ever think when choosing church leaders that our first line of wisdom is to see how well they manage their own homes. The Greek here is actually talking about ruling, directing, and leading in the home first. It carries with it the understanding that we are "to take care of, be concerned for, and care for" our own homes. When we do that, then it is proof that we can lead the church with the right heart. How can we love those who aren't blood related, if we ignore those who are? I keep an autographed picture of the famous Billy Sunday in my office for one reason. I loved the work he did for God. I admire his charisma and boldness for Christ. But that is not the reason his picture hangs in my office. It hangs in my office to remind me every day that I have a choice. I have a choice to place the discipleship of my children ahead of the discipleship of every other living being in the world. All of Billy Sunday's boys died alcoholics.

The word *child* in this passage refers to children still under age. It implies children not yet of age, living in subjection, subordination, and obedience to their father's authority. It is true that the character of young children reflect the character of their father's leadership.

E. **1 Timothy 3:6-7:** "He must not be a new convert, or he might become conceited and fall into the condemnation of the Devil. Furthermore, he must have a good reputation among outsiders, so that he does not fall into disgrace and the Devil's trap."

The only way to ride a bike is to get on one. Leadership in the church is a serious decision. We must be very careful to guard the prudence of seasoned leaders in a world that lusts for youth. I don't care how much training you have had, or how much college or army training you have gone through, if you are young, there is no way for you to have the seasoned wisdom of someone who has faithfully served the Lord for many years. It's simple; we gain wisdom from experiences in life. When you are twenty, you have only so much life experience to call upon to make future decisions. When you are older (hence the word *elder,* implying white-bearded), you have earned wisdom through many of life's trials. I am a great advocate of young leaders, and especially young Timothy's call to pastor old churches! The difference between Timothy and many young people today is that Timothy had a Paul—a mentor that he listened to and revered.

Timothy knew that he was out of his league and needed the seasoned wisdom of previous saints.

> Last year, on two different occasions, I walked through the city he pastored. I saw the Christian graffiti on the remains of the church where Mary, the Mother of Jesus, attended. I saw the cross, carved into the head of the Roman Emperors at the museum in Ephesus. And it hit me that Timothy had succeeded. Nero was after him. He had to have been a nervous wreck following John the disciple of Jesus and Saint Paul as their pastors. But he succeeded, and today the rocks still cry out his victories.

What was the difference? Timothy had gained wisdom from a seasoned mentor. Choose carefully the leaders of your church.

1. **"He must not be a new convert":** The way to ruin the respect and dignity of the office of an elder/ bishop/pastor is to place a novice in its teaching chambers. Paul is giving us the requirement of maturity. These leaders are not to be "new converts." The Greek that means our leaders must not be newly planted, or newly converted to Christianity. The root of this word gives us the word "germinate." Leaders are not people who have recently "sprung up." The leaders you are looking for are seasoned and lovers of wisdom. This phrase is actually a Greek way of suggesting that a novice is not to be considered for the level of leadership. Novice leaders have not had time to be truly disciplined by afflictions and temptations.

2. **"Or he might become conceited and fall into condemnation of the Devil."** The purpose of this statement is to explain why novices

should not be considered for this level of leadership. This verse suggests that such novices when trusted with major leadership often become conceited. This is a Greek word meaning "wrapped up in smoke." It is an exaggerated idea of our own importance. It implies that it is easy for novices to become conceited. To be conceited means to be blinded to the point that it blunts our spiritual alertness. Paul is warning us that novices must not be placed at this level of leadership, because the position of the office can easily blind them with pride, thus blunting their ability to lead.

Proud people become blinded to Satan's agenda. There is a phrase here that refers to falling into condemnation of the devil. The real Greek word here is judgment. But when has the devil ever had the power to judge? There is only one righteous Judge. The word in this passage refers to the reason for the judgment. Satan was judged by God for pride (Ezekiel 28:17).

3. **"Furthermore, he must have a good reputation among outsiders, so that he does not fall into disgrace and the Devil's trap."** You don't value character until you lose it. When we lose our reputation, it takes us a lifetime to gain it back. Paul is telling us that as we discern God's leadership gift on someone, we must look for a good reputation, not just the reputation of the body of Christ, but those outside the body of Christ. There are many so-called Christian leaders who work very hard to keep up an "appearance" of godliness to those inside the church. However, while the church may not know about their secret lives, the unsaved surely do! This verse is challenging us to choose our leaders from

the ranks of those who have a good reputation among those who do not know Christ—meaning to have an excellent testimony from the outside. When an old life is still secretly lived through the false pretense of conversion, the world usually knows it. Drug dealers know their customers, and prostitutes know theirs. Businessmen know well those who pay their bills and those who do not. The wicked know the unsavory. We are all shocked when a double life is revealed about a church leader. Choosing a church leader requires strategic thinking. Here, Paul is looking ahead when he uses the word "reproach." The one in danger of possible reproach is the church, when we choose leaders who do not have a good reputation with outsiders. We all know the damage that a fallen leader can cause the local church when they fall. Choose your leaders carefully, because "perception is reality."

God's wisdom is proactive and protective. What so many church people do not realize is just how much God has to say in the Bible about church life. He tells us, rather clearly how to choose important church leaders.

F. The additional wisdom of Titus 1:5-8.

Unlike the office of deacon, the Scriptures contain additional wisdom for the local church regarding the office of the elder/bishop/pastor. Titus 1:6-8 says:

> The reason I left you in Crete was to set right what was left undone and, as I directed you, to appoint elders in every town: someone who is blameless, the husband of one wife, having faithful children not accused of wildness or rebellion. For an overseer, as God's administrator, must be blameless,

> not arrogant, not hot-tempered, not addicted to wine, not a bully, not greedy for money, but hospitable, loving what is good, sensible, righteous, holy, self-controlled, holding to the faithful message as taught, so that he will be able both to encourage with sound teaching and to refute those who contradict it.

We will not take the time to repeat the directions here that have previously been explained. We will look only at the directions in Titus that are not found in Timothy.

1.  **"Blameless."** The words may look the same in English, but the Greek word is slightly different. The Timothy version of being blameless carries with it the concept that my life is beyond rebuke. Here the word is actually *unimpeachable,* which means, "I am free from legal charges." No one can legally pin unsavory ways on me. It means I am not accused in a court of law.

2.  **"Children"**: Both Timothy and Titus tell us that an elder must have his home in subjection. Titus uses a few more descriptive words to help us. He says **"Children not accused of wildness or rebellion."** Paul uses the word "accusation." We are told that church leaders must have children who cannot be incriminated. This is not a judicial word, but a word noting public condemnation. Paul says that a leader's child must not be accused of **"wildness."** This word means that an elder's child must not be a prodigal. The passage in Timothy is also referring to those children still under the authority of the home. Such children are to be safe, not living in extravagant squandering, debauchery, and drunkenness. The word **"rebellion"** is used to imply that such children are not to be undisciplined, disobedient, or

immoral. It is important to realize that God doesn't expect something of an elder's child that he isn't expecting of you as well.

3. **"Not Self-Willed":** Elders should not be pleased with themselves while they despise others. They are not to be obstinately maintaining their own opinions while being reckless with the rights of others. Our leaders are not to be overbearing or inflexible with their own opinions. They must be considerate of the opinion of others. Look for leaders who are not self-pleasing, arrogant, or full of self-indulgence.

4. **"Not quick-tempered."** Not wrathful or prone to anger. This is actually a rare Greek phrase meaning "not soon to anger." It is referring to those people who do not have their anger under control. The issue here is emotional maturity.

5. **"Loving what is good."** This means, "to love goodness and be benevolent." It is not just a word that likes being kind, but it places actions behind its thoughts. This person loves to practice kindness. This person has a positive attitude. It is related to the word for merciful and compassionate. This is a late word and used only in the New Testament.

6. **"Just."** This is how a person should relate to his fellowman. It means, "to be right with regard to human laws." It is important for an elder to have a right relationship with people; without it, community is impossible. The word *just* means, "to act honestly and equitably."

7. **"Holy."** Leaders are to live a life of holiness. They are to be pure from sin. The word *holy* implies that our lives are relating to God's law. We are fulfilling our duties to live a sanctified life.

8. **"Temperate."** The word *temperate* means that leaders should have the inner resources to control their bodily desires—to have the proper self-restraint in regard to indulgence.

The office of an elder is important for the protection, government, and freedom of the local church. In 1 Thessalonians 5:12-13, Paul tells us to respect them and to hold them in high regard. Hebrews 13:7 tells us to remember them and consider their way of life. It also tells us to obey them and submit to their authority, because they keep watch over our souls. It goes so far as to remind those of us who do not, that in the long view of eternity, it will not go well for us. Elders are here to protect your soul and build you up in the most holy faith. The offices of the bishop/elder/pastor are all held to the same standards in Scripture.

## PRECEPT FIVE:
### Ethical Requirements for Deacons in the Local Church

One of the main reasons that churches struggle for new leadership is because we have lost the biblical art of mentoring. A close second reason is because we have lost the biblical structure that naturally trains and prepares new leadership. Paul says in 1 Timothy 3:8-13:

> Deacons likewise, should be worthy of respect, not hypocritical, not drinking a lot of wine, not greedy for money, holding the mystery of the faith with a clear conscience. And they must also be tested first; if they prove blameless, then they can serve as deacons. Wives, too, must be worthy of respect, not slanderers, self-controlled, faithful in everything. Deacons must be husbands of one wife, managing their children and their own households competently. For those who have served well as deacons acquire a good standing for themselves, and great boldness in the faith that is in Christ Jesus.

The office of deacon follows the office of elder/bishop/ pastor in the scriptural account of leadership. What are the ethical responsibilities for the ministry of a deacon? Whereas the elder/bishop/pastor leads the local church as an overseer, the deacon is to take care of the physical and logistical needs of the church so that the elders can concentrate on their primary calling. We see this distinction in Acts 6:1-6 as seven men were chosen to handle the more practical matters of ministry. This is the only passage that mentions the qualification of deacons. This is an official list, but it is not meant to be exhaustive. The similarities of the qualifications for deacons and elders/bishops/pastors are important to note. The ethical characteristics of deacons are as follows:

A. **Deacons, likewise, should be worthy of respect, not hypocritical, not drinking a lot of wine, not greedy for money, holding the mystery of the faith with a clear conscience. And they must also be tested first; if they prove blameless, then they can serve as deacons" (1 Timothy 3:8-10).**

The word *deacon* is a word meaning, "to serve." Both elders and deacons are called to be servants. We see this in Philippians 1:1 where Paul writes: "Paul and Timothy, slaves of Christ Jesus: To all the saints in Christ Jesus who are in Philippi, including the overseers and deacons." Deacons are precious gifts to the body of Christ, without them the local church would never prosper. Many of the deacons at CCC operate with the pastoral gift and serve as conduits for prayer and care to thousands of people. They are immensely valuable to our church, and I know to yours as well. The following are ethical requirements for this office:

1. **"Deacons, likewise should be worthy of respect."** The ethical requirements of an elder/ bishop/pastor are, in many instances, the same

as the ethical requirements of the deacon. The list in 1 Timothy 3:8-13 contains seven of the same instructions given to elder/ bishops/ pastors. This is the reason that the ethical list for elder/bishops/pastors is followed by the phrase "deacons likewise." It is interesting that Paul speaks of the elder/bishop/pastor in the singular and of the deacons in the plural. The word here implies that a deacon must be serious, respectful, above reproach, having good character, honorable, and dignified. Paul's last admonition about elders included having a "good reputation among outsiders" (1 Timothy 3). His first admonitions to deacons were about guarding a good reputation. Deacons, as we shall see, will require a good reputation and well-known character. Reputation refers to the position one occupies or the opinion others may have of the individual, while character is the combination of moral and other traits. The word here is related to the same word used for elder/bishops/pastors in 1 Timothy 3:2 when we are told that they must be "respectable."

2. **"Not hypocritical"**: This is the word for being "double-tongued." It won't take long for a double-tongued deacon to be exposed. It implies that our deacons must not be insincere, untrustworthy, or indulging in harmful gossip. This word instructs us to choose leaders who do not say one thing to one person and another thing to someone else. Our leaders must mean what they say. They must be in full control of their speech. A deacon's actions and speech, whether they realize it or not, speak to the greater church. If a deacon is negative, full of hateful, critical speech against a leader, a subject, or someone else, then

it will appear that the church is against these things as well. Deacons must realize that their behavior reflects on the greater church and that even the smallest comments can damage the reflection of the church. Jesus said, "My church" (Matthew 16:18).

3. **"Not drinking a lot of wine."** Here again one of the same rules for elder/bishops/pastors applies to deacons (1 Timothy 3:3). A deacon is not to be a lover of wine. This means that they are to be in full control, temperate, not addicted or overcome by anything.

4. **"Not greedy for money."** A deacon is not to be out for shameful gain. They are not to be part of dishonest gain. Deacons must set a great example as to how money is handled and how it influences our hearts. The word means that deacons should not be known for obtaining money in disgraceful ways. Deacons set the example for giving and tithing, just like elders/bishops/pastors. The longer I serve God, the more tithing makes sense to me. God doesn't need my money. I need to honor God with my money so idolatry doesn't set itself up within my heart. Deacons must love God above money, and their lives should set an example. When money is the price for doing wrong, then it becomes filthy, according to Paul. Look for deacons who love to give and who live lives of obedience to Christ in the areas of their wealth. When God has a man's money, He then has him—wholly kept from idolatry of all sorts. Where your treasure is, there your heart will also be! (Matthew 6:21).

5. **"Holding the mystery of the faith with a clear conscience."** Paul is saying this mystery of the gospel is a gospel obtained by faith. He begins

with the word "holding." This word in the Greek means that "one has hold of something continually in his possession." It is an ongoing governing force in their lives. Paul loves to refer to a man's conscience (Acts 24:16; 2 Corinthians 1:12). Deacons must have an inner guide for life. It is Paul's way of saying that orthodoxy is important, but when "right beliefs" are accompanied without holiness then our beliefs have no power. You must choose church leaders who hold firm to the true faith without wavering. Unstable leadership is worse than no leader at all.

6. **"And they must also be tested first."** I will be the first to admit that I hate trouble and trials as much as the rest of you. However, a little age, a lot of suffering as a young man, and the survival of trials that should have absolutely killed me have given me a gift called endurance (James 1:3). Paul makes it clear that we should not choose leaders who have faith experiences not tested by trials. It is so important that we take the time to know those who labor among us. This wisdom comes directly from the first book written in the New Testament—1 Thessalonians 5:12. We must examine a potential leader. At CCC, we allow 30 days for anyone to write to the leader a grievance and copy the lead pastor's office. This helps the potential leader to feel the gravity of the office, and at the same time, the body to sense the seriousness of the task. We have to give time for such appraisal of men.

Paul uses a word for testing that implies a testing over a period of time. The idea is that the local church would have an available, worthy group to pick potential leaders from a stock of survivors! This passage insists on an orderly and careful evaluation.

7. **"If they prove blameless, then they can serve as deacons."** Paul says that when we find nothing against a potential deacon—no specific charges of wrongdoing—then the individual is ready to be a leader. The test of public scrutiny is God's idea delivered to the church from the lips of the apostle Paul. The point is not "after they have been scrutinized…then…." The phrase in the Greek tells us that this achievement is not conditional. This passage is literally saying, "Then let them…." It is predictive in nature. The word *blameless* is actually the Greek word for "unimpeachable." It means that the person is not accused as a result of public investigation. Your blamelessness has been proven. The idea here is to investigate the lives of our leaders so that we can prohibit an unsavory character from such a worthy office. What safety is given to the community of a local church when our leaders have been tested and proved blameless BEFORE we place our hands on them for office! A tested life is the best credentials for ministry.

B. **"Wives, too, must be worthy of respect, not slanderers, self-controlled, faithful in everything."**
Major fights have broken out in churches and denominations over the role of women in church leadership. I find it difficult to know that the first people to whom Jesus revealed His resurrection and the first to preach the Resurrection gospel were women, and for some reason we exclude them now. The one area that many people do agree is that the Bible does allow for women to serve in the role of "deacon." In the first 1,000 years of church history,

there are literally 10,000 women called "deacon." There are at least forty-seven deaconesses mentioned from the church region of Asia Minor (Revelation 2). Pliny, in a letter to the Emperor in A.D. 111, mentioned that he had recently arrested two Christian women who held official positions that he called "deaconesses." It is recorded in Luke 8:1-4 that women joined the ministry of Jesus. And while Phoebe (in Romans 16:1) is called a servant, it is the exact same word for deacon; and in all probability, she was a deaconess. Paul mentions more than 18 women who were in leadership positions in the New Testament church. Paul distinguishes wives from wives of deacons (1 Timothy 3:11). The problem here is the word for wives. The Greek actually says "woman." It is also important to point out that no word existed in the Greek language for female deacons. In other words, Paul had no other words to use here but "woman." It can refer to both single and married women. So at best, there is a certain amount of ambiguity present in the Scripture toward this subject. We will treat these next phrases as instructions for women deacons or ethical requirements for women in ministry positions.

1. **"Wives, too, must be worthy of respect."** It would be wise to note that Paul wrote nothing to the wives of elders/bishops/pastors. So why would he write to the wives of deacons and not elders? What Paul does write in the Greek is the word "likewise." This word is the same word in 1 Timothy 2:9 to say "in like manner" (NKJV). It denotes transitions of another class of individuals. It connects the previous ethical requirements with these he is introducing. To be "worthy of respect" means the same here as it did for all deacons. They are to be dignified, temperate,

sober, and all of the other instructions we have uncovered in the preceding verses related to the same word. Deaconesses must be trustworthy. There should be a modest dignity to their countenance. They must be grounded and grave.

2. **"Not slanderers."** Women must have the same depth of character as men for the office of leadership. This issue is not mentioned as the recent qualification of deacons although it most certainly applies to them as well. A church leader must not be a malicious talker. The Greek here is "slander"—the word often used for Satan. This word implies "those who say harmful things about other people." Our leaders must use their speech to unite, not divide. Community is protected by words.

3. **"Self-Controlled."** This is the word again for sober. It is the same word that is used in 1 Timothy 3:2. It is a call for women in leadership to remain in control of themselves, to be calm, dispassionate, circumspect, and free from excessive passion. Women in leadership must be clearheaded, not violent, but gentle.

4. **"Faithful in everything."** Our leaders must have a sense of fidelity. They are to be especially trustworthy and dependable. There are some who think that this passage is a caution toward the proper use of church funds since many women aided the poor and the children with church resources. It certainly means we are to discern which people are ready for a long-term faithful calling.

> There was once a man who desired church leadership, which is a good thing. I always had the thought in the back of my mind that he desired it for prestige. He was high maintenance,

and he had to have the pastor's time and attention on a regular basis to feel validated. The pastor thought he was a friend and suggested his presence on the elders team. This man, once elected, became a loose squirrel in the church. It was immediately obvious that he did not know how to lead, nor did he see himself in the proper light of a biblical elder. To him, he was an investigator. His immaturity was amazing. When confronted by the pastor with Matthew 18, it was obvious that he was clueless to his commitment to the people he was called to lead.

This might sound simple, but to Christ, oversight in His church is a grave concern. There was a reason why elders who abandoned their posts in the ancient world were put to death. God's offices require fidelity. I am not suggesting capital punishment for the wayward, but what I am saying is that God takes it very seriously, and so should you.

C. **"Deacons must be husband of one wife, managing their children and their own households competently. For those who have served well as deacons acquire a good standing for themselves, and great boldness in the faith that is in Christ Jesus" (1 Timothy 3:12-13).**

Paul repeats the title "deacons." The domestic issue for a deacon is just as important as the domestic duties of the elders/bishops/pastors.

1. **"Deacons must be husband of one wife."** This phrase means a deacon must be a "one-woman man." He is to have no girlfriends in the closet. This is the same word used in 1 Timothy 3:4-5 and needs no further explanations.

2. **"Managing their children and their own households competently."**

This passage is covered as well in 1 Timothy 3:4-5. Here again, choosing a church leader requires the presence of an orderly home. Spiritual training begins in the home. It is the first institution of only two which God personally started. The second being the church that is dependent upon the health of the first!

3. **"For those who have served well as deacons acquire a good standing for themselves, and great boldness in the faith that is in Christ Jesus."** This is an encouragement to those who would serve as deacons and then aspire to the office of an elder/bishop/pastor. While some make the point that such a division and step system did not exist at this writing, I would have to argue otherwise. They certainly had strategic foresight, because even the office of bishop eventually evolved into a regional position. History clearly bears this out by simply following the gravesites of many of the twelve disciples. The word which implies "served well" is actually the word "step or threshold." The Greek actually says, "are acquiring a step." It can mean "grade" or "mark." This passage goes further by suggesting that the ones who do so gain great confidence and boldness in the faith. It means that service to God increases and enlarges our faith. I have said often that you never really grow until you become a leader. Leadership has a way of requiring one to search for doctrinal positions, defend one's faith, and to encourage others from your own overflow with God. To those who are worthy of such a position, they should expect great growth in their personal lives. They, too, need to be encouraged, because Paul is saying that their reward will be rich.

Leadership is an art and requires the discerning of reality. You have a divine requirement to pray and fast before you select church leaders. Once you do, it is important that you support them wholeheartedly until, God forbid, the day comes when three witnesses bring credible charges against their lives—this would include improper doctrine. Hopefully, your church will be mature enough to handle that trying hour correctly. And, it is my great hope that those things never happen in your local community of faith.

The Scriptures have been clearly laid out for you to use as you discern church leadership. Support them, love them, and give them the grace you want and expect. Care for them, protect their children, and submit to their leadership, and watch your church grow!

# THE LAW OF FOLLOWERSHIP

## The Knowledge Box

**The Law of Followership:** It is the capacity of an individual to actively follow a leader. It is a role held by certain individuals or groups; it is the reciprocal social process of leadership where people have a willingness to follow a leader.

**The Precepts:**

1. We Need Followers Who Can Self-Manage.
2. We Need Followers Who Are Competent.
3. We Need Followers Who Have Courage.
4. We Need Courageous Followers Who Act by Faith.
5. We Need Courageous Followers Whose Courage Produces Prosperity.

No one leads all the time. Even your pastor is accountable to others, usually a district overseer or superintendent, which would mean that they too, would at times, follow. Pastor's councils and local church elders often follow a fivefold office. It has been said that a great leader has first learned to be a great follower. All of us are, after all, followers of Jesus Christ. So each and every member of the local church must become a great follower. Jesus said in Matthew 16:24 and Luke 9:23: "If anyone wants to come with Me, he must deny himself, take us his cross and follow Me." The word for "follower" as used here is a word that suggests that you come and go with me as my attendant. I am the teacher, and you will follow me as my students or disciples. It is a Greek tense that implies that the call to follow is a repetitive action; thus, you must "keep on" following me. As disciples, we are all called to follow Him. To do so, we must *cleave* (an old word suggesting we "stick close") to Him. This will require believing and trusting Him. All leaders, all saints, and all body members are first called to "follow Him." When we decided to "cleave" to Him, we were all making another decision to "follow" the leader—Jesus Christ.

As we have already learned, Jesus delegated His leadership to certain offices and functions in the local church. In 1 Corinthians 11:1, Paul tells the Corinthian church to "imitate" him. The word means to follow him, be an imitator of his actions, examples, and patterns. There is a reason why the last two chapters were full of God's requirements for local church leadership. These leaders are held to a higher level of accountability, because they are to set the example. And thus, you are to follow that example and honor those leaders with obedience to God's Word, but if you decide not to, as Hebrews 13:17 says, "that would be unprofitable for you."

Just as there is a biblical structure and mandate for leadership, there is a biblical structure and flow to followership. We are all called to be followers first. We start with total engrafting (John 15:7) by cleaving—embracing the lordship of Jesus Christ. This followership then, through obedience to Christ, submits to the godly leaders whom Christ has placed over us in our lives. The writer of Hebrews says, "Pursue peace with everyone" (12:14). The word "pursue" was used in both a bad and a good sense in the times of Jesus. It is also used to mean "follow." To pursue implies intent and obtaining a goal as if you hunted for it. It was a moral pursuit where one runs swiftly in order to catch some person, as in running after them. It also means to run swiftly to obtain the goal. It carries with it a great sense of urgency with passionate intensity. Thus, we can see the concept of pursuing/following something with a purpose. Jesus extends this invitation to come and follow Him, so followership must be a very important subject to Him. Success and failure in your local church isn't dependent only on how well your leaders can actually lead you, but also on how well the followers follow!

So, what kind of followers do we need to be producing in the local church? Do we need to build an army of mindless robots who cannot think for themselves or a team of cowards who follow tyrants? Is it possible that we need an insubordinate soldier who cannot take direction from his leaders in war? No, we need followers, who can: (1) self-manage, (2) be highly committed to the cause and the community which holds it, (3) be individuals who are competent in their calling, and (4) be people who have the courage to do something about it. The scientific field of followership owes a great deal to the scholar Robert Kelley who suggests that these four qualities are actually the four keys to effective followers. We will examine them through the eyes of Christianity and the local church.

## PRECEPT ONE:
### We Need Followers Who Can Self-Manage

The local church is not a spectator sport, even though we have done an excellent job of making it into one. We are a community. In biology, *community* means "a group of interacting, living organisms sharing a populated environment."[1] The biological definition makes for a perfect understanding in church. We are living organisms, and we share a populated environment. For example, Creation began as two individuals. Then through the development of two healthy individuals, God created two institutions to manage these individuals—the family and the church. Institutions are, therefore, only as strong as the individuals who make up the institution. Therefore, self-managing is critical to the success of any organization. Most of church life is not elder meetings or fivefold leadership, but individuals in community working interdependently. The greatest responsibility any church member has is to manage himself or herself! The reason that the Bible sets up a very limited structure of leadership is because Christianity is set up to predominantly exist as a followership model. To have an excellent local church, you must have an excellent belief in the power of a follower! Robert Kelley, in his book, *The Power of Followership*, makes a great point about leadership. He writes, "The current debate raging in leadership circles today is: Who is more important, leaders or managers? . . . The mediators say both are needed. Followers, the 80 to 90 percent who actually do the work, don't even get mentioned."[2]

You can't talk about followership without addressing the danger of being abused by leadership. Robert Kelley has a different take on that statement. He says, "A nation of sheep begets a government of wolves."[3] If you want healthy leaders in your church, you have to be a very self-managed, alert lamb. After all, wasn't it Jesus through-out the Gospels who constantly talked about staying awake lest a leader arise who was anti-Christ? (Matthew 24:22). Is it possible that the real antidote to spiritual abuse is healthy sheep? Furthermore, is it possible that building a great church has as much to do with building great followers as it does finding great leaders? We need followers to self-manage, so the church can be completely whole. If leaders are the only ones involved, then abuse is always possible. Not leadership alone, but an active and thinking laity built the church. Just take a look at the American political system and notice how many millions of Americans are not involved in the political process. The arrival of an illiterate electorate will be the downfall of our great country if we don't activate the followers. Simply look back into American history to prove this point: the Pilgrims with the Queen, the Mayflower, the Boston Tea Party, the Revolutionary War, the two Great Awakenings, and the Black Civil Rights Movement. They all had great leaders. But their leaders would have never succeeded had there not been an army of dedicated followers marching behind them. Leadership and followership "are complementary, not competitive paths to organizational contributions. Neither role corners the market on brains, motivation, talent, or action. Either role can result in an award-winning performance or a failure. The greatest successes require that people in both roles turn in top performances. We must have great leaders and great followers."[4]

### Wisdom Point A

*We have to create environments that support the development of self-management.* Ron Ritchhart in his book, *Intellectual Character,* believes that ability should be transformed into meaningful action. He believes that belief has to be acted out if we are ever going to see the value of education. He also believes that we need to be developing students' dispositions to act and use the knowledge, ability, and skills they have acquired, or education is worthless. He deeply believes that it is the operation of our disposition that most affects our behavior. He states that we must "Recognize an opportunity is a complex enterprise because it is a subtle endeavor."[5] Ron says that a disposition has four aspects to its behavior, and I believe that these qualities can help us to see our responsibilities as followers in a local church. These four qualities are: (1) awareness, (2) motivation, (3) inclination, and (4) ability. Building a great environment in your local church is, therefore, first dependent upon the dispositions of its followers.

1. **Every great environment begins with a wonderful disposition.**

   To have a great disposition means that you have an unusual state of being. It can refer to order and final arrangement of how one acts. We often talk about someone's disposition during trying times; whereas, when we are describing people's behavior, we say, "Their disposition is happy." The word *disposition* means "arrangement," so, it can mean the arrangement of our personalities. The disposition of an usher can speak volumes about the friendliness of a local church. Greeters with bad breath or unkempt appearances are loud voices of dispositions. So then, to understand dispositions, we must first begin with awareness.

   a. **Awareness**

      As leaders, all the children of God are called upon to be aware of their dispositions. When you think about the ethical requirement for elders/deacons, you are really looking at the qualities of their dispositions. Followers must be aware, conscious of their behavior, and how it affects others. We must always be aware that we too are ambassadors for Christ (2 Corinthians 5:20);

therefore, we must remain aware of our environment and how our actions affect the people within these places. Great followers are aware that their behavior influences the overall disposition of the church. Great followers are mindful of their dispositions.

### b. Motivation

Why we do what we do is very important. I have met my fair share of people who wanted to sing on Sunday because of who was in those chairs. We all know of famous stars who sold out their faith, even leaving it, who at one time swore they wanted to sing to the masses to glorify Christ. I am not saying that singing music other than gospel is a sin, but I am saying that singing with the wrong motive surely is a sin. Motivation is the reason or desire why we do something. It is crucial to achieving goals, especially self-control. It is the process that initiates. Colossians 3:23-24 says: "Whatever you do, do it enthusiastically, as something done for the Lord and not for men, knowing that you will receive the reward of an inheritance from the Lord. You serve the Lord Christ." We need followers who are motivated to build the community, not their own agenda or kingdoms. Motivation moves us toward action. We need followers with a disposition of a motivated person. The first time I traveled to the state of Utah, I did not understand all the emblems of bees. I asked my friend: "Why all of these symbols of bees?" He told me that the symbol of the bee was a reflection of the work ethic of the Mormon people. The body of Christ must have motivated people to spread the gospel around the world. We must be motivated to build and guard the community. We must be motivated to keep a motivated disposition! As Ron Ritchhart says, "Acting on opportunities requires a commitment of time, energy, and resources."[6]

If only we could truly grasp that Christ is about to return for His church, then motivation would never be an issue. Just as the ten virgins had to keep their lamps trimmed and burning, we too must stay sober in our motivation for the Kingdom. Great followers must have a motivated disposition.

c. **Inclination**

"Motivation has a primary effect in heightening awareness, as well as acting as a driver to push us into action. To distinguish these two functions, we can refer to this advanced primary nature of motivation as inclination, reserving the word motivation to designate the more situation-specific driver of action."[7] We all should have an internal witness to create a healthy disposition for our local church. I know we don't realize this, but it doesn't take a visitor long to realize that not everyone in your church is not getting along. They sense poor dispositions. I can pick it up immediately at a funeral. I can walk in, survey the chapel, observe where people are sitting and not sitting, and know the disposition of the room. We must have the desire to have a healthy disposition in a church, and that means followers need to be aware that their very lives are giving off good or bad messages.

d. **Ability**

Great followers are keenly aware of their abilities. Our skills do play a very important role in our followership, and it is important that we create an environment that develops the abilities of individuals. This disposition is extremely important to the health of your local church. I can spot a dead church a hundred miles away. Simply tell me how many people out of 75 are working in their giftings! In dead, unproductive churches, followership sits and soaks. Church is a spectator's sport to them. "It is the *preacher's* job to do that," they exclaim. In a healthy local church, the abilities of individual followers are developed and deployed. I realize that there are too many churches where the pastor isn't mature enough to release the saints into ministry. "A lack of awareness might, in some cases, be a factor of weak ability. Not having a rich knowledge base of specific actions and behaviors to draw from might make it more difficult to see occasions for employing the limited abilities one does have."[8] A healthy environment that releases the abilities of followers must be developed to create a healthy local church. A church with the disposition of a community of bees is a great sign as to what they are all really motivated to do!

2. **How do we facilitate dispositional development?** Here again, Ron Ritchhart, in his wonderful book, *Intellectual Character*, writes that there are several ways to develop a follower's disposition for greatness.

a. **A Salient Model**

Followers need a model of proper dispositions. This is one of the roles of biblical leadership. Paul says in 3 John 1:11: "Dear friend, do not imitate what is evil, but what is good. The one who does good is of God." The way we learn to do good is to watch other people do good. If my children see me pray, they will pray. If they see me tithe, they will tithe. They mimic me. The word for imitate here is the Greek word that gives us our English word for mimic. Paul says, "Therefore I urge you be imitators of me" (see 1 Corinthians 11:1). In our Western world, that sounds like a tough thing to say to someone, but that is exactly what Paul is saying here. The Greek leaves the sentence open to interpretation in broad ways. We must remember that there were no preceding examples to coach these new Christian leaders. So Paul says "copy me." And he does so in several passages within the New Testament (Galatians 4:12; 2 Thessalonians 3:7-9). If our goal is to create followers with a good disposition, then we should start with a salient model of behavior.

b. **Consistency of Expectations**

My children read the environment of my home and pick up on certain unconscious expectations. As a parent, I have learned the tremendous power that consistency with expectation can bring to me. There is an old saying that says, "You get what you expect." The reason that we have labored through so many laws of community in this book is because it sets the standard of expectations. People know what you will allow and what you will not allow.

> Over the last 14 years at CCC, I have had to make some very painful calls to terminate different individuals—many of whom I actually liked as individuals. The termination sent a clear message to our entire church as to what would be tolerated and what would not be tolerated.

You cannot develop the right dispositions or environments when the expectation is inconsistent. "When the implicit message contradicts the explicit message, the implicit message is likely to win out."[9] Can you imagine with me what your local church could do in your community if you built an intellectual disposition of faith where godly values were lived out because they were expected? Saint Augustine, in his book, *The City of God*, actually argues this point well. He told Rome that had they lived by the consistent values of Christianity, Rome would still be standing today. The hearers of this report had to have known the professed, actualized values of which he was speaking. In other words, early Christians lived out consistent values that were expected of all Christendom, which in turn, created an environment of tremendous dispositional power.

## c. Explicit Instructions

> I don't want to give the impression that dispositions somehow magically appear when conditions are ripe. Although dispositions may develop out of the natural interactions with appropriate and significant role models, there also exists a need for explicit instructions…Although dispositions aren't formed through such direct instructions, the presence of explicit instruction within supportive cultural context over time supports their development.[10]

There is a great strategy in the thinking of God to give Moses a law, because without it people would generally forget its principles. When the law is written down, then you can take it and run with it (Habakkuk 2:2). You can even go back to it and refer to it again.

## PRECEPT TWO:
### We Need Followers Who Are Competent.

Young pastors often ask me what has been the hardest part of building a great church. I answer, "The pain of learning through the school of hard knocks." Early in the development of CCC, I was horrible at choosing major leaders, both full-time and volunteers. It was a hard lesson to learn when I realized that I loved some people much more than they ever loved me. When you have a gift, which enables you to see the best potential in people, that gift has a way of blinding you from their real motives. This precept is so important to church health that I really can't emphasize it enough. The thing that keeps most churches behind and underperforming is the quality of people who attend them. The Barna Group, in 2003, released a survey titled, *"Small Churches Struggle to Grow Because of the People They Attract."* As someone who has spent over 30 years formally studying church growth, I reluctantly must admit it's true. The competence of the people who are members of your church is a crucial element to your productivity for Christ. While the research is pointing to smaller congregations staying small because of the type of people who attend them, I am referring to this research to prove a larger point of the competence needed in all followers. As it relates to smaller congregations, Barna found that they often "draw people who are not college graduates and are more likely to appeal to people with lower household incomes. . . . The data revealed that small churches have a lower participation of attenders who are spiritually active."[11] They, in other words, attract more people who just "sit" and "soak." They attract people with low levels of commitment to God's Word, prayer, and faithfulness to working in their spiritual gifts. According to research, the average person in a small church goes about his/ her spiritual journey believing that it's the "preacher's job" to do the work of ministry. Such a belief system leads us to this truth—the wrong people in your church are worse than no people in your church. The skills and aptitude necessary to complete the task God has assigned to you requires individuals of high quality, who pursue knowledge, and are constantly upgrading their own life skills.

## Wisdom Point A

*Competence begins in your church when each individual becomes personally responsible.* We need another American Revolution, but this time one that awakens the followers of Christ to their personal responsibilities. Bob Dylan said: "I think of a hero as someone who understands the degree of responsibility that comes with his freedom." Newton Minow, former Chairman of the FCC gave some prudent advice to the church when he said: "We've gotten to the point where everybody's got a right and nobody's got a responsibility." In the church world, we all are quick to blame others—the preacher, the executive pastor, the nursery workers, the elders, or deacons—but we are slow to take responsibility. I heard about a lady one time who became irate at the fact that her church did not show up to the hospital for her minor surgery. When the staff looked into the matter, they found out that this lady never told anyone she was going to the hospital and assumed that the church leaders would find out through "the grapevine." She refused to take her responsibility. Church leaders are not mind readers. We blame the teacher for our lack of daily Bible study, we blame the children's pastor because our children are ignorant of the Scriptures; we blame the usher because we couldn't find the bulletins; but on Judgment Day, the blame will not fall on anyone but ourselves. We can't blame others or our environment for the choices we make. "The hallmark of personal responsibility is our willingness to accept that we are accountable for the results of the choices we make."[12]

I love the poor and the uneducated. We are building a great outreach that extends to the poor at CCC, more so than ever before in our history. However, I realized that I needed people of a higher caliber to do so. The local church needs to develop a new set of followers. These followers must have a higher aptitude for learning. Learning has nothing to do with a college education. My mother constantly studies and has never been to college. Many of my mentors have no formal degrees, but read constantly, attend seminars yearly, ask questions constantly, and have developed the wisdom of Solomon—a wisdom that will far exceed some people with Ph.Ds. I am not talking just about accomplished people in academics, but followers who love learning and who want to be their best. Studies show that these people are more likely to attend a large church than a small one. Those same studies tell us that it's the mentality of the people in small churches that keep them unproductive. Not all small churches are unproductive, but those that are unproductive are that way because of the types of people who attend them.

What would your church look like if every member became personally responsible for his or her choices? We are living in a different world today. No one wants to take personal responsibility. If I kill you as I drive drunk in my car, it's not my fault, it's because I was raised in a wealthy home and was not taught correctly. It's the fault of "affluenza." If only my mother had been a better person, if only my schoolteacher would have been a better teacher . . . always the blame game. Yet the potential to activate the kingdom of God lies within the body of Christ taking personal responsibility for themselves, and the overall mission of the church. Responsibility is an emotional competency and an essential element of integrity. Adults show responsibility by controlling their impulses, keeping their promises, and meeting their commitments. If this is true, then we know that spiritual maturity is when people act responsibly, show up on time, and keep their commitments. Competence begins when we take responsibility.

1. **Take Responsibility for your own walk with God.**
The old saying goes: "I can give you a fish, and you will eat for a day; or I can teach you to fish, and you will be able to eat for a lifetime." I want to enable my people to walk with God in a personal way. It is not the church's job to train your children biblically. It is not the pastor's job to do the work of ministry for you; it's his/her job to equip you to do the work of ministry (Ephesians 4:12). A great pastor can tremendously enhance your understanding of the Scriptures, but it is your job to study them out in a daily way (Luke 9:23; 2 Timothy 2:15). The biblical historians are telling us that we are living in the most biblically illiterate generation in the history of Christianity. In a recent CBN report which interviewed people in this generation, "sixty percent could not name half of the Ten Commandments or the four gospels."[13]

> I will never forget the day I took a walk with a pastor friend in Toledo, Ohio, named Tony Scott. He had built a great church after many years of toiling in great faith. As we were walking through his new complex, he made a statement that shook me to my bones. He said to me, "Michael, for years I led a church as if it were a revival center. Then, one day I looked up and noticed that the area churches were full of people who once attended this church. They were here only for the high experience. They hopped from church to church, revival to revival, from emotional experience to emotional experience. I made up my mind that day that I was no longer going to be a revival center, but a teaching center that grounded people in the Word of God. I was going to build a local church, not a revival center. There is a difference." I left his presence that

> day knowing that I had made the same mistake. I
> went home determined to make CCC an anoint-
> ed teaching center of intellectual Charismatics. I
> am not saying that we don't want the "move of
> God," because God only uses people who move!
> His Spirit is always welcome in our church at any
> time or place. However, while America may be
> biblically illiterate, I determined deep within my
> heart that the people I pastor will *not* be illiterate!

Have you ever thought that it might be your own spiritual maturity that's holding your church back from its divine destiny? Your church is only as good as its members. I tell people all the time that CCC is a great church because of its members! We have good people. We have faithful people. We have people who love the Word of God, and they all know, "You can't obey what you do not know!!" The more you study, the more you pray; the more you grow up and begin to work in your gifts, the more mature the church will be. This requires you to be personally responsible for your spiritual competencies! The science of church growth is very clear on this subject. The best way to keep a church ineffective—with an exhausted pastor and stubborn sheep—is to fill it with people who are small-minded. Small-minded people in church don't have much of a personal relationship with God outside of their pastor's weekly sermon. They ride an emotional experience each week at an altar or by "their kind of music" stirring them up. In no time, they are like a Tupperware bowl that has been constantly overheated in the microwave. They live lives that are unbendable, out of shape, and without the original form that their Creator intended for them. Small-minded people don't want to grow the Kingdom, because deep down they feel that the "church" is "theirs." They fear new people, because they fear losing power. They seldom live consistent lives outside of church. They know their church is small-minded, and they wear such belief as a badge. Remember, anything in nature that doesn't reproduce and grow is considered to be unhealthy. And, even great people can be greatly misguided. We are too close to the coming of Christ to let small-minded people demand we build a smaller ark, when we all know the earth is about to flood. It is time for you to mature; it is time to know the laws of community; and it is time to know what God expects of your spiritual life. We must master the Word and practice the consistent use of our giftings.

2. **Take Responsibility for the personal commitments you make.**

It is amazing how some people treat a "gift of the Holy Spirit" in their lives. The God of the universe is giving you a gift (1 Corinthian 12:11), such as teaching or mercy to be used for Him. So when you commit to teach a class, usher on the fourth Sunday of every month, serve at the coffee bar, or agree to register children at sign-in, you are actually being a steward of a gift from God. How do you think God feels when you show up late to your class, unprepared, or do not even call in to report your absence on the fourth Sunday? Do you think He might feel disrespected? Maybe He even senses you are unappreciative of the gift He gave you. Most of us would never treat our "secular" work like we treat our "spiritual work." And while your marketplace ministry is crucial to the health of a local church, you can only take with you what you have done for the kingdom of God! You are not going to be rewarded in eternity for what you accomplished at IBM. You are going to be rewarded only for what you have done for the kingdom of God. First Corinthians 10:31 says, "Therefore, whether you eat or drink, or whatever you do, do everything for God's glory." In Proverbs 12:26, we are told to be "more excellent than [our] neighbors" (KJV). Paul tells us in Philippians 2:5 to "Make your own attitude that of Christ Jesus." It should be a shame to be more diligent and proficient at work than you are in your calling in the kingdom of God. I know that our occupations are our lifelines to providing biblically for our families. However, what you do in the coal mines, your job at Apple, IBM, GE, or for the government will not go with you to the afterlife. I love marketplace ministry. And ministry happens through our God-called occupations outside the local church. But, when we respect temporal things more than we respect spiritual things, then there is a major problem.

Honor the commitments that your giftings bring to you. Do not underestimate their importance to you or to someone else. They are an eternal investment and important for your spiritual development. God cares greatly about your competence in His house. God cares greatly about your competencies for HIM at your place of employment. Christians should be the best workers, the most faithful employees, and serve with the highest of dedication and excellence. You will be rewarded one day for how you treat your calling on this earth. Why do you think the Bible refers to multiple believers being given "crowns" in heaven? (1 Corinthians 9:25-27; 1 Thessalonians 2:19; James 1:12; 1 Peter 5:2-4; Revelation 2:10; 2:17). Revelation 3:11 tells us that we are to "guard" these crowns. Take responsibility for the personal commitments you make. If you are going to be an usher, show up on time, stick a breath mint in your mouth, comb your hair, put on some deodorant, and usher with great excellence! If you are going teach a children's class, Google the age characteristics of the age group you are going to teach, know how to teach them, study your lesson plans, think deeply about how your lesson could become more alive to the children you are about to teach. If you are going to teach, then teach them with excellence. If you have agreed to be an elder, then know your doctrine, know what your church believes and doesn't believe! Know the needs of your pastoral staff and know how to pray and address people with biblical mercy.

Study the laws of community in which you were elected to protect! Bring back excellence to the local church. There is an old joke that absolutely infuriates me when I hear it. It says, "When is a school not a school?" The answer is, "When it's a Sunday school." Where do they think Sunday school originated? It came about in a time long before the development of child labor laws in London. Children would literally have to work all week and thus miss the opportunity for education. Then, one day Robert Blake started taking these same children on Sundays and used the Bible to teach these children to read and write. I firmly believe that the teaching in a local church should be better than the teaching found in the public school system. I will go to my grave demanding a greater level of intellectual capability on Sundays and Wednesdays than can be found in any other teaching institution! So be faithful, competent, and consistent with the call of God on your life every week.

3. **Take Responsibility for Each Other.**

   In the Bible, the greatest lie told by someone is recorded in Genesis 4:9 when God asks Cain: "Where is Abel thy brother?" and he replies, "Am I my brother's keeper?" (KJV). While we cannot be responsible for other people's actions, we are responsible for one another's care and spiritual journey. The Hebrew people cherished community and demanded solidarity. The Hebrews presupposed mutual responsibility, because it was the foundation to their covenant commitment (Leviticus 19:18; Galatians 5:14). To them, "Community responsibility took priority over individual preferences or rights."[14] The church is a collective body (1 Peter 2:9-10), hence the many body metaphors from Paul (Romans 12:3-8; Ephesians 4:12). Cain was the first murderer. He was also the first recorded person to selfishly break a human relationship. Thousands of years later, we see the fruit from his selfish seed when Jesus says in Matthew 24:12: "Because of the increase of wickedness, the love of most will grow cold" (NIV). You don't have to just spot Cain's lie ("I don't know") to know that his heart wasn't right with God (Genesis 4:9). But deeper into this passage, we see the depth of his sin—his lack of love. Leon Morris said: "But real love is impossible for the lawless person. By definition, the lawless person is motivated by personal, selfish concerns, not by any regard for others as far as the rules that govern our intercourse with one another. So with the upsurge of lawlessness, there is a cooling off of love. The one necessarily involves the other."[15]

4. **Take Responsibility for the Financial Integrity of the Church.**

   Keeping any nonprofit solvent is a magnificent feat. God has set up a way to run His church financially through sacrificial giving and tithing. Please save me the rhetoric that tithing was only part of the Mosaic Law. Cain and Abel tithed, why do you think Cain killed Abel? Jesus spoke of tithing (Matthew 23:23). But my argument here is not tithing, but giving. The Scriptures are full of admonitions to believers, regarding tithing and giving sacrificially to the work of the Lord (Leviticus 27:30-32; Deuteronomy 23:4; Matthew 23:23; Luke 2:41; 12:48; 1 Corinthians 16:1-2; 2 Corinthians 8:2-3; 9:7; 1 Timothy 5:17-18). The higher ideal is to consistently, cheerfully, and joyfully give to the work of Christ (2 Corinthians 9:7). Do you think that we should sacrifice less than the ancient patriarchs? We have more revelation and greater blessings than any before us. I have learned that the people who gripe the most about giving never give. The people who talk the most about how the church handles money never give. *I wonder how those who don't believe in giving to a local church actually think ministry goes forth without sacrificial giving.* The construction paper your child comes home with every Sunday isn't free. The lights you sit under, the air conditioning you enjoy, the insurance for your family's safety, the video screen that communicates the gospel to you, the microphones that amplify worship, or the tens of thousands of dollars in curriculum, all cost money and require resources. The resources you faithfully and consistently give help in protecting your pastor and church leaders from burnout.

I don't think the average follower understands how faithful stewardship serves as a tremendous encouragement to the church leadership. Honestly, very few pastors "milk the ministry" to become rich; most are sincere, hardworking, precious individuals. They all carry the final burden of your church's financial integrity. And, this responsibility does not end just because its spring break or the Fourth of July. God has blessed you to be a blessing, so assume responsibility for making your church a house overflowing with resources for ministry. Don't let your pastor carry the financial burden of your church alone! Electricity for a nonprofit is the same cost as any secular business. And, once again, you can't take it with you. Give out of love, and give to win souls (John 3:16). Give with consistency (1 Corinthians 16:1-2), and give without expecting to get something in return. Give sacrificially (2 Corinthians 8:1-13; 9:6), and give to make a difference! Give to defeat idolatry in your life. Give to master greed; give to change a life; give to send an invitation; give to rebuild a home; and give to protect the financial integrity of your church and the name of Jesus. Give willingly (2 Corinthian 8:11-12). Give expectantly (Luke 6:38)! Give cheerfully (2 Corinthians 9:7). Give . . . it is how the gospel started! "For God loved the world in this way: He gave His One and Only Son, that everyone who believes in Him will not perish but have eternal life" (John 3:16).

Some people object to tithing based on the New Testament as an Old Testament practice. If you believe this, then you had better hope and pray that tithing is an Old Testament issue. Here is the reason why. In the Old Testament, all God asked from you was ten percent—a tithe (Genesis 14:20; 28:20-22; Leviticus 27:30-32; Nehemiah 12:44; Amos 4:4; Malachi 3:8-10; Matthew 23:23; 18:12; Luke 11:41-42; Hebrews 7:5-9). There is a huge difference between the Old Testament's direction on giving and the New Testament's directions on giving. In the Old Testament, God required a tenth (Leviticus 27:30-32). In the New Testament, God asks for much more! (Luke 18:22; Acts 11:27-39; 1 Corinthians 16:1-2; 2 Corinthians 9:7). God hates a few things

(Proverbs 6:16-19). One of the things the Bible says God hates is greed. Greed is a sin and completely contrary to the character of God (Mark 7:22; Luke 12:15; Romans 1:29; 1 Corinthian 6:10; Ephesians 5:3). So, children of God, give and give cheerfully as God uses you!

## Wisdom Point B

*It takes relational competence to build a community.* All of us are still maturing on some level. None of us has reached perfection (Philippians 3:12; James 1:1-27).

> I once knew a man who led a massive amount of people. He tirelessly traveled the road of reaching the academic apex. He held an earned doctorate and was one of my favorite speakers. He showed maturity in discerning the "times we live in," just as the children of Issachar "knew what we should do about them." (1 Chronicles 12:32). He could take any audience into ecstasy with his mastery of words. Yet, while he showed great maturity in these areas of leadership, he still lacked great maturity in biblical community. This "giant of the faith" did not even know the basics in the laws of community. When confronted with a relational virus in his organization, he resorted to childlike relational behavior. He refused to "play" with other "classmates," because they were "playing" with his former "friends."

Such immaturity in the laws of community becomes a deadly poison. Its venom flows through our blood, affecting everyone in the church. When unity is lacking, oxygen is lacking. When community in your church is sick, your church is sick. Community is the sign of health. That is why church hoppers are more dangerous than the bite of a Brazilian wandering spider. Their bite usually causes death by asphyxiation, thus causing a loss of muscle control. In some cases, their bite causes priapism in males. A church hopper cannot mature; it's impossible. They walk away from every fight. They are afraid of commitment. Just like the Brazilian wandering spider, when church members can't get along with each other, it spreads a deadly poison that literally takes their breath away. They fight against each other, not for each other. Community is the oxygen of the local church, because the Holy Spirit has breathed life into each individual member. When we are living in deep community, there is freshness in the air. Unity gives the body oxygen to breathe. But when we fight each other, the oxygen—the life of the Holy Spirit (Acts 2:42)—is asphyxiated. We literally choke. When we fight and fuss with each other outside the boundaries clearly set by Scripture, we become impotent. The Word of God is our powerful sword. When we ignore what it has to say about living a competent life, relationally, the body will suffer.

Fighting stimulates many believers, for it is their reason for existence. This "over stimulation" exerts itself needlessly until the ability to truly reproduce in a healthy manner has vanished. We are called to reproduce, not waste our precious human resources in battling each other; but we should direct our energies in uniting each other for the correct battle. Those who waste their energies on strife and church gossip, do so at the expense of misunderstanding their call. Divisive people often think that they are to protect and guard the church from the pastor! Show me a church always fighting, and I will show you an impotent church; a place where procreation always ends in a miscarriage, abortions, or worse yet, infanticide!

The Holy Spirit is the giver of life through His breath (Genesis 2:6-7; John 20:22). He is our teacher and guide (John 14:26). He brings life (Matthew 1:18; John 3:5; 7:37-39; Romans 1:4). Our bodies are His temples (1 Corinthians 6:19). John 14:16 tells us that the Holy Spirit is given to us as a comforter. In Romans 8:9, we are told that if we don't "have" the Spirit, we do not belong to Him. The word, *have* means "to possess." The Holy Spirit lives in us. In Acts 1:4, we are told to "wait" *with one another*. In Acts 2:4, *"they"* were all filled with the Holy Spirit at the same time. The power of the Spirit began with *being together*, and according to Acts 2:42, the power of the Spirit birthed a deeper form of community. The Holy Spirit works individually and in corporate ways. How can we defame one another and not realize we are defaming an image of God? (Genesis 1:26). How can we divide a body that the Holy Spirit himself brought together (Acts 1:4, 8; 2:4)? How is it possible to believe that the church is full of the Spirit if there is division among us (Jude 1:19)? The writings of John in chapter 15 tell us that when we connect to the Vine, we bear "much fruit" (Galatians 5:22). It is not possible for the Spirit of God to divide His body! We are one body. It is time for the local church to mature enough to discern what the Scriptures are telling us about our relational lives. It gives direction on the rules of community, and nowhere does it give us permission to blame another "playmate" for the actions of "other playmates." It is time to become competent in our interactions with "one another." The only exception would be if the "playmate" was living in unrepentant sin. My point is simple. We know what the Scripture says about divine healing, seed-faith giving, and prophecy, but when are we going to learn what it says about how we all should go about living together in church life? When are we going to become spiritually mature enough to become competent in our relational lives? It is time for the church to become competent in its relational life. What would it mean to become competent in our relationship with one another?

*Competence*, according to the *Merriam Webster Dictionary*, means "readiness of bacteria to undergo genetic transformation; the ability to do something well; the quality or state of being competent." There are four stages of competence, or as psychologists refer to it—"the conscious competence learning models." This model, according to

Wikipedia, relates to the psychological states involved in the process from incompetence to competence in a skill. As stated, there are four stages of learning to become competent in something.

The first stage is called the *unconscious stage*. In this stage, we do not understand how to do something, and we may not even realize we are inept in this particular knowledge. For example, many pastors do not cognitively realize that they do not understand the structural mechanism involved in church growth. One cannot structure a group of 50 the way one must structure a group of 250. Yet, we might not consciously realize that we do not understand this principle; therefore, we are unconscious of our incompetencies in the structures of church growth. To become spiritually competent in the relational life of church, we must have an awareness that God's laws speak to this subject with a depth of which we are presently unaware. We must recognize our deficit in the laws of community. We must recognize the value of acquiring these new skills. The first step to becoming competent in community is to recognize our own incompetence in this area, and furthermore, to grasp the importance of learning these skills. Then, we must begin to make a new commitment to address this deficit of knowledge in our spiritual lives.

The second stage is the *conscious incompetence*. I do not know how to sing, and I know I don't know how to sing. I am aware of both the fact I cannot sing and that I don't know how to sing. Furthermore, I know that I would need to develop new skills to do so, thus addressing this deficit in my life. This is a conscious incompetence. This second stage requires making a new commitment to address this deficit in our lives. Once we realize that we don't know the laws of community (stage one), then we can make a commitment to address the deficit (stage two).

The third stage is a *conscious competence*. As a landscaper, I know how to plant a flower garden. I know that certain colors must be placed in a certain order for the eye to follow, and I realize that there is a law of how we number the planting of flowers in sequence. This understanding and awareness is demonstrated by the knowledge and skill of landscaping. When you know the steps and can focus on each of them in a chronological pattern with ease, you are consciously competent. To become consciously competent in community is to learn the laws of community so well that we know how to address a relational virus in our church without straining to know what to do. It is in us so deeply that we don't have to think about it, because we have so internalized the scriptural laws of community that they flow out of us naturally. For example, if someone—a member of your church—said to another member in your church that he "heard" that your pastor was seen by another person coming out of a hotel room with a woman other than his wife (he was sure it was not his wife), you should automatically know that gossip will be sent by Satan to destroy your church. You should know the Scriptures so well that you automatically recall the law of community that relates to accusations against an elder. This law is found in 1 Timothy 5:19. To be consciously competent would mean that you instantly ask if there is more than one eyewitness. This law not only protects the church from wayward leaders, but it also protects godly leaders from wayward believers! To be consciously competent in community is to understand how to do something. You know that there is a biblical law of community, informing us how we are to address such accusations against an elder.

The fourth stage is called *unconscious competence*. This is like tying your shoes; you don't even think about the skill you have mastered, you just perform the skill with great ease. It is like driving home or riding a bike, you just perform the function without thinking about how to do it. You have refined the skill so well that you don't have to concentrate on performing the task. To become unconsciously competent in community is to arrive at a place where your church knows the Word so well that they immediately quote the Scripture as their guide in any situation. For example, another member in the church has constantly stirred up malicious gossip about the leader who teaches the boys on Wednesday night. To be unconsciously competent in community would require that we instantly recognize this person is acting in the flesh (1 Corinthians 3:3). We know that envy and strife are the signs of carnality. We have become so unconsciously competent in community that we know what to do, where the scripture is found, and it takes little or no thought because it resides deep within us.

It takes a relational competence to build a community. Community just doesn't happen; it takes hard work—work that is oftentimes emotionally exhausting and relationally challenging. But the payoffs are out of this world!

## PRECEPT THREE:
### We Need Followers Who Have Courage.

I always live my ministerial life by a certain set of rules. One such rule I go by is this: Choose your fight. Ask yourself what hill would you be willing to die on and what hill will you refuse to die on? The one hill I will always charge is disunity. Don't get me wrong, I am not looking for a fight. I don't want to fight. I want unity, so we can win the world for Jesus. However, I know that when the Enemy stirs up disunity, I am either going to have to choose to be a coward or charge a hill. Charging any hill takes competence. And, it is hard and often unappreciated work. However, I know that all of the competence in the world doesn't matter if you don't have the courage to live by your convictions. In the Bible, Daniel is one such example. He lived a pure and blameless life as a leader, yet he was a loyal follower at the same time. He was diligent in all his duties, and he excelled in the kingdom of Babylon. His competencies were known throughout the kingdom of Nebuchadnezzar. Yet, this competent servant-leader refused to compromise his convictions! He knew what was right and lived his life by placing first things first. When confronted unjustly, it did not change his decisions. He did not "give in" because he wanted "peace." Giving in to your adversary can never bring peace. Only following God's laws will bring the assurance of peace. Daniel lived by a set of values and principles that were not for sale; they were fixed. But all of the "convictions" in the world are worthless if you don't have the courage to take a stand for them. I think it is important to remember that Daniel was a follower with courage.

## Wisdom Point A

*Great followers have the courage to follow.* It takes a great deal of courage to follow someone else. There can be no leaders without followers, because leaders cannot accomplish their goals without effectively leading followers. Every leader is at some point a follower, due to the fact that every leader usually has a leader over him or her. I like how Kelley describes such a follower:

> A follower is one who pursues a course of action in common with a leader to achieve an organizational goal. Effective followers make an active decision to contribute towards the achievement of the goal and demonstrate enthusiasm, intelligence, self-reliance, and the ability to work with others in pursuit of the goal. Effective followers recognize the authority of the leader and limitations that imposes on their own actions, consider all issues on their merits, make their own decisions, hold their own values, speak their minds and hold themselves accountable for the consequences for their actions.[16]

I sincerely believe that Daniel exemplified this type of leadership as a follower. Ira Chaleff, in his book, *The Courageous Follower: Standing Up, to and for Our Leaders,* says there are five forms of courage that every follower needs.

> First, *courageous followers have the courage to assume responsibility* for themselves and the organization. Daniel was the administrator of the satraps. He ensured that the king would not be defrauded (Daniel 6:1-2). He assumed his responsibility as a follower to his leader so well that his enemies had to make up false charges on him. He was said to have had "an extraordinary spirit, so the king had planned to set him over the whole realm" (Daniel 6: 3-5). Second, courageous followers *have the courage to serve.* They are not afraid of hard work, and they assume additional responsibilities to unburden the leader. In Daniel 6:3, we can see the great trust that Daniel's leader held for him as a follower. Courageous followers stand up for the leader and the tough decisions that they make as a leader. Third, they have the *courage to challenge the process,* behaviors, or policies, when they believe such actions violate their values. They are not afraid of rejection or to initiate conflict and correction. While Daniel obeyed God over his leader's edict, he also continued to honor his leader (Daniel 6:21). Fourth, courageous leaders have the *courage to participate in transformation.* Daniel did not run from tough times (Daniel 6:10-11, 16, 19, 21). These types of heroes challenge the process and embrace change like a kid embraces a stick of cotton candy. They stay committed to their leaders during the unstable climates of change. They too are not afraid of change or to examine their own need for transformation. Nowhere does the Scripture state that Daniel ever blamed his leader, but instead, he continued to be exemplary in his followership. Fifth, they have the *courage to take moral action.* They are not afraid to take a stand when the majority refuses to arise to the occasion. When everyone else is hiding, refusing to tell the emperor that they are naked, they are not afraid to do what it takes to not only bring about change but also to live by their

professed value systems. It takes a lot of courage to be a follower.[17]

Daniel stood up when everyone else refused to stand (Daniel 6: 10). He wasn't afraid to obey God before man or his leaders. He knew his Supreme Authority and refused to replace him for the sake of convenience, political power, or wealth. The world will tell you that if you do what is right, you will suffer for it. Sometimes this is true, but in Daniel's case, he prospered because of it! (Daniel 6:25-26).

We must have courageous followers in the local church—followers who love their leaders like Daniel did. We need followers who are not so quick to misjudge their leaders or too slow to go against the flow of the crowd. Daniel taught us that courageous followers are leaders, and courageous leaders are great followers!

## Wisdom Point B

In the face of an unknown future, followers are made secure by the presence of a capable leader!

> When I was a little boy, my father used to take my cousin and me hunting for raccoons! I don't know if you understand the concept, but let me explain it. You go into the woods at the pitch-dark of night. You take two "coon dogs" that bark like a wolf howling at the full moon. Add a mean boar raccoon to the mix that has no intentions whatsoever on giving in to you or the dogs in the cold, dark-pitch of night, and then add some sound effects that would make any make-shift haunted house a grand success. At least, now you have a basic concept of "coon hunting" in western Kentucky. So, here I am with my cousin "Stevie," both of us under nine years old, away from the comfort of home, looking at a full moon while two dogs howl like ferocious animals bent on killing something. The adults in the group chase the dogs that in turn chase the raccoons! Now, these adults are old men (at least to two nine-year-olds) who are usually more concerned

about chasing the dogs that are chasing the raccoon, than keeping up with two, nine-year-old boys. This dreadful event takes place in the pitch-dark of night, under the glow of a full moon, where branches hit you in the face, water fills your shoes, and the cold air floods your veins like a bucket of ice. Does this sound like fun? I didn't think so, but the point here is this: I know what it is to be afraid. Add to this crazy scenario the fact that I am staying up late at night watching old horror movies with my mother and documentaries about Sasquatch roaming the countryside, and you have the possibilities of a circus sideshow on your hands. I know what it is to be scared. But here is my deeper point. My fear was in direct proportion to the distance of my earthly father. I still remember being so scared that the only solace I had was the absence of fear on my father's face. Somehow, Stevie and I conquered our fear, because of the lack of fear on our leader's face—in this case, our fathers' faces.

Confident leaders have a way of making followers feel secure in the future. Courageous followers must be confident leaders. There is an Old Testament story recorded in Deuteronomy 31:6; Joshua 1:9; and 1 Chronicles 28:20; we will use Deuteronomy 31:5-6 to make our point. All three passages, in essence, give us the same instructions. "Be strong and courageous, don't be terrified or afraid of them. For it is the Lord your God who goes with you; He will not leave you or forsake you." Consider the following breakdown, which hopefully will help to enhance the security of our followers.

1. **Moses publically endorsed Joshua as the leader**. How many times do you publically endorse your leaders? Do people know where you stand? Deuteronomy 31:7 says, "Then Moses called Joshua and said to him in the sight of all Israel" (NKJV). It is important to publically endorse your leader so people will know you are unified with him or her. Don't assume that your local church knows your

position. Unfortunately, the only time most church leaders know where you stand is when there's a fight!

> My wife's family helped me to understand the importance of expressing where I stand at a recent birthday party for the matriarch of the family. Rather than wait for her death, they each wrote a very heartfelt letter to this wonderful lady. The uniqueness of these letters was that they all publically read their letters to her as she sat and listened. It was a beautiful moment. I thought to myself as I watched: *I want all my loved ones to know what I think about them while they are still living. I don't want to wait until they are gone to reminisce and praise them.*

Your leaders need to know that you support them. Every week I get a letter from a member who does nothing but encourage me. This member praises the sermon, the church, the church people, guest speakers, new colors in the lobby, and anything else found to be praiseworthy. It literally makes my day and gives me more energy to build a better church than any other element. The power of words is amazing, because, after all, the entire world was made by words. Followers need to know what their leaders think about them; leaders need to know what their followers think about them. Don't reserve your words for only criticism. Speak up; build a local church by praising your leaders. Confidence in the leader will in return build great confidence in the followers.

2. **Divine Encouragement is expressed through human encouragement.**

God wanted to encourage the people of Israel. But in these passages, He used his human leaders to express His divine encouragement. Multiple times

Moses uses the expression, "the Lord your God" in relaying a message. God needs your mouth, not only to encourage His leaders, but also to express His encouragement to other followers. You speak for Him whether you realize it or not. When a courageous follower speaks faith-filled words, it lights up the environment. When you praise three times quicker than you ever thought to criticize, you will change the atmosphere in your church. You will build each other up like Paul told us to do (1 Thessalonians 5:11). This building up includes you in building up your leaders. I am tired of church people placing a qualifier in front of a complement that warns the recipient that the positive thing they are about to say is not to increase that person's pride. When was the last time you praised a sports star and said: "Now, I don't want you to get the big head but that was a great pitch"? The answer is never! You would never meet a famous sports star and say such a thing, because I believe we all know that it takes more humility to receive a compliment than it does to reject one! God wants to encourage His people through your lips! Let God use you this Sunday and go through your church looking for courageous followers and leaders to compliment and praise.

3. **Take courage in the presence of the Lord**.

Daniel had no one to encourage him. It's a hard and difficult fact that success in your life is often hated by others. They are too much of a coward to tell it to you publicly. They would never admit it for fear that their weakness might be revealed. They secretly work behind closed doors as they manipulate the system with the goal of your demise. Daniel 6:10 must have been a very lonely moment. Living out your principles when times are tough builds character in your life (Romans 5:4-6). But it doesn't make it any easier when you have to do what is right alone. So what should a courageous follower do in times that he/she is required to stand alone? Take courage in the presence of the Lord. In Deuteronomy 31:6, we are told to be "strong and courageous" because "the Lord your God who goes with you; He will not leave you or forsake you." How many times have you heard it said, "Had the Lord not been on my side where would I be?" The presence of the Lord brings courage.

4. **A Follower's past can bring courage to him or her**. In Deuteronomy 31:4, it says, "The Lord will deal with them (your future enemies) as He did Sihon and Og, the kings of the Amorites, and their land when He destroyed them." The reason that competence is so important in a courageous follower's life is because past experiences serve as teaching moments, thus enabling him or her with a knowledge not previously known. Had we not had a past fight with a dark night, we would not know how to handle the dark night in which we presently find ourselves. The past gives us valuable experience that we will need for tomorrow. God reminded Israel that He had already defeated Sihon and Og for them in the past. He was telling them that this new enemy could be taken care of just like He took care of the last enemy that tried to destroy them! To be a courageous follower only reminds us of the countless times when God has shown up for us. Recall the enemies in your past and remember God's faithfulness to you! Your past can bring you encouragement.

5. **As a courageous follower, never be intimidated by the menacing opposition of your present enemy!**
   God said in Deuteronomy 31:6: "Don't be terrified or afraid of them." Courage oftentimes has to break through intimidating circumstances. It takes courage to go to the next level. And the next level is usually guarded by the hounds of hell that use the spirit of intimidation to keep you from the gates of your future destiny!

   > My mother and my Aunt Peggy took me and my cousin Stevie to a haunted house when we were young. I know this is beginning to sound sadistic; it does to me as well. However, we were scared out of our wits by ghosts and goblins, witches, and a mad scientist. That was until my mother told me that they were only people dressed up as frightening figures. Then, all of a sudden, what once paralyzed me with fear now had no hold on me. What was the difference? The absence of fear.

   God has said not to be terrified or afraid of your enemies! He has exposed the Prince of Darkness for the defeated foe he is. Colossians 2:15 says, "He disarmed the rulers and authorities and disgraced them publicly; He triumphed over them by Him." So what is there to fear? Nothing. Only be strong and courageous!!!

6. **Courageous followers realize that God is faithful in times of transitions.**
   Moses was leading the children of Israel in a great time of transition. Joshua was newly appointed as their leader. They were in a new land, preparing to take new territory. Change can be unnerving, just ask the cowardly lion in the movie, *The Wizard of Oz*. He agreed to start walking on the Yellow Brick Road in hopes of change. It wasn't too long before

frightening mystical creatures flying through the air met that walk. Sometimes when we are changing, success can look a lot like failure. Joshua was human too. However, he held on to the dream of reaching the Promised Land, no matter the cost involved in possessing it. It is going to take a courageous follower and a fearless leader to help change your church into a loving community of faith. Don't be afraid!

7. **Courageous followers do, at times, become discouraged.**

> I have worked for months on an event, and only 12 people showed up. I have preached my heart out, only to barely muster one "amen." I have trusted people who betrayed me. I have dealt with moral failure in the lives of people I loved. I have prayed for a financial breakthrough, fasting for 30 days, only to lose my building. I know what it is to be discouraged.

In Deuteronomy 31:8, it says to us, "Do not be afraid or discouraged." Courageous followers encourage one another (1 Thessalonians 5:11). It is important to remember that the Christian life is the overcoming life. John 16:33 says, "You will have suffering in this world. Be courageous! I have conquered the world." Paul says to us in 2 Corinthians 4:16:

> Therefore we do not give up. Even though our outer person is being destroyed, our inner person is being renewed day by day. For our momentary affliction is producing for us an absolutely incomparable eternal weight of glory. So we do not focus on what is seen, but on what is unseen. For what is seen is temporary, but what is unseen is eternal.

You know the saying, what doesn't kill you, can only make you stronger! Think about how many times you assumed the worst possible outcome. How many times have you said, "This is it; this is where I am going down!" And has it ever happened to you? The answer is nothing that the adversary has thrown at you thus far has prospered long term! God has delivered you out of them all! We all can get discouraged from the emotional challenges of life. But 2 Kings 6:16 is an antidote for the sickness of human discouragement. It says, "Don't be afraid, for those who are with us outnumber those who are with them." First Samuel 30:6 says, "David was in a difficult position because the troops talked about stoning him, for they were all very bitter over the loss of their sons and daughters. But David found strength in the Lord his God." Leading people can be tough and following great leaders can be an even tougher call sometimes. Both take tremendous courage. Courageous followers will become discouraged, but God has left you alone to form the most effective arsenal against your adversary—the power to encourage yourself!

In the face of the unknown, future followers need the presence of capable leaders. Such leaders often extinguish the fiery darts of doubt and unbelief by their demeanor. Courage has a price that is often called upon for payment at a moment's notice. Courage is often for specific times and seasons. Courageous followers secure such faith in unexpected seasons when nothing is seemingly happening. Yet, when the moment comes, they arise to the occasion and conquer in their finest hour.

## Precept Four:
### We Need Courageous Followers Who Act by Faith.

Do you have enough faith to build an ark in a day when it had never rained? Would you swallow your pride and dip in a pool seven times, looking as foolish as possible, for the possibility of a healing? Hebrews 11:7 says, "By faith Noah, after being warned about what was not yet seen, in reverence built an ark to deliver his family." How much faith does it take to become a courageous follower? In the arena of courage, there is no room for people pleasing. Nor is there time for worrying about your public image. Courage requires selling completely out to God regardless of what the masses are saying about you. Noah wasn't crazy; the people who were drowning were. Naaman who had leprosy did not want to wash in the Jordan. He thought Elisha was irrational. But, God operates by a different set of rules. He wants His followers to place their foot in the Jordan River, THEN it will divide. God requires faith, and it takes courage to live in faith. When you mingle your faith with the encouragement of God, miracles happen. If you are going to be a courageous follower, you too will be called upon to activate miraculous times with uncommon faith.

## Precept Five:
### We Need Courageous Followers
### Whose Courage Produces Prosperity.

When the Hebrew children gained the courage to cross the Jordan River, they inherited the Promised Land. When Noah garnered the courage to build an ark in a world that laughed at his expense, he saved his family from total destruction. When the woman with the issue of blood mustered up the courage to press her way through the crowd, she found favor. You can't exhibit courage in God's house without finding prosperity. First Chronicles 22:13 says, "Then you will succeed if you carefully follow the statues and ordinances the Lord commanded Moses for Israel. Be strong and courageous." In Deuteronomy 30:7, it says to us, "Be strong and courageous, for you WILL go with this people into the land the Lord swore to give to their fathers. You WILL enable them to take possession of it. The Lord is One who WILL go before you. He WILL be with you; He WILL not leave you or forsake you. Do not be afraid or discouraged." Courage in faith activates the hand of God. Courageous followers know that faith will require a moment of courage. Courageous followers are confident, not in their ability to move mountains, split the Red Sea, or heal diseases such as leprosy, but in the promises of God. He has promised to go with you. He has promised to be with you. He has promised not to leave you alone on the battlefield. He has promised not to leave. If that's not enough to encourage a frightened soldier, then I don't know what will.

# END NOTES

Chapter Ten
The Law of Followership

1 "Wikipedia Community," Wikipedia, www.wikipedia.org/wiki/Community.

2 Robert Kelley, *The Power of Followership* (New York: Currency Doubleday, 1992), 30.

3 Kelley, *The Power of Followership*, 34.

4 Ibid., 41.

5 Ron Ritchhart, *Intellectual Character: What It Is, Why It Matters, and How to Get It* (San Francisco: Jossey-Bass, 2002), 34.

6 Ritchhart, *Intellectual Character*, 36.

7 Ibid., 37.

8 Ibid., 37.

9 Ibid., 47.

10 Ibid., 47-48.

11 "Small Churches Struggle to Grow Because of the People They Attract," The George Barna Group, February 10, 2014, September 2, 2003, www.barna.org/barna-update/article/5-barna-update/126small-churches-struggle-to-grow-because-of-the-people-they-attract#UwQLEHmklds.

[12] Doug Lennick and Fred Kiel, *Moral Intelligence: Enhancing Business Performance and Leadership Success* (New Jersey: Wharton School Publishing, 2005), 95.

[13] "Know Your Bible? Many Christians Don't," CBN, February 27, 2014, July 24, 2009, www.cbn.com/cbnnews/us/2009/June/Do-You-Know-Your-Bible-Many-Christians-Don't/.

[14] Kenneth A. Mathews, *New American Commentary Volume 1A Genesis 1-11:26*, logos Software, ed. E. Ray Clendenen (Nashville: Broadman and Holman, 1996).

[15] Leon Morris, *The Pillar New Testament Commentary: The Gospel According to Matthew*, logos Software, ed. D.A. Carson (Grand Rapids: William B. Eerdmans Publishing Company, 1992).

[16] Robert Kelley, *The Power of Followership* (New York: Currency Doubleday, 1992).

[17] Ira Chaleff, *The Courageous Follower: Standing Up, to and for Our Leaders*, 2nd ed. (San Francisco: Berret-Koehler Publishers, 2002).

## CHAPTER ELEVEN

# THE LAW OF SPEECH

## The Knowledge Box

**The Law of Speech** is the faculty or act of expressing or describing thoughts, feelings, or perceptions by the articulation or words in such a way that it lifts up the people of God. It not only refuses to speak words that destroy human lives, but it is also highly committed to speaking life to oneself—a life that was created in the image of God.

**The Precepts:**
1. Your Words Carry Within Them the Power of Life and Death.
2. The Words of Community Make or Break Your Community.

Our speech is a religious issue to God. James, the half-brother of Jesus tells us, "And the tongue is a fire. The tongue, a world of unrighteousness, is placed among the parts of our bodies. It pollutes the whole body, sets the course of life on fire, and is set on fire by hell" (James 3:6). He even went further with this warning in James 1:26: "If anyone thinks he is religious without controlling his tongue, then his religion is useless and he deceives himself." James, the half-brother of Jesus said that "religion"—belief in God—can be directly related to speech! Jesus himself said, "I tell you that on the day of judgment people will have to account for every careless word they speak. For by your words you will be acquitted, and by your words you will be condemned" (Matthew 12:36-37). Words are, after all, a faithful index to one's soul. In Matthew, Jesus says that our words are an estimation of our character. They are mirrors into one's heart, which reveal the heart's true intentions. Jesus actually uses the word *idle*, which means "a word spoken insincerely with no moral usefulness, a word that is hurtful and unproductive." This word literally means "without work." We are admonished by Christ not to speak words that do not give us productive work. Just as fruit is a product of its tree, words are a product of one's heart. In fact, the Scripture says, "For the mouth speaks from the overflow of the heart" (Matthew 12:34).

We all tend to believe that God doesn't pay close attention to our words. After all, the average man speaks around 7,000 words a day, while the average woman speaks nearly 20,000 words each day. That would mean that every year a man speaks over 2,555,000 words each year, while a woman would speak close to 7,280,000 words per year. Now there are currently 3,589,563,409 (billion) women on earth today speaking on the average of 20,000 words each day, which would mean that in just one day, the women of the world have spoken over 71,791,268,180,000 (trillion) words. There are 3,641,675,801 (billion) men in the world, and if each one is speaking an average of 7,000 words a day, it would total 25,491,730,607,000 (trillion) words each day. Together that would equate to 101,282,998,787,000 (trillion) words spoken every single day in this world. It is mind-boggling to think that God hears each word we speak, and He is going to judge us by our words. So, be careful what you say.

Why should we watch what we say, and why are the words we speak so important to God? In Proverbs, the Bible records seven things God hates: "The Lord hates six things; in fact, seven are detestable to Him: arrogant eyes, a lying tongue, hands that shed innocent blood, a heart that plots wicked schemes, feet eager to run to evil, a lying witness who gives false testimony, and one who stirs up trouble among brothers" (vv. 16-19). All of these things require a direct violation to the laws of community. Yet, three of them directly require the misuse of the tongue, and a fourth requires the use of the tongue to plot an evil scheme. Our words really do have power.

## Precept One:
### Your Words Carry Within Them the Power of Life and Death.

In Proverbs 18:21, we find this vital bit of wisdom. "Life and death are in the power of the tongue, and those who love it will eat its fruit." Few people would say that the local church isn't on earth to bring life. Fewer people would admit that the same local church is not on earth to bring that life to those who are perishing. But here is the problem: we are so focused on abortion, homosexual marriage, and drunkenness that we now quite possibly have thousands of local churches on earth with adherents guilty of murder. Let me explain. The ancient rabbis took this passage very seriously. The rabbis in the Talmud note "that if one embarrasses someone in public, the victim's face often turns white." They compare that to the pale face of the dead, so they say that embarrassing a person is akin to killing him or her. In fact, they go further: such a remark also "kills" both the speaker and the listener. The rabbis, therefore, call slander "the third tongue" (*lishan telitae*), because "it slays three people: the speaker, the listener, and the one spoken about" (Bablyonian Talmud, *Arakhin* 15b). Not only do speech violations cause death, but they also deprive a person of a place in the world to come."[1] The concept that our words carry with them—the power of life and death—are poignant. The Bible teaches us clearly that our words have the power to heal or kill, to encourage or discourage, to bring life or death to one's spirit.

## Wisdom Point A

*A good tongue has power.* The writer of Proverbs 10:11 says that "the mouth of the righteous is a fountain of life." Our mouths should be wells from which others may draw refreshing water for life. The righteous, those who stand in right position before God, are to be the kind of people whose words refresh others. A negative word can make one's spirit weary, but "A word spoken at the right time is like gold apples on a silver tray" (Proverbs 25:11). When God blessed Solomon, He did so based on a unique principle. Solomon could ask God for anything in the world, yet he asked God for wisdom (2 Chronicles 1:7-10). Proverbs 10:31 tells us that such wisdom is produced from the mouths of the righteous. Therefore, wisdom is directly connected to our mouths and the speech that comes out of it. When Solomon requested wisdom from God, he gained the favor of God. It was the words he used with God that brought him favor.

1. **God used His words to create the universe and set its atmosphere.**

   Without words, our thoughts can never become a reality. Words have vibration and sound to them. They go forth and have the power to create life. John says from the very beginning of time, the Word existed. Not only did God create the heavens and organize nature, but the Word also created man and everything in this world. Jesus himself, the Ancient of Days, is actually called by John, the Word (John1:1). There is tremendous power in His words, for God used words to create man. Man was thus created like His Father as a speaking human being.

   You were created in the image of God (Genesis 1:26) by words. These words were used to create a positive atmosphere for you. In Genesis 1, we see multiple times where God spoke words and created something beautiful through them. But there is a deeper truth still. Notice that after He spoke and thus created, He observed and watched the results of His words. Consistently, the Bible records, "And God saw that it was good" (Genesis 1:12). He knew, and Scriptures teach, that words not only create an atmosphere, but also individuals have a responsibility over the words they speak—they are to be good stewards over them. The Lord told Jeremiah: "I watch over My word to accomplish it" (1:12). God set this principle into the Rock of Ages. Notice in the first chapter of Genesis how many times God "saw" the results of His words as good. My question for you is this: How would the atmosphere of your church change if you took responsibility to speak "good" over its creation?

2. **Good words protect.**

In Proverbs 12:18, we learn that "the tongue of the wise brings healing." Proverbs 15:4 goes on to say that the kind of "tongue" that heals is actually called a "tree of life." The kind of words that a "healing tongue" brings, according to Proverbs 15:26, are "pleasant words [that] are pure." These words serve not only the hearer but also the speaker, since Proverbs 14:3 tells us that "the lips of the wise protect them." The Bible tells us to, "Stay away from a foolish man; you will gain no knowledge from his speech" (Proverbs 14:7). But in Proverbs 15:2, we are told that, "the tongue of the wise makes knowledge attractive." The benefits from holding a "good tongue" exceed the attraction to knowledge, because "Truthful lips endure forever. . . . Whoever speaks the truth declares what is right" (Proverbs 12:19, 17). We must ensure that our words are working for us, not against us. This is not "charismatic, positive confessions" that ignore and refuse difficult times. This is the principle of a good life that the Creator planned for you a long time ago.

There is something to positive speaking. Dr. Norman Vincent Peale made positive thinking popular in 1952, when he taught that we should shut out negative thoughts and focus on positive thinking, and success would naturally follow. Many hyper-faith ministers have built the "Word of Faith" movement on this teaching. However, positive psychology understands the "benefits of mindfulness, which means accepting both the positive and negative emotions and then acting consciously, while staying true to personal values and goals."[2] Positive emotions are linked to positive words. We have already seen clearly that our words—our speech—

create "healing," "life," both "pleasant" and "pure" emotions, "protection," and an "attraction to wisdom." According to Harvard Medical School, "Positive emotions have been linked with better health, longer life, and greater wellbeing in numerous scientific studies. On the other hand, chronic anger and hostility increase the risk of developing heart disease, as people react to these feelings with raised blood pressure and stiffening of blood vessels."[3] That is why Proverbs 15:23 says, "A man takes joy in giving an answer; and a timely word—how good that is!"

3. **Bad words destroy.**
   We learn in Proverbs 15:4, "The tongue that heals is a tree of life, but a devious tongue breaks the spirit." We are reminded that while a good word brings life, the power of death too is found in the tongue (Proverbs 18:21). We find that a "harsh word stirs up wrath" (Proverbs 15:1). That such a mouth actually can't help "blurt[ing] out foolishness" (Proverbs 15:2). We see in Scripture that our words not only "condemn us" (Matthew 12:37), but also when we use words "rashly," they are like "a piercing sword" (Proverbs 12:18). James 3:8 tells us plainly that the tongue can be full of poison. Poison is a substance that causes disturbances usually by chemical reactions in the body. Our tongues can cause a negative reaction in the body of Christ when it spits out poisonous words. Speaking negative and hurtful words actually hurts the speaker more than the intended victim, because the Bible says that a "lying tongue [will endure only for] a moment" (Proverbs 12:19). Poisonous words bring death to the environment. That is why throughout the *Laws of Community* we have stated repeatedly the importance of language to other believers. We are called

to "build up" one another (1 Thessalonians 5:11). Many believers do not realize how much work church volunteers actually put into their calling. A good teacher puts in hours of preparation, worship personnel have weekly meetings, the nursery staff must practice patience, and the least critical word can steal their moment of joy. A word spoken in due season can bring life to a weary soldier in the army of God. A word spoken with the wrong motives, with a harsh spirit, can crush the mightiest of warriors. "A gossip's words are like choice food that goes down to one's innermost being" (Proverbs 26:22).

4. **Characteristics of a tongue that speaks wisdom.**
It doesn't' take long to spot a fool, but often wise people are overlooked. The Bible says, "The mouth of the righteous produces wisdom" (Proverbs 10:31). God's people should be known, not by gossip, but by words of wisdom. Our greatest evangelistic effort could simply be the building of a local church where our tongues make "knowledge attractive" (Proverbs 15:2). Here are biblical characteristics for speaking in the house of God:

a. *"A soft answer turns away wrath"* (Proverbs 15:1 KJV). A virtue of wisdom is to know how to live in harmony with one another. It is not the issues we fight over in church, but rather the temperament of the people involved who actually cause the fight. Old Testament words are best understood through pictures. The picture here is not one of a fire being put out, but the stirring up of the fire, thus causing the fire to grow. A "mild" answer puts out a fire with such power that its "gentle tongue can break a bone" (Proverbs 25:15). There is power in kindness; it soothes. It puts out the "fire" that anger brings. Consider how you might give a softer answer to members of your local church.

b. *"A man slow to anger calms strife"* (Proverbs 15:18). When we cause strife, we do so, according to this passage, because we are hot tempered (18a). When we are slow to anger, we quiet contentions. How many local churches would still be alive had they simply understood this one principle? When we are slow to anger, we remain in control, and thus our actions calm contentions. We fight strife with calmness according to the Bible. "A patient person shows great understanding, but a quick-tempered one promotes foolishness" (Proverbs 14:29). The power behind such a person slow to anger is humility. That person is not readily offended at insults. Patience and gentleness are the greatest tools for calming strife. To do this, an individual will need to remain humble.

c. *Guard your mouth and protect the life of your local church* (Proverbs 13:3). A fool speaks quickly and without thought, but a wise man "guards his mouth," thus protecting his life. Half the battles in your spiritual life could be avoided if only you could stay quiet! Keeping quiet is not easy, but it is possible, even when you are innocent! (Matthew 27:11-14). Wise people keep a guard on their mouths, thus literally protecting their physical lives, according to this passage. "A fool gives full vent to his anger, but a wise man holds it in check" (Proverbs 29:11).

d. *Wise people speak fewer words (Ecclesiastes 10:14).* "The words from the mouth of a wise man are gracious, but the lips of a fool consume him. The beginning of the words of his mouth is folly, but the end of his speaking is evil madness. Yet the fool multiplies words." The Word tells us that "The intelligent person restrains his words, and one who keeps a cool head is a man of understanding" (Proverbs 17:27). The refraining of words and the self-discipline to speak fewer words are signs of wisdom. After all, the Bible says, "Even a fool is considered wise when he keeps silent" (Proverbs 17:28).

e. *Your tongue is reflective of justice* (Proverbs 14:25). Today, there is much talk about social justice, but unfortunately the word has been robbed from the right by the left. Moses stood up for the Israelites and spoke for them, becoming a mouthpiece against injustices. As a Christian, you are to speak up for those who cannot speak up for themselves, because God does care deeply about injustice. Proverbs 14:25 actually says, "A truthful witness rescues lives." How trustworthy are your words? Do you show up on time? Do you keep your leadership appointments and projects in trust under your stewardship at church? The trustworthiness of your words is needed by God for an appointed time when you will be called on to right an injustice. Proverbs 12:17 says, "Whoever speaks the truth declares what is right, but a false witness, deceit." Such lips endure forever; they are trusted and used mightily by God. So, your character is directly tied to the words you speak. God knew this principle well. He said that when your words match your actions, you will develop a character that can be used to speak up when lies are being told on others. Then your character, because of the history of your words, will carry so much weight that when you do speak, people listen.

f. *Godly words justify you.* Matthew 12:37 says, "For by your words you will be acquitted, and by your words you will be condemned." To Matthew, words play an important role in our lives. Notice in Matthew 7:13-27, the great role "words" actually play in our discipleship. In verses 15-21, words are attached to our relationship to Christ. False prophets speak like sheep. The concept of fruit is connected to what we do; what we do is connected to what we say. Take a look at Matthew 7:21, "Not everyone who says to Me, "Lord, Lord! will enter the kingdom of heaven, but only the one who DOES the will of My Father in heaven."

Words can be very deceptive. Every wolf in your church knows what to say, because he is an expert at acting like a sheep. A wolf is always polite. He said, "Lord," which was the equivalent of "yes sir" in Bible days. Yet, this word was also a divine title which would tell us that all wolves can use words to seem orthodox. The phrase, "Lord, Lord!" is particularly interesting, because it shows us that wolves will use words fervently and with great emotion behind them. Decibels are never a sign of sincerity, just like the lower decibel in our speech is not a sign of true piety. Wolves speak passionately, and they also speak up publically for Christ. The difference is this: They don't obey the words they speak. The terrifying issue here is that we can fool ourselves by the words we speak for Christ! Our lips claim loyalty in the hopes that our outer works will hide the true inner realities. What is even more fascinating to me is the fact that these wayward people, when confronted with the lack of continuity between their words and their actions, revert back to their words as proof of their obedience to Christ! Here in the Greek, it is implying that one has used words to deceive someone about his or her true character and has used these words, "Lord, Lord," to advance one's own cause rather than the kingdom of God. The words, "I never knew you," is a Greek phrase requiring experiential knowledge to know someone. In the ancient world, this was considered to be the "law" of the Eastern "ancient of origins." This law of identity was very important for knowing a person. This is why this phrase in Scripture literally means, "I do not know you, where are you from?"

People can often speak kind words—"Lord, Lord," and still be a very deceptive person (see Matthew 7). Jesus is saying that our words can be deceptive, but the true test of our knowing Him is found in the obedience and correlation of our words with what we actually do. Outward behavior is like inspecting vegetation on a tree. However, it's the fruit that inevitably discloses the species!

Matthew 12:37 is the last phrase of a passage dealing with fruit and trees! Notice Matthew 12:34-35: "For the mouth speaks from the overflow of the heart. A good man produces good things from his storeroom of good." Likewise, a tree is to its fruits what your heart is to your speech. When Matthew quotes Jesus as saying, "every careless word they speak," it implies a morally useless word. The simple fact is that living a life with a "good tongue" will actually pay off, not only for your church, but also for you personally. On Judgment Day, one of the ways in which we will be judged is by our words.

Think about how God established the moral code through the foundation of the Ten Commandments. Exodus 20:7 says, "Do not misuse the name of the Lord your God, because the Lord will not leave anyone unpunished who misuses His name." Proverbs says: "For as he thinks in his heart, so is he" (23:7 NKJV). Your thoughts are the fruits to your spiritual tree. Our thoughts precede our actions. Our words justify us, because they bear witness to the true condition of our hearts.

g.  *Godly lips will endure forever.* In Proverbs 12:19, the writer tells us: "Truthful lips endure forever." That is a way of saying that a "truthful tongue is consistent." Any good psychological assessment will ask the same question, repeated in different forms, in order to find the truth about what one really is thinking. When you speak words of truth, you never struggle with trying to remember what was said in the first place. Truth is the reliability of our words. The word *endure* means "to establish forever." What our local churches need are truth tellers—people who speak reliable words that are consistent with their character. Our speech has a lasting quality to it. It empowers people because it is trustworthy. What does it mean to be the kind of person in your church who is trustworthy? People also judge us by our words. When we don't keep our word, they believe that we are untrustworthy. However, a trustworthy person watches every word. Truth is authenticity. Psalm 15:2 says that we "acknowledge truth in [our hearts]." Psalm 51:6 says, "Surely You desire integrity in the inner self." The words of William Faulkner are very applicable here:

"Never be afraid to raise your voice for honesty and truth and compassion against injustice and lying and greed. If people all over the world... would do this, it would change the earth."[4]

## Wisdom Point B

*A wicked tongue can wound, kill, and destroy human lives.* I know a few habitual liars. They, of course, have some very admirable qualities about them as well. But I don't trust what they say. I want to be careful not to paint a "hopeless" picture to the character of every habitual liar. However, the root of their "habit" is extremely dangerous. John 8:43-44 says:

> Why don't you understand what I say? Because you cannot listen to My word. You are of your father the Devil, and you want to carry out your father's desires. He was a murderer from the beginning and has not stood in the truth, because there is no truth in him. When he tells a lie, he speaks from his own nature, because he is a liar and the father of liars.

One of the most decisive testimonies brought against our adversary by Christ is that he is never consistent with his words. He is a liar and the father of all liars, according to Christ himself. He too can speak only from his own internal resources! What is so sobering is how Jesus started this passage as an answer to those who did not understand His "words." Jesus continues to say that those who are liars are children of the devil, because we are of the lineage of his ethical fatherhood. Why? He does not tell the truth, and he is a liar. As we learned earlier in the power of a good tongue, our good ethics unite us with our heavenly Father who speaks good words over us (Genesis 1). However, here is a tongue that is bad; it cannot speak truth, is used to pull down others, and is a direct sign of a person's fatherhood—in this case Satan.

In James 3:5-6, it says, "So too, though the tongue is a small part of the body, it boasts great things. Consider how large a forest a small fire ignites. And the tongue is a fire. The tongue, a world of unrighteousness, is placed among the parts of our bodies. It pollutes the whole body, sets the course of life on fire, and is set on fire by hell." The half-brother of Jesus said that unrighteousness is a product of an uncontrolled tongue, and that this tongue actually has the potential to set a life on fire. And then he says that the person who strikes this "match" is from hell itself. The tongue, he says, is like a "small spark" or a "rudder" on a ship, implying that small things can turn large objects (see James 3:3-5). He is suggesting that a small part of our bodies—our tongues—can cause massive damage if left uncontrolled. Our tongues can kill and destroy other people.

1. *A wicked tongue can bring potential ruin.*

> I know a young lady in a local church who left the local church because someone said "she was gay." I know a youth pastor whose credibility was endangered because he was accused of adultery with a girl he never touched! I know a pastor who had to leave his church because of false words spoken about him by an elder. I know about great harm coming to a local church, because an immature believer accused his leaders of an appropriation of funds that never happened. I know of a business that had to close, because the townspeople accused the owner of murdering a wealthy lady. He didn't.

The tongue can cause a spiritual forest fire. It can engulf your congregation like sparks engulfing a dry, arid sequoia forest. Our tongues are like James said—the match that starts the fire. It is the most unruly part of our bodies. (Why do you think on the Day of Pentecost the Holy Spirit took over the

275

tongue?) Proverbs 13:3 says: "The one who guards his mouth protects his life; the one who opens his lips invites his own ruin." Proverbs 18:7 says: "A fool's mouth is his devastation." Our tongues can wound and kill others and ourselves as well. If you want to invite ruin to your life, run your mouth. We must remember that our tongues can heal or wound even at church.

2. *A wicked tongue will almost always invite strife to your church.* I love people, but I hate the behavior of gossips. I will not give them a moment of my time. Proverbs 18:6 says, "A fool's lips lead to strife." Proverbs 15:1 says, "A gentle answer turns away anger, but a harsh word stirs up wrath." Proverbs 17:28 tells us, "Even a fool is considered wise when he keeps silent, discerning, when he seals his lips." Proverbs 10:19 says: "When there are many words, sin is unavoidable, but the one who controls his lips is wise." As I think about the many times I have seen people fight in the church, I can trace such childish behavior back to a foolish person who couldn't control his or her own tongue, thus lighting the spark upon the dry heart of an angry believer.

Each time I have to have a difficult conversation with a church employee or member, I do so with great care, research, and accountability. Even when the employee has to go, it is important to reply with a soft answer. A soft answer to an aggravated person is a truth of psychology. And since all truths are His, this fact is also a truth of God. When we raise our voices, we naturally place the other person in a defensive mode. An angry voice can be contributed often to a lack of patience. We become frustrated by those things into which we have invested. So, take a frustrated person who feels defensive and slighted, add a dose of inflection, and you have the potential for an explosion. The Bible says that a soft answer turns away wrath, so remember that the control of your voice is largely dependent upon emotional control (Galatians 5:22). Our emotions of fear and excitement will automatically tighten around our voice box. The hearer will notice this inflection and respond likewise. Through the years of ministry, I have encountered dissension and strife many times, but I could not place my finger on the reason. This usually happened in times of confusion where untruths were everywhere in the air, but no one was seen propagating them. When you encounter times and seasons like these, you should be sober and alert, because there is a liar in your midst. Oftentimes, a bad tongue hides its face. These people seldom use their bad tongues in front of authority; it is usually used away from authority in the presence of sincere people in order to spit their poison into the hearts of pure people. Their intention is that the seed of suspicion would take root and cause others to question their leaders through the conduit of unbiblical means.

3.  *A wicked tongue can destroy the hope in you*. Have you ever thought about the power of the tongue? For example, you can receive a dozen compliments about your new haircut, but it takes only one negative comment about your hair to make you want to shave your head! The psalmist said in 55:21: "His buttery words are smooth, but war is in his heart. His words are softer than oil, but they are drawn swords." Words have the power to wound us. No matter how big you are, the small power of words can bring you to your knees.

    Satan knows the power of words too; after all, he was present when God formed the world and all that is within it by the power of His words. He saw the Word become flesh and dwell among us lowly servants. He heard Jesus speak to the dumb, deaf, and blind, and witnessed their healings by the power of His words. While Satan has no ability to create with his words, he can destroy with them. He creates destruction in our lives by using the words of other people. After all, he is the master of it. Hear him say, "Did God really say that if you eat of...?" He deceives with his words; he destroys with his words; he misleads with his words. The Bible says all liars are only acting like their father — the "father of lies." God's people use their words to build up people and create atmospheres of expectancies. On the contrary, the followers of darkness use their tongues to deceive, wound, attack, mislead, destroy, and discourage. Proverbs 18:21 said: "Life and death are in the power of the tongue and those who love it will eat its fruit." A bad tongue is full of poison. It hinders people's ability to strive for greatness. A bad tongue can paralyze your will to do well; it can hinder your vision and weaken your eyesight. The Bible says in Proverbs 25:18: "A man giving false testimony against his neighbor is like a club, a sword, or a sharp arrow." The Word of God is telling us that the power of the tongue can be an instrument of death.

4. *A wicked tongue has the power to defile the speaker and the hearer.*

   Matthew 15:10-11 tells us: "Listen and understand: It's not what goes into the mouth that defiles a man but what comes out of the mouth, this defiles a man." Matthew 15:17-18 says:

   > Don't you realize that whatever goes into the mouth passes into the stomach and is eliminated? But what comes out of the mouth comes from the

heart, and this defiles a man. For from the heart come evil thoughts, murders, adulteries, sexual immoralities, thefts, false testimonies, blasphemies. There are these things that defile a man.

Again, the ancient rabbis called slander the "third tongue." It "slays three people: the speaker, the listener, and the one spoken about"[5]

> I remember a time in my ministry when I was having trouble with a staff member who could not help stirring up trouble within our staff. I love and believed in this person so much that I became blinded to their real motives. I never realized that you could love a snake, but you can. It wasn't until I sat quietly by and listened to a phone conversation that this person was having with another leader in our church that I realized his defilement. Their words broke my heart, but they also opened my eyes to the impurity and insincerity in this person's life. I personally heard one venomous lie right after another. Many people had warned me of this individual's character, but I refused to listen to the many "eye witnesses" of this person's behavior. What I do remember is how I felt about this individual after my friend hung up the phone. I listened to myself be slandered, knowing that he too had slandered me to everyone else in the room. But my mind was on the "fact" that he had destroyed himself in the process. He could no longer pretend to be something to me he was not.

5. *A wicked tongue will conceal violence.* It's not easy to trap a bad tongue, because it acts like a slippery snake. These individuals are crafty and strategic with their lies. There is one way that can help you spot a bad tongue in your church. The Bible says in Proverbs 10:11: "The mouth of the wicked conceals violence." Proverbs 10:6 says the same thing

to us. In Scripture, deceitfulness marks the lives of wicked people. This passage gives us tremendous insight into wicked people and how we are to identify them. Wicked people conceal violence, because evil has hidden itself from day one. Satan did not enter the Garden as Lucifer; he entered it as a snake. Evil hides in the words and thoughts of evil people as Matthew 15:18 told us. Evil men hide their true thoughts and go to great lengths to cover up the violence their hearts have planned for you and your church. Evil people conceal evil more than the church believes. We all have met people whose lips testify to something other than what their lives profess. Wicked people conceal violence through their words. As a friend of mine has taught me, "The best predictor of future behavior is past behavior."

6. *A wicked tongue will ambush you with words.* The Bible says in Proverbs 12:6: "The words of the wicked are a deadly ambush." The Hebrew here is very helpful to our understanding. The Hebrew for *word* implies an expressed design. This means that wicked tongues design wicked moments. They literally lie in wait and thirst to shed your blood. Ancient Hebrew rabbis believed firmly that lying on someone was akin to murdering the person. The strategic principle here is the fact that wicked people "lie in wait." They are cunning, for they hide and deceive until the right movement comes that will cause the most bloodshed. A person with a wicked tongue always waits to attack until the most damage can be done. I hate to be caught off guard by an attacker. It is nauseating to me. Wicked people make plans to attack the righteous. There are no mistakes with their timing. If there is a person in your life who is questionable, stay alert, be sober, and watch for the

most opportune time to cause you damage; then you will know the calendar of your enemy.

7. *A wicked tongue that tells a lie about you actually hates you.* The Bible says in Proverbs 26:28: "A lying tongue hates those it crushes." No one wants to admit that they are hated, but even Jesus said, "You will be hated by everyone because of My name" (Matthew 10:22). Most Christians and church leaders are good, God-fearing people just like you. Unassuming people and unorthodox ways often lead them like sheep to the slaughter. It will be a defining moment in your life when you realize that the person lying on you actually does so out of hatred for you. The person will most certainly deny it, but God's Word clearly says otherwise. In ancient Judaism, the one who lies was also considered a thief, because he/she is stealing another person's thoughts. There has been some discussion among theologians whether this passage is saying that a liar hates the truth. However, the Hebrew is pointing to the liar hating "the crushed victim." A lie injures the person; it crushes that individual with a tongue of deception. The liar cons himself into justifying his action by his hatred. The liar thinks, *because I hate this person, my actions are justified.* The person who lies on you in church is not your friend, not today, not now, not ever.

8. *A wicked tongue will always reveal your secrets.* I believe a disclaimer is needed here. Good people can have bad problems. A good person can make bad decisions. A good person can speak poorly for a moment. But the best predictor of future behavior is bad behavior. In other words, we are all going to have times in our church life where we are going to be hurt by people who profess to love us. We are dealing with imperfect humanity, and because

of this, we are going to be hurt by people who do love us. Jesus, Paul, and Moses were, and you will be too. Maybe you have been, but here is wisdom: When the same person constantly exhibits such wicked behavior, you are not with a friend but a foe.

> I hurt one of my closest friends, and he hurt me. It was all a big misunderstanding, actually caused by a gossiping friend who cared! He really did care, but the pain doesn't discern the motive of care. I sat on my back porch for literally hours as I poured through the Scriptures on community. After the stars had been out for hours, in a still moment before God, I realized that this behavior was not only normal, but I could not define it as completely illicit either. I had to resign my fears and feelings to God's Word, which led me to a stronger friendship. I also had to ask for forgiveness for the pain I caused by my fear of being betrayed again. So, there are good people who do love you, but who will hurt you.

The laws of community will help to guard and discern those kinds of friends at church.

If someone has a repetitive pattern of always betraying your trust, the person just might be considered a wolf in sheep's clothing. The key is the first noun in Proverbs 11:13—"A gossip goes around revealing a secret." The word for "gossip" is *slanderer*. It literally says "Worker of slander." When someone's full-time job in the church is slandering, watch out! They pedal scandal, and as the Septuagint says, they are "The [men] of double tongue[s]." This verse tells us that these workers of slander speak to us with the intent that salivates to tell secrets. These peddlers of scandal lack self-control with their discreet ways. You know you are in the presence of wickedness when it reveals, discreet-ly, the secrets of others. They exhibit the fruit of their patriarch, the father of lies, as they show no self-control. Truth isn't afraid to be heard from atop the roof; however, a slanderer is a coward with a discreet tongue. We all have shared secrets and said unkind things about other people. But when there is a pattern of discreet gossip by someone who is constantly working the church, pedaling lies, and telling half-truths, you are in the presence of wick-edness.

Lest we throw caution to the wind, a simple closing may be in order. Matthew 25: 31-33 says, "When the Son of Man comes in His glory, and all the angels with Him, then He will sit on the throne of His glory. All the nations will be gathered before Him, and He will separate them one from another, just as a shepherd separates the sheep from the goats. He will put the sheep on His right side and the goats on the left." Since I am a shepherd, I can't help but end this section by adding a little seasoning called mercy. We are all human; we all have a sin nature; and we all make mistakes. And most of us are not mature enough biblically to know, at least not yet, what the Scriptures require of us as we live out our church life in deep community. Indeed, there are those who are wolves in sheep's clothing (Mat-thew 7:15). We are told in Matthew 7:16, "You'll recognize them by their fruit." So, it is possible to properly identify a wolf in sheep's clothing by the bad fruit. The issue to keep in mind is all apple trees produce good and bad fruit.

> I remember as a child, my papaw would pick me up and place me on his shoulders so I could pick the choice fruits from his tree. Even as a child, I quickly knew that good trees do at times produce a bad piece of fruit. But never in all of those years did a good tree produce a harvest of bad fruit.

When you see the presence of consistently bad fruit, mark such a one and keep your eyes wide open. Pay little attention to what they are saying to you and a lot of attention to what they are doing! (Romans 16:17). Be careful to judge in a biblical way. As we learned in the chapter titled, "The Law of Judging," judging is not wrong. However, judging wrongly is dangerous to the health of your local church. It is best to leave the separation of sheep and goats to the ultimate Shepherd.

## PRECEPT TWO:
### The Words of Community Make or Break Your Community

Words are so important to Christ that He actually said, "Heaven and earth will pass away, but My words will never pass away" (Mathew 24:35). Jewish rabbis knew the power of words because on Yom Kippur (the Day of Atonement), the holiest day of the Jewish year, "Jews recite a long litany of sins for which [they] ask God's forgiveness. A large portion of that list involves sins we commit through speaking."[6] The Hebrew people take speech very seriously. To a Jew, a slanderer was worse than one who commits incest. It was the equivalent of murder to a Jewish person, because speech could cause a death. There were moral qualities to words. The question is: How do we use words?

### Wisdom Point A
*You can misuse words.* God forged the heavens and earth by His words. He has promised that the products of His words will pass away, but His words will never pass away. Good words have the power to heal and stifle strife. Bad words can wound deeper than any dagger could ever reach. Words have power. Satan cannot create; he is not

Jehovah Elohim, the Creator and Sustainer of life. Therefore, he hasn't the power to use his words to create. His words can only "kill, steal and destroy" (John 10:10). It is then within reason to conclude that the one who is the father of liars, who cannot create with words, would then strategically use them to destroy. When we use words to destroy others created in His image, we are dancing with the author of wickedness.

1. *Filthy Language is a sign of disrespect to God.* I hate to hear God's name used in vain. I cringe to hear my Lord and Savior Jesus Christ have His name blasphemed. In fact, all foul language is an insult to our Holy God. We are all created in the image of God, and when we swear at someone, we are swearing at His image. These things are prohibited by ancient rabbis as they saw the degrading of another human being through words as an insult to God himself. Because of this belief, we must treat others with respect as we communicate with them, even when we disagree or are very upset with them. To say a curse word is to express how you are upset about a situation by the use of stronger words. Cursing every day, at all times, takes away the meaning of those words in the first place. Rabbi Elazar ben Jacob said, "A person who uses rough language is like a pipe spewing foul odors in a beautiful room."[7] Since our bodies and our sexual organs have been formed and created by a Holy God, we blaspheme God when we curse with sexual words, and/or use foul words. Ancient rabbis considered "swearing and listening to it as a prostituting of the mouth and ear." Moses Hayyim Luzzato writes:

   > With regard to prostitution of the mouth and the ear, that is, speaking words of prostitution or listening to them, our Sages "screamed like

cranes," that is, emphatically denounced in saying, "Let God not find anything unseemly among you' (Deuteronomy 23:15), that is, unseemly words," which is befouling one's mouth...If one would gain your ear and tell you that the Sages said what they did about obscene speech only to frighten you and to draw you far from sin, and that their words apply only to hot-blooded individuals who, by speaking obscenities, would be aroused to lust...obscenities constitutes the very "nakedness" of the faculty of speech and was prohibited as an aspect of fornication along with all other such forms of it.[8]

We curse what we do not respect. When we curse each other in church (yes, this does happen more than you would ever want to know), we are cursing at God even when we are not directly using His name. Man is created in His image (Genesis 1:26). We are living, finite beings created by a living, infinite Creator. The laws of speech require that we carefully guard the words we speak to one another for that reason.

2. *Lying destroys the foundation of community.* Telling the truth is required in your church for a lot more reasons than the average churchgoer can realize. The Bible says, "The truth will set you free" (John 8:32); but, How does truth set us free? It takes truth to enable community, because without truth, social cooperation is impossible. It takes trust to build the inner social workings of your church. Even the marketplace requires truth, for without it, no one can be trusted in his or her transactions. Lies, however, destroy trust and tumble the walls that protect community. I have always had a heart for the underdog, the down and out, or the one looking for a second, third, or fourth chance.

I once worked with a young adult who had a very troubled past. It wasn't the problem of turning one's life around that stopped our relationship. It wasn't his spread sheet, the gossip about his former life, or the weaving of social dysfunctions that former addiction brings to one's life that destroyed our relationship; it was his lies.

A liar destroys community and trust, because when individuals constantly tell lies, they tear down all confidence. As the Hebrew says, they are *shaima shav*, literally, "worthless words to be heard." The Levitical law says, "You must not steal. You must not act deceptively or lie to one another." "The liar did not think enough of you to tell you the truth, and so you rightly feel dishonored and molested."[9] When you speak the truth in love in your church, you are protecting it in many ways. Because the church is a living organism, it can't exist without living things. It is impossible for a church to "live" when truth is not present, because Jesus said: "I am the way, the truth and the life" (John 14:6). All of life—from our families to our friendships—is impossible without truth.

The Book of Proverbs says: "A false witness will not go unpunished" (19:9). Being a liar is hard work. While liars can cause a tremendous amount of discernment and work to identify them, they will eventually trip up over their own words. Proverbs 12:19 says, "A lying tongue (will last) only a moment." Proverbs 11:6 says, "The treacherous are trapped by their own desires." It's hard to discern who is being deceptive, but it is easy to catch a liar. When you lie, you have to keep telling lies to protect the lie you told previously. The Bible says that eventually you will end up trapping yourself in a lie. Trapping yourself is a consequence of sin. People who were once lost are often frustrated when they first give their lives to Christ, because they think that people should all of a sudden trust them. Not so. Trust is earned, even for the righteous! Character is developed, not given. While we have a new nature (1 Corinthians 15), that new nature must be nurtured and developed. There are consequences to lying, one of which is that no one ever trusts what you say. In Ephesians 4:31, Paul says, "All bitterness, anger and wrath, shouting and slander must be removed from you, along with all malice." Colossians tells us: "Do not lie to one another, since you have put off the old man with his deeds and have put on the new man who is renewed in knowledge according to the image of Him who created him" (3:9-10 NKJV).

We have a personal responsibility to "remove" character flaws like lying. Proverbs 19:22 says: "Better to be a poor man than a liar." Paul told us in 1 Timothy 1:10, "...for kidnappers, liars, perjurers, and for whatever else is contrary to the sound teaching based on the glorious gospel of the blessed God that was entrusted to me." Paul links Christian maturity and sound doctrine as contrary to being a liar or perjurer. When we lie, we hinder our ability to grow up in the "truth," and lying makes sound doctrine (truth) impossible. It is said of God that He hates seven things, one of which is a liar (Proverbs 6:17). The basis of all moral law is the Ten Commandments. It is the lowest level of morality on earth. One of its foundational principles is to not "bear false witness" (Exodus 20:16). Telling a lie is so serious to God that He even includes this sin in those listed which are easily discernable to lead one to everlasting punishment in the "lake of fire" (Revelation 21:8). Why does God hate lying so passionately? Because He is Truth (John 14:6). Proverbs says:

> Smooth lips with an evil heart are like a glaze on an earthen vessel. A hateful person disguises himself with his speech and harbors deceit within. When he speaks graciously, don't believe him, for there are seven abominations in his heart. Though his hatred is concealed by deception, his evil will be revealed in the assembly. The one who digs a pit will fall into it, and whoever rolls a stone—it will come back on him. A lying tongue hates those it crushes, and a flattering mouth causes ruin" (26:23-28).

3. *Gossip is a sinful misuse of words.* There is a fantastic book that you need to own called, *The Way Into Tikkun Olam (Repairing the World)*. Few books have made a more forceful impact on me. It has served not only as a guide for this section but also it has placed a holy fear in my heart about my speech and how serious God is about my speech! I have always hated the behavior of a gossiper. I actually feel sorry for anyone who literally feeds on such sewage. Proverbs 18:8; 26:22 says, "A gossip's words are like choice food that goes down to one's innermost being." The words of a whisperer penetrate the heart. To be a gossip is to struggle with perverted lust. Anytime you feed your "spirit" on demonic sewage, the result of such a diet cannot yield any type of spiritual health.

We get our Hebrew word for *gossip* from the word that means "peddler." In the beginning of the Levitical law, one can find all kinds of laws about speech and its effect on community. "You must not go about spreading slander among your people: you must not jeopardize your neighbor's life: I am Yahweh" (Leviticus 19:16). It was a foundational code in the moral law (Exodus 20:16). Gossip is the misuse of words. "What is a talebearer? It is someone who claims things and goes from one person to another saying, 'This is what so-and-so-said,' and 'This is what I heard about so-and-so.' Even if it is true, such speech destroys the world."[10] Gossip destroys the world, and it doesn't matter if it is true. Christians are called to *Tikkun Olam*—they must repair the broken world in which we live. The way to begin is to rid our churches from gossips, peddlers of half-truths, horrible truths, and outright lies. Here is wisdom from the Scriptures about Satan's peddlers.

a. *Proverb 16:28 says, "A contrary man spreads conflict, and a gossip separates friends."* You can expect ONLY conflict from a gossiper; they literally live for it. Gossips destroy community, because they separate friends. An immature gossiping Christian has destroyed more local churches than fornication ever thought possible. (In the Law of Unity chapter, we discussed in detail how to handle a gossiper or backbiter. In this chapter, we warn ourselves of the consequences of breaking the laws of speech, which will result in conflict and enemies.)

b. *Proverbs 20:19 says, "The one who reveals secrets is a constant gossip; avoid someone with a big mouth."* The Scripture is never bashful in directing us to avoid certain "immature believers" because of the danger they present to the rest of the body. It is one thing to gossip and be repentant about what you have said. We all struggle with controlling our tongues. However, it's quite another thing to be in the presence of a peddler of murder who will not be accountable for his or her crimes. I will not give a gossip my time. The danger of gossip in the church is the difficulty of pinpointing the original place of slander. If someone is peddling secrets in your church, your "sin alarm" needs to be going off. There is a right way and a wrong way to address negative situations in your church. Peddling gossip is never one of them. You can spot a consistent gossiper, because they are constantly revealing the secrets of others.

c. *Proverbs 26:20-22 says, "Without wood, fire goes out; without a gossip, conflict dies down. As charcoal for embers and wood for fire, so is a quarrelsome man for kindling strife."* You can kill gossip by simply closing your ears. Gossip can only mature into full conflict when there are ears to receive the lies and damaging truths. We are to address issues biblically as we have spoken about in numerous laws. However, we are to squash, walk away from, refuse to listen to, and ignore a church gossip. Many people say to me, "I didn't want to appear rude." So, in effect, you are saying you would rather save face with a peddler of sin than to honor the Word of God! It takes wood to build a fire. Conflict dies when there is no one to stir it up. I have met many people in my 30 plus years of ministry who ran to the scene of every church fire, right in the midst of the smoke, ashes, and causalities from those inhaling the poisonous fumes. People who love conflict are sick. Our world is full of it. We have entire programming on television driven by it. We can't even watch the news without it leading the way with two talking heads who hate each other. This is not the world our Father has created for us! The world that He created for us was a peaceful and loving place. A utopia is not possible now, thanks to the two pieces of forbidden fruit that tumbled across the ground in the Garden of Eden thousands of years ago. But thanks be to God, He has left us a manuscript with laws to govern our relationships as we wait for the restoration of all things (Acts 3:21). We must guard our communities of faith from such peddlers of the flesh. The easiest way to put out a fire is to starve it of any oxygen. Don't listen; walk away. Kill strife and gossip by refusing to listen to those who tell it.

d. *A constant gossip is corrupt and rebellious to authority; in fact, Jeremiah 6:28 says, "All are stubborn rebels spreading slander. They are bronze and iron; all of them are corrupt."* The prophet Jeremiah didn't mince words and neither did God about what kinds of people Jeremiah would be called to as a prophet. Remember in Matthew 7:15-20 that Jesus reminded us about the importance of fruit (Galatians 5:22) in our lives. A constant gossip cannot produce any other fruit but the fruits of the flesh (Galatians 5:19-21). You can't get fresh water and salt water from the same cistern (James 3:11). A bad tree cannot give good fruit, and a good tree cannot give bad fruit. Sometimes, it's good to call it what it is—a peddler who follows Satan and will constantly "accuse" the brethren by living in their flesh and feeding on the filth of this world. There are some gossipers who are good at heart, while there are others who are rotten to the core. The difference can be found in their consistency in slander and their accountability to authority.

e. *Whispering peddlers spread fear of harm. Psalms 41:7 says, "All who hate me whisper together about me."* It's a tough road to travel when your life is surrounded by constant whispering. Friends will wound you with their words as they look you in the eye (Proverbs 27:6). Gossipers will whisper behind your back, and therefore can be considered enemies of God who prove their hate for you by not honoring your identity in person. A gossiper is a coward who masquerades as a salesman. David said in Psalms 41:5-6, "My enemies speak maliciously about me: 'When will he die and be forgotten?' When one of them comes to visit, he speaks deceitfully; he stores up evil in his heart; he goes out and talks."

Real friends are NEVER malicious. Real friends never speak difficult words to wound, only to heal. Real friends are not deceitful, because they live by the laws of true community. When they come by your house or office, it is to find out how you are really doing, not to sniff out some crisis. Gossipers have stored up evil in their hearts, and they can't help but go out and talk.

Your local church can be full of fear by letting a gossiper go unrestrained or accountable for their words. The church is a hospital for the sick (Mark 2:17). Sick people have problems, and all sick people should be treated with dignity and respect, regardless of their illness. All sick people have certain rights to privacy. It's none of your business how many times they messed up. Were they accountable, repentant, and brokenhearted? Did they make their wrongs right where applicable? How can your church heal the sick when their privacy cannot be protected? Many new believers "worry" enough about their past, they don't need us to add to their constant fears. Perfect love casts out all fears, and when you love someone you would never hurt them on purpose with your words.

f. *Proverbs 25:23 says, "The north wind produces rain, and a backbiting tongue, angry looks."* Gossip and slander infuriate people. However, the righteous can hold their tongues! They stifle slander by having the self-control to ignore it. A church is not supposed to be an angry place. Slanderers in the house of God make God's house a manufacturer of bitterness. When we stop slander, we ensure peace.

g. *Paul wrote the following passage in the Book of Romans:*

> And because they did not think it worthwhile to acknowledge God, God delivered them over to a worthless mind to do what is morally wrong. They are filled with all unrighteousness, evil, greed, and wickedness. They are full of envy, murder, quarrels, deceit, and malice. They are gossips, slanderers, God-haters, arrogant, proud, boastful, inventors of evil, disobedient to parents, undiscerning, untrustworthy, unloving, and unmerciful. Although they know full well God's just sentence—that those who practice such things deserve to die—they not only do them, but even applaud others who practice them (1:28-32).

It is interesting that at least seven of the things that God considers morally wrong are somehow connected to slander and gossip, which He insinuates is the fruit of a "worthless mind." It takes a debased mind to gossip and slander. The Greek actually says that all these things are "improper." To have a slandering spirit, one must have a "worthless mind." The Greek word here implies, "notwithstanding the test." It was an ancient word used to describe sub-standard coinage. Coins give us our English understanding of character. A person's image was engraved on a coin—a character. If the coin had been diluted or shaved from its precious metal, it was considered to have no "character" and was then deemed substandard. A slanderer's mind has not withstood the test of righteousness, nor could the slanderer withstand a trial by God. The Greek here implies "a second trial." It is saying that these kinds of people will never make it in a trial by God.

h. *Slander is the fear of all church leaders, because they know its power.*

> For I fear that perhaps when I come I will not find you to be what I want, and I may not be found by you to be what you want; there may be quarreling, jealousy, outbursts of anger, selfish ambitions, slander, gossip, arrogance, and disorder. I fear that when I come my God will again humiliate me in your presence, and I will grieve for many who sinned before and have not repented of the moral impurity, sexual immorality, and promiscuity they practiced"(2 Corinthians 12:20-21).

Every mother loves to see her children enjoying each other's company. Every dad loves to see the order of his home and enjoys the pride it gives him. All shepherds love to see the unity in their churches. When there is unity, there is love. When there is an attack on unity, there is an attack on love. Paul was no different as he addressed the city of Corinth. I recently took a tour through the old city of Corinth and saw many of the places Paul personally stood. When I read the verses above after having seen these places, my heart aches for him, because I know the heartbreak of every pastor when slanderers and peddlers of unrighteousness disturb the sheep. Paul rebukes this local church for the embarrassment they are placing in the city because of all the "gossip, slander, and quarreling." It is fascinating that he links these sins of community with promiscuity by calling them "unclean." Unity encourages the shepherds. Disunity embarrasses them, and as Hebrews 13:17 says, "For that would be unprofitable for you." Slanderers and peddlers of the flesh in your local church cause your leaders grief. Philippians 2:1-4 says:

> If there is any encouragement in Christ, if any consolation of love, if any fellowship with the Spirit, if any affection and mercy, *fulfill my joy* by thinking the same way, having the same love, sharing the same feelings, focusing on one goal. Do nothing out of rivalry or conceit, but in humility consider others as more important than yourselves. Everyone should look out not only for his own interests, but also for the interests of others.

Slanderers stop the joy of your leaders. Gossipers suck the life out of your teachers, prophets, pastors, evangelists, apostles! Help take away the fear of battle from every pastor, stop gossip in its tracks.

i. *Mature church leadership must be mature with their words.* In 1 Timothy 3:9-11; 5:13-14; 3:8-13, Paul gives us the lists that we are to use as a requirement for the appointing of bishops, elders, deacons, or members of the Ephesians 4:11 fivefold giftings. All require the fruit of self-control.

Slanderers do not have self-control. Paul tells Titus in a passage about the qualifications of an overseer to "rebuke sharply" those who are idle talkers (Titus 1:12-13). Paul tells Timothy: "Remind them of these things, charging them before God not to fight about words; this is in no way profitable and leads to the ruin of the hearers" (2 Timothy 2:14).

Maturity in church leaders is crucial because of the laws of unity, discipline, and judging. If your church leaders are not spiritually mature (Hebrew 5:13; 1 Peter 2:2), then the danger of chaos during times of social dysfunction are heightened. Church leaders who walk through biblical principles to safeguard the church must remain alert and sober as they constantly search the Scriptures for solid biblical wisdom on how to discipline, judge, or unify a matter. When leaders are not biblically mature, they leave only smoke and ashes for the members to sift through as they find due north. Mature church leaders can cut off gossip, slander, miscommunications, and half-truths by methodically following the process of the laws of community. A leader in your church with mature words becomes a tremendous safeguard for community.

j. *The last days will produce the breakdown of deep community through the conduit of words (2 Timothy 3:1-5).* This passage reads like the hall of shame it is. Notice that all the vices mentioned predominantly require another person to be involved in order to commit the violation. Many of them are committed through the sins of slander and peddling the things of the flesh with their tongues or demeanors. The most shocking line here is found in 2 Timothy 3:5: "Holding to the form of godliness but denying its power. Avoid these people." The Greek means that these "religious" people are saying no to the reality they profess! Slanderers and peddlers of the flesh are people who literally say "NO" to the reality of God! They denied its power—the living, regenerative, transformative power—that the gospel brings to our lives! The great news here is that you don't have to live your life as a slanderer of God's people one more second. You can be transformed by stopping the peddling you have been doing and accepting the transformative power you have been denying! Take a good look at 2 Timothy 3:4: "Lovers of pleasure rather than lovers of God." In fact, a gossiper takes pleasure in spreading gossip! They hunger to fill their innermost beings with trash (Proverbs 18:8). This passage effectively separates those who love pleasure (gossip, slander) from those who are "lovers of God." You are what you eat! The problematic issue here is the debilitating fact that Paul isn't talking about the "world" in the last days, but rather those who are in the church! We need the laws of community to prepare effectively for the return of Christ!!

k. *It's your job to protect your local church by guarding your own tongue! Psalms 34:13 says, "Keep your tongue from evil and your lips from deceitful speech. Turn away from evil and do what is good; seek peace and pursue it."* Even a soft answer from someone like you can turn away great wrath, since your tongue too has the power of life and death. I think one thing that is so important here is the unfortunate fact that a soft tongue is required whether you are the accused or the guilty accuser. The blame and the blamer, the hurt and the hurter, the truthful and the liar, all have the same responsibility: put the fire out for the betterment of the kingdom of God. It is not easy to keep your tongue. It's not easy to seal your lips.

> Today, I found out that a person I really did love and deeply cared for called me Kool-Aid. I have never been called Kool-Aid before! When you are insecure and do not know who you are, the words of other people can be dangerous to your self-esteem. But when you know who you are and you are secure in your identity, then it doesn't matter what people say.

There are times when you are attacked by the very people you helped and loved. You can love a snake. You can fall in love with a wolf in sheep's clothing. Even when you are innocent of the slander, you must react with a soft tongue, because as the Scriptures have told us, it puts the fire out.

1. *James 4:11-12 says, "Do not criticize one another, brothers. He who criticizes a brother or judges his brother criticizes the law and judges the law...But who are you to judge your neighbor."* The laws of judging are clear, and as we have learned, the Bible does not tell us not to judge issues. But when we judge the motives of someone else, when we criticize our brothers, we assume that our critical analysis is better than God's ability to discern the case. Slander destroys the trust that community demands of us. Slandering people or judging people is acting as if you are the law of God. Only God has the right to be the final arbitrator of judgment. We can discern and judge behavior through biblical laws of judging;

however, this particular passage is referring to the judging of someone's soul, not his or her behavior. There is a huge difference. Only God, James says, is the Judge of a man's soul and his or her final spiritual destiny.

4. *Our words are never to oppress others. Leviticus 25:17 says, "You are not to cheat one another, but fear your God, for I am Yahweh your God."* "The foundation for this prohibition is two verses in the Torah that assert we must not wrong one another: "When you sell your property to your neighbor, or buy anything from your neighbor, you shall not wrong one another" (Leviticus 25:14); and "Do not wrong one another, but fear your God; for I, the Lord, am your God" (Leviticus 25:17)."[11] The Rabbis believed that the first part applied to those wronging people through goods and services while the second verse actually referred to people wronging others through the use of words. We are told in Exodus 22:21: "You must not exploit a foreign resident or oppress him, since you were foreigners in the land of Egypt." We can better understand this belief by looking deeper at the Jewish tradition.

> The Jewish tradition demands quite a lot of someone who had harmed another person by requiring wrongdoers to complete the process of return (teshuvah) described in Jewish sources. That the process includes acknowledgement of one's wrongdoing, remorse expressed in words to the harmed party, compensation to the victim to the extent that is possible, and, ultimately, better behavior is even harder than serving time in prison, for some convicts never acknowledge that they have done anything wrong, let alone try to make amends to the people they have hurt. Once a person has completed the process of teshuvah, however, this Mishnah demands that people in

society not even mention the person's former troubles with the law, for that would be to engage in oppressive speech.[12]

Our words are not to be used to oppress, but to free (Isaiah 61). It is time that the local church, in a mature way of biblical confrontation, begins to hold people accountable for their words. We should practice complete forgiveness as well, for once a member of your local church works the process of Matthew 18, the matter must be finished forever.

## Wisdom Point B

*You can bless with words. First Peter 3:8-9 says, "Now finally, all of you should be like-minded and sympathetic, should love believers, and be compassionate and humble, not paying back evil for evil or insult for insult but, on the contrary, giving a blessing, since you were called for this, so that you can inherit a blessing."* Harmony requires humility to function; love moves both down the field to victory. In Luke 6:27-29 it says, "But I say to you who listen: Love your enemies, do what is good to those who hate you, bless those who curse you, pray for those who mistreat you." To bless people with your words is not an easy task, but Peter explains to us why. When we bless those who curse us and we don't "pay back evil for evil or insult for insult," we are actually asking for God to shine His favor on our enemies. We are asking for God's favor on the person who conferred injury on us. This means that we are calling on God to bless them to the point that they are blessed eternally. We are asking for them to be blessed in every kind of way—both temporal and eternal—with all benefits. After all, Peter has already told us: "And who will harm you if you are deeply committed for what is good? But even if you should suffer for righteousness, you are blessed. Do not fear what they fear or be disturbed" (1 Peter 3:13-14). In other words, no railings against you can injure you. Peter is reminding us that we don't put out fires with fires, but with cold, cool, water. The water we douse fire with is a water mixture of humility and kindness. We are to look at the slanderer's soul in the long term by praying a blessing that he or she would make it to eternity. Peter said, "We inherit a blessing." That is a nice way of reminding all of us that we did not "earn a blessing." We all inherited it by grace. So remember that your tongue is a fire hydrant with tremendous power to put out the most dangerous of all flames. John 1:16 said, "Indeed, we have all received grace after grace from His fullness." How do we as mature believers walk out of our world with the wisdom of kind words with great humility?

1. *We need to walk with the wisdom of tactfulness.* If you can't control your tongue and use it to send a soft answer, I doubt you have the discipline to be tactful. To be tactful requires discipline. As a friend of mine told me recently, "A lot of people want deliverance all along, but God wants only discipline." It takes self-control to be tactful, and local church leaders are going to need a healthy dose of it. "When there is no practical purpose requiring the truth and those hearing it will have only their feelings hurt, the rabbis tell us to choose tact over truth, especially when the truth is a matter of judgment in the first place."[13] We are, after all, to speak the truth in love (Ephesians 4:15). Being rude is not a spiritual gift. Being cruel is oppressive speech and thus forbidden by the Levitical law. In Proverbs 25:15, we learn that, "a gentle tongue can break a bone." We need the wisdom of the town clerk in ancient Ephesus who said, "You must keep calm and not do anything rash" (see Acts 19:35-41). Tact is a major ingredient in unity.

We need Christian diplomats! Paul, in 1 Corinthians 10:32-33, says, "Give no offense to the Jews or the Greeks or the church of God, just as I also try to please all people in all things, not seeking my own profit, but the profit of many, so that they may be saved." Jesus said in Matthew 18:7, "Woe to the world because of offenses. For offenses must come, but woe to that man by whom the offense comes." Offending people is not an act of ministering. Ministry requires tact and diplomacy. True tactful leaders seek to maintain peace and stability. Gamaliel was tactful (Acts 5:38-39). The wisdom of being tactful is the power to live humbly and not take things personally. Daniel returned his answers with "tact and discretion" (Daniel 2:14). Church leaders need a smoothness and skill while dealing with members. There is a difference in smoothing over issues with kindness and humility and being a "smooth talker." *Tact* is the ability "to speak with delicate perception." Tactful people are people who look out for others. You cannot be tactful and be self-absorbed. I believe that is why Paul says so many times, "Do nothing out of rivalry or conceit, but in humility consider others as more important than yourselves. Everyone should look out not only for his own interests but also for the interests of others" (Philippians 2:3-4). It takes a seasoned leader to be diplomatic. We are, after all, "ambassadors" for Christ (2 Corinthians 5:20; Ephesians 6:20). Tactful people keep a close watch on their words. Poor words produce bad situations. Good words from tactful leaders calm the deliverer of poor words, which ignite bad situations.

2. *You bless people with words of hope. "Realize that wisdom is the same for you. If you find it, you will have a*

*future, and your hope will never fade" (Proverbs 24:14).* All Christians become weary at times, and an uplifting word truly is like Proverbs 25:11 says: "A word spoken at the right time is like gold apples on a silver tray." Paul said in 2 Thessalonians 2:16, "May our Lord Jesus Christ Himself and God our Father, who has loved us and given us eternal encouragement and good hope by grace, encourage your hearts and strengthen you in every good work and word." Hopeful words strengthen our hearts and our speech. You can use your tongue to start a fire or start a revival. You can speak life into your local church by simply being positive with your words of hope. First Peter 1:3 tells us that He is a "living hope." First Corinthians 13:13 talks about the lasting impact of believing and hoping: "Now these three things remain: faith, hope, and love. But the greatest of these is love." Love builds hope; love encourages hope in you; Love protects the desire for hope in you; and love hopes all things. We must help people find hope INSIDE the church. Our tongues can bring dread or hope. We can speak hope or failure. It is a choice. Hope is a choice we make. Hope is so important to God that it remains forever. Build hope into someone today.

3. *Use your tongue to bless people with words of gratitude.* How can you identify a new convert who is going to last? Which members really love their church, and how can you truly discern it? They are the ones who are grateful. Never give to an ungrateful man; you are wasting your gift. Hebrews 12:28 says, "Therefore, since we are receiving a kingdom that cannot be shaken, let us hold on to grace." Paul was grateful to the Ephesian church (Ephesians 1:16-18). In Luke 17:11-19, one out of ten returned to Jesus with gratitude for his healing. David was

grateful (Psalms 118:1-29). Wise Christians will use their tongues to praise long before they use them to criticize. We need to become stewards of gratitude. In the old Webster's Dictionary of 1828, *gratitude* is described as follows:

> An emotion of the heart, excited by a favor or benefit received; a sentiment of kindness or good will toward a benefactor; thankfulness. Gratitude is an agreeable emotion, consisting in or accompanied with goodwill to a benefactor, and a disposition to make a suitable return of benefits or services, or when no return can be made, with a desire to see the benefactor prosperous and happy. Gratitude is a virtue of the highest excellence, as it implies a feeling and generous heart and a proper sense of duty.

What could anyone add to that?

The law of speech has tremendous power to do good or bad. Our words can build or destroy. We can use them to heal or kill. The entire world began with the expressed tones of God's vocal chords. Words are so important to God that He named His Son "The Word." Use yours today, inside your local church, to create life.

# END NOTES

## Chapter 11
## The Law of Speech

[1] Rabbi Elliot N. Dorff, *Tikkun Olam: Repairing the Broken World* (Woodstock, Vermont: Jewish Lights Publishing, 2007), 69-70.

[2] "The Psychology of Wellbeing: Musings on the Science of Holistic Wellness," *Psychology of Wellbeing* (March 6, 2014, September 4, 2012), *www.psychologyofwellbeing. com*.

[3] Ronald D. Siegel, "Positive Psychology: Harnessing the Power of Happiness, Mindfulness, and Personal Strengths," ed. *Harvard Health Publications* (Boston: Harvard Healthy Publishers, 2013).

[4] "Quotes About Truth Telling," *Goodreads, www.goodreads.com/quotes/tag/truth-telling*.

[5] Rabbi Dorff, *Tikkun Olam*, 69.

[6] Ibid., 69.

[7] Ibid., 72.

[8] Ibid., 73-74.

[9] Ibid., 75.

[10] Ibid., 78.

[11] Ibid., 86.

[12] Ibid., 88.

[13] Ibid., 92.

# The Law of Loyalty

 —— **The Knowledge Box** ——

### The Law of Loyalty

**Loyalty:** To be loyal is to be faithful to a person, organization, commitments, and/or obligations. It carries with it the philosophical idea of doing the best you can do for others. Spiritually speaking, it is a fidelity to a greater cause than your own, unswerving in one's allegiance to someone or something. It is the legal understanding that we are contractually obligated to our final authority—Christ Jesus—and to one another.

**The Precepts:**
1. Loyalty Begins With an Adherence to the Laws of God.
2. Loyalty Is an Environment.
3. The Characteristics Possessed by Loyal People Are to Be Valued.
4. Disloyalty Is a Process.
5. How the Law of Loyalty Guards Your Church.

Peter gets a bad rap if you ask me. Yes, he sank in the sea, but at least he had enough faith to get out of the boat in the first place. He denied he ever knew Jesus, cursed God while a rooster crowed, and ran off weeping into the night. Furthermore, it is interesting that Peter, in John 13:36-37, was the one who demanded that if Jesus was leaving, then so was he. And, this is the same Peter who later would take a sword to a soldier's ear who was trying to take his friend from him. In the judge's chamber, we may level the gavel on Peter as being a hothead, but in reality, he was the only disciple who fought for Jesus in that final hour. Rooster or no rooster, he was loyal to the very end.

Roosters in Palestine actually crow late at night between the hours of 12 and 3 a.m. in the morning. As the Church of Jesus Christ, we all know about Peter's adamant declaration to never leave Jesus. None of us can ever forget the story about a rooster crowing three times as Peter denied the One He so loved. Yes, it was that decision that I am sure produced the bitter taste of tears that come to all of us when we make the wrong choice. Peter failed his Lord in a test. He ran off into a crowd. But, why do we miss the foundation of his radical loyalty? He may have failed a test, but he didn't miss graduation. This same Peter may have run off into the darkness of the night when a rooster "ratted" on him, but it's this same Peter who returned on the Day of Pentecost that blesses me so much. He took his failure and made fertilizer of it. He was proven to be a known liar; yet, he did not let this failure define his future. He got alone before he got up. He must have made a place of prayer and repented in ways that led to fruit—the real meat of true repentance. We must not forget that it was only Peter who stayed deathly loyal in the darkest part of Jesus' night.

Why do we not see this kind of loyalty in the church today? When your enemies start betraying you, when the rooster crows on you, when you weep bitter tears, that is the time for true friends to arise and be counted. That takes a sacrificial kind of love which prefers one's brothers and sisters to one's own safety. It may go against human nature, but it doesn't go against Scripture. Resolve yourself to loyalty today. Stop running from church to church because you didn't get your way during the Christmas play. Stand up; grow up. Let the Holy Spirit bring you to a place of deep commitment to the people with whom you attend church every week. They need you, and you need them. The truth is, we all need each other in the body of Christ more today than ever before.

Most people want to support their leaders, but few really know how to do it. Being faithful, no matter what, is the greatest gift you can give your pastor and church. Don't ever think that they don't know it, because they do! Your silent action speaks volumes to your church leadership. I am convinced that the greatest hindrance to church growth is a dysfunctional, disloyal body of Christians. Furthermore, I am convinced that deep loyalty will outlast and overpower any weapon that Satan tries to throw at your local church. What could your church accomplish for Christ if your congregation became extremely loyal to its leadership and "one another," creating a culture of allegiance? The law of loyalty protects the mission of God.

## PRECEPT ONE:
### Loyalty Begins With Adherence to the Laws of God.

The word *loyalty* defined in a law dictionary means: "That which adheres to the law; that which sustains an existing government." The word *loyalty* actually comes from the old French word *loial,* from Latin *legalis,* which has as it root word *lex* or "leg," meaning law. Many people believe that this is why the word "loyal" is often viewed as binding or obligatory. When individuals declare their loyalty to the government, they take an oath called the "Loyalty Oath." These oaths are made by various classifications of public officials and people who work in sensitive positions. Many people in our military will take this oath, especially during times of stress, war, or threats. In corporate law, there is a title called "duty of loyalty," and it is used to describe a fiduciary's fidelity to do his/her duty.

In our world, "loyalty has become an old-fashioned word. My grandparents were loyal to the brands of their childhood. For example, they did not go to the store and buy what was on sale; instead, they went and specifically purchased a certain brand. "Close-Up" was not "Colgate" and "Folgers Crystals" was not the same as the "knockoff" brand. They were loyal to their brands. Saints of God I knew in my early Christian development were loyal to their denominations. For example, if you were to pick up my childhood Sunday school teacher and place her in another city far away, she would find a church within her denomination. Not today and probably not ever again will we see this kind of brand loyalty. However, I do believe that loyalty is a virtue for the twenty-first century. No sensible pastor is going to argue that the Christian body is not in war today with the culture at large. War and loyalty have always remained two conjoined ideas, because after all, loyalty is a legal, ethical principle.

As a Christian, where does loyalty begin? Josiah Royce, in his famous book *The Philosophy of Loyalty*, said:

> Loyalty is the willing and practical and thoroughgoing devotion of a person to a cause. A man is loyal when, first, he has a cause to which he is loyal; when, secondly, he willingly and thoroughly devotes himself to this cause; and when, thirdly, he expresses his devotion in some sustained and practical way, by acting steadily in the service of his cause.[1]

The person to whom we must be devoted is Jesus Christ. The cause to which we are devoted is the mission of God to win the world. The practical way in which we show this devotion is loyalty to His local church.

Proverbs 3:3 tells us: "Never let loyalty and faithfulness leave you. Tie them around your neck; write them on the tablet of your heart." The word translated *loyalty* is actually *chesed*, and it implies a faithful covenantal love. To be loyal as a Christian begins first with being loyal to one's covenant with God. In this passage, "loyalty" and "faithfulness" are two of the qualities of God himself. An essential element of this loyalty is love. Jesus Christ said, "If you love Me, you will keep My commandments (John 14:15). Without loyalty to God's laws or His Word, there isn't the slightest chance of unity or proving our love to Him. There has to be a fidelity and fierce loyalty to the laws of God. No community can be built outside the laws of loyalty. All communities require proper environments to function.

## PRECEPT TWO:
### Loyalty Is an Environment.

God painstakingly created the proper environment for humans. He took His great time when He methodically pulled this world together with its order and beauty. Yes, before man could be created or placed, He meticulously designed a world of order, which He himself later called "very good." The beauty we see today is a result of the order, structure, and laws God created so that man might have the perfect conditions in which to live and thrive. The local church wasn't created to be in a disloyal, unloving environment; therefore, it demands an environment of community in order to be successful. Leadership and laity have the responsibility to guard the church with furious loyalty.

**Wisdom Point A:**

*The culture of allegiance in the twenty-first century is quite different than in the past.* Today, we are sadly more committed to our favorite sports teams long before the thought of loyalty ever enters our thoughts regarding religion or commitment to our houses of worship. No NFL, NBA, or NBL, can survive without committed fans. Fans are usually more committed than average Christians, because they come early (tailgate), they are involved until the end (they don't leave during the last few minutes of the game [altar call]), they pay (season tickets [tithes and offerings]), and they support their teams during extreme weather conditions (they show up regardless if it's sunny or snowing). God is looking for people who are willing to give up their own will for a specific cause. David said in 1 Samuel 17:29: "Is there not a cause?" (KJV). How do we create an environment that builds loyal people?

1. *Understand that loyalty is more than mere emotion.* Loyalty must express itself; it must act; it must spiritedly reply. Loyalty is not carefully guarded feelings; instead, loyalty speaks up; loyalty acts on the behalf of others. Loyalty is not silent in the midst of trouble or persecution. It is a vocal ally, so find people who prove their loyalty out of action, not emotion.

2. *There must be a cause!* A loyal person looks to the cause to guide his or her behavior. The "cause" has its own values outside of self. You can't be loyal without a cause! There must be something to which you can devote yourself. A cause is larger than self. It has its own value into which the loyal place their belief. Loyalty directs itself to a cause greater than oneself.

3. *Ironically, it is a sort of restraint of your natural desires.* It is a submission of our desires for the betterment of a specific cause. Loyalty requires an individual

to have self-control, because it does not follow by impulse alone. People must be loyal to something outside them, and to do so, requires self-restraint. It is being loyal to something much larger than our own desires. I am amazed at how many times humility is required to advance the Christian mission. To be unified to a cause requires humility, because loyalty requires self-restraint of desires, and then places the desires of the people ahead of one's own individual wishes. I challenge you to lose yourself into something larger than your own dreams.

4. *Value your cause.* A cause has a value, and this value implies that a person believes. We deeply believe in the values of the cause.

5. *Individually, decide to be a union.* The cause is about the individual good of others, and thus the cause requires loyalty. To create a culture of allegiance means that we build members who are loyal to something outside of themselves. Loyalty is important for the good of individuals. Loyalty is intensely personal at first, but then we realize that our cause is not only personal but also interpersonal. This individual cause is personally a passionate subject to us, which as Josiah Royce would say, "awakens our heart; only such a cause can unify his outer and inner world. When such unity comes, it takes in him the form of an active loyalty."[2] Before we can become loyal, we must first become individually passionate about a cause. When we value the cause deeply enough, we will sacrificially give ourselves to this cause. This unity of loyalty, however, doesn't negate individual responsibility. It actually enhances loyalty to the cause by impassionate action—taking responsibility for our passionate cause.

6. *Individuals whose faces are set like flint.* The power of a facial expression is worth a thousand pictures. Facial expressions can tell the story of displeasure or pleasure. When I hear gossip or negativity, my facial expression will show that I am not interested in their conversation. Your face can show a gossip or church dissenter that their disloyalty is not welcome in your presence. No fire can exist without oxygen.

7. *We need a culture where disloyalty is not tolerated.* We should simply get rid of it. Don't try to coddle it; get rid of it. Disloyalty must be expelled immediately. Remove disloyalty quickly and create a culture where it is constantly being rooted out. It is important to remember that the opinions and insights of others, which are different from your own, is not a sign of disloyalty. Welcome diversity and different opinions. Weed out disloyal people who undermine your strategies and are unfaithful to you as the leader or your leaders!

8. *Create an environment where people are promoted before their rightful time.*

> I have a problem that happens to be a virtue. I can easily see the best in people and their potential for greatness. My problem is that they oftentimes refuse to look at what I can see in them. In my passionate vision for transformation, I become such a fan so quickly that I have not allowed them the proper time to prove themselves. Sometimes, I am like many other pastors, anxious that if I don't get people placed quickly, they will never take root in our church. I have learned that roots take time to grow. And those real leaders will stick with you when the times are tough and welcome the process of approval. I will never forget the first set of elders I developed in a local church. What a mess I made! At the first sign of

trouble, these "men of God" where nowhere to be found. They abandoned ship at the first sign of turbulent waters. I trained them in Matthew 18 for a year. I taught them how to handle relational viruses and troubles in a church. Yet, the first hint of trouble that came from the relational problems of lightning sent many of them running for cover. Their loyalty was with their egos and reputations, not the betterment and protection of the body of Christ. Yet, in their midst were real soldiers of God—men who were not afraid of an attack from the Enemy. They were seasoned for warfare and competent in battle—people who are still with me today.

What was the difference between the two types of early elders? It was loyalty to a cause.

9. *Create an environment of "want-to" people.* I used to talk people into staying who wanted to leave or resign. I don't do that anymore. I make a way for them to leave. If you are going to create an environment of allegiance or a culture of loyalty, then you should make a way for resignation so they can exit in peace. The apostle Paul wrote in 2 Corinthians 8:12: "For if there be first a willing mind" (KJV). How true. Surround yourself; build into your church a culture of leaders who have willing minds.

### Wisdom Point B:

*How a disloyal environment is birthed.* Warning: The devil doesn't need an outside demonic "imp" to destroy your church: All he needs is a spiritually immature Christian from within.

The lethal weapon in any church body is the disloyalty of its members. Lucifer, Absalom, Joab, and Judas were all disloyalists. In America, we are fond of saying, "You are a Benedict Arnold"—a phrase originating all the way back to the American Continental Army. Just like David and Jesus, George Washington and early Americans also had their betrayers. Benedict Arnold sold out his American comrades to the British forces for money and prestige. He was a major military leader in the early days of the United States. He often reported directly to George Washington himself. It seems that traitors always have a history of being right by your side, looking you in the eyes, before they stab you in the back with their tongues or knives? All traitors are jealous. Ironically, traitors are trainers for Christian leaders. The bad news is that all great leaders suffer some form of betrayal. The good news is you can create a culture of allegiance. It is possible to be aligned with other people who are firmly committed to each other and your leadership. However, this kind of culture doesn't happen by accident and certainly doesn't take place overnight. Guarding your church from disloyalty takes the same commitment to diligence. Here is how to spot an environment which births disloyalty.

1. *Absenteeism*. My eyes are always on the late people to the room. It can show a certain level of disrespect. I am not talking about being in a traffic jam or an emergency call from work while heading out the door to the meeting. I am talking about the one who "swaggers" in as if he were on his own time. People who are purposefully late or people who don't show up to services, major church events, or important meetings need to be watched. It is the little foxes that spoil the vineyard; and when people loudly disrespect your time and leadership by silently not showing up, watch them because they are sending a message of disloyalty.

2. *They will poison you before others*. People who don't defend you in private are not your friends in public either. Be on the watch for those people who act like your friend in front of the masses but quietly

question your authority and decisions privately. They place little doubts about you in the minds of loyal people. They are really cowards, because they always attack you when you appear vulnerable. They love to look like a "messiah" or "the Lone Ranger" who is here to "save the day." Watch for those people who poison the mission in front of people. There is a proper way to address disagreements and air out problems. Solving disagreements should be done privately, outside the group, but only when the leader is present.

3. *They hang with the few and never mingle with the masses.* Loyalty is an issue that requires commitment to others. It is a loyalty to a cause greater than ourselves that truly unites us. When you see people building cliques to the left when the rest of the church is on the right—watch out! Disloyal people create small groups who never unify with the larger body. Disloyal people hang with other people of poison. They carry an offense virus into a small group of people. They avoid the critical mass of positive people heading the organization into a greater future. This is the reason disloyal people hang with the few; it is much easier to become the "messiah" of a small group.

4. *They stand by the disloyal person.*

> I will never forget the day that an elder I trusted stood by a convicted felon who lied. I thought this elder loved me and my family, but he seemed to be more interested in the filth and gossip of a liar than standing in loyalty with his pastor— something he promised to do. It shouldn't have been a surprise when he poisoned a small group of people, all of whom were disloyal all the way out the door.

(Of course, they were silently being led by God.) Disloyal people attract one another. If you think about how Absalom and Adonijah, the two sons of David, tried to exalt themselves onto the throne, it was always by standing with the disloyal person who stood against their father, the King of Israel.

**Wisdom Point C:**
*Disloyal people have struggles with honoring spiritual authority.* To be loyal requires self-restraint, which requires humility. It is amazing that so many people have trouble participating in the praise of another human's accomplishment. A disloyal person will vote against you when they can do so silently. They struggle with submission to spiritual authority. They would never admit it; in fact, they often talk about humility and submission, but they never actually show such behavior in their personal lives.

## PRECEPT THREE:
### The Characteristics Possessed by Loyal People Are to Be Valued.

Loyalty today is in short supply. You cannot be loyal and not express loyalty, because loyalty involves a cause, and this cause has to be valued enough by someone for them to act on their loyalty. Loyalty, in other words, demands action. What characteristics do loyal people possess?

**Wisdom Point A:**
*Loyal people ultimately look to the lordship of Jesus Christ.* Disloyal people always seem to play the "God card" in church work. They blame "God" for their poor conduct, lack of commitment, church hopping, nondiscipleship, and lack of servanthood. However, a truly loyal person is first loyal to Jesus Christ and His Word. Paul says in 1 Corinthians 11:1:

"Imitate me, as I also imitate Christ." There is this sense that Paul has an order to his mimetic model. Model me, because I am modeling the life of Christ. Our loyalty to Christ, according to Luke 14:25-33, supersedes all other relationships. The cost for full allegiance to Jesus is everything. Serving Christ requires faithfulness, allegiance, fidelity, wholeheartedness, and devotion. Loyalty is indeed a big concern to God.

The first place for loyalty to Jesus Christ to penetrate is in our hearts! Repeatedly, we are told to serve Him with our whole heart, soul, and mind. In Matthew 22:37, we are told, "Love the Lord your God with all your heart, with all your soul, and with all your mind." There is no better definition of loyalty to God. It is interesting what the half-brother of Jesus said in James 1:5-8. It reminds us that a double-minded man should not expect anything from God. Such disloyal behavior is condemned throughout both the Old and New Testaments. Paul was admonishing the Corinthian church for its lack of loyalty in the second Book of Corinthians. He even suggested that disloyalty to his apostleship was disloyalty to Christ himself. They were being disloyal to the truth of Scripture.

Here is the next point: "The Christian's devotion to God is inseparably bound up with his loyalty to the mystic union of the faithful in the church...loyalty itself, as a devotion to a cause which unifies many human lives, is, as we shall see, profoundly religious in spirit."[3] To be loyal to God is suggesting that we must also be loyal to "one another." Both loyalties are connected. Think about it. What was the "sin" of Judas? It was disloyalty. God is faithful to us as an example. Therefore, we too must be faithful to our fellow brothers and sisters. Wise leaders create loyal environments by first being loyal themselves. What are they loyal to? They are loyal to the personhood of Christ, the gospel He preached, the Word He gave us, and the church

He is building! We are expected to be loyal to Christ—that is exactly the reason He uses the metaphor of marriage and speech of betrothal. We are His and expected to be loyal to Him. Yet, we are ONE bride to Him. Mark said: "If a house is divided against itself, that house cannot stand" (3:25). Look at Mark 12:29-31 and notice the first command is great loyalty to Christ; "the second is: Love your neighbor as yourself. There is no other command greater than these." Loyal people are first loyal in their relationship to Jesus Christ. If they fail to be loyal to Him, they will fail in being loyal to you. The mature ones realize that being loyal to Him and to the members of His church are one in the same.

**Wisdom Point B:**

Loyal people set their faces like flint toward the disloyal.

> I revered my grandpa. He looked like a Hollywood Baldwin with his jet black hair, crystal blue eyes, and six-foot figure. When I was a young child, I used to sit at the kitchen table and drink coffee with him. I loved it, and he laughed constantly through the ordeal. One morning I began telling him a dirty joke. I didn't realize that I was telling him a dirty joke. His kind blue eyes turned to eyes of an instructor as he informed me that I had just told him a dirty joke. My heart froze with fear. While he remained kind, his look was stern. I knew never to bring up that joke again in his presence.

In Isaiah 50:7, the prophet Isaiah talks about setting "[our] face like flint." This sentence means one's face should be expressionless, impassionate, or hard. I do not laugh off disloyal statements, look at my feet, or ignore slander. My face clearly shows displeasure with such behavior. This may sound rather simple, but it works. Loyalty is serious business in the Scriptures, and it must be to all of us as well.

## Wisdom Point C:

*Loyal people will not withhold information.* There are several scriptures in Corinthians that may be easy to dismiss on most occasions. Paul says in 1 Corinthians 5:1: "It is widely reported that there is sexual immorality among you." Paul said, "It is widely reported," or someone actually told me that you.... In 1 Corinthians 1:11, Paul wrote, "For it has been reported to me." This is not about being "a rat." It is about a loyal structure working to ensure the health of an organization. "A good and loyal structure works: faithful people inform the top leaders about anything that is out of order."[4] Notice that Paul never condemns the people who reported poor behavior. Paul knew that one person's disloyal behavior could possibly wreck the entire Corinthian church. Paul makes it clear that there were loyal people reporting information to him. They were loyal to Christ and His body. Loyal people are loyal to the organization—the cause.

## Wisdom Point D:

*Loyal people are fully persuaded to their cause.* Paul said in Romans 4:21: "Being fully persuaded" (KJV). You don't have to send out a search party for loyal people. They are always there, positive, and accounted for. When you value something, you support its value through your faithfulness to it. Jesus loved the local church so much He gave His life for it. He worked diligently building its leadership on the grassroots as His primary work here on earth. We need loyal people to the purpose and mission of our local churches. This kind of loyalty is fully persuaded to the cause, and nothing can dislodge it from its foundation. Be more loyal than the gossip; more loyal than the dissidents; more loyal than the critics; and more loyal than the status quo. Such persuasive loyalty can move the gates of hell. Such loyalty can move mountains. This kind of furious loyalty, combined with the mass strength of the body of Christ can accomplish much for the kingdom of God.

**Wisdom Point E:**

Loyal people are characterized by long-term relationships.

> I started fifteen years ago with a small group of people as we dreamed of building a great church in Western Kentucky. Today, when I look at the thousands of people who attend this church, I get seriously sentimental about those people who started with me fifteen years ago. Their longevity has proven their loyalty to this church, the mission of God, and me. The longer they stay rooted, the more power they have in influencing the world for Christ.

In Ecclesiastes 4:12 it says, "A chord of three strands is not easily broken." Satan is attacking the church on all sides. If ever the body of Christ needs to stick together, it is now. The Baptist church down the road is not my competition. I am at war with the Adversary. To go to war, we need faithful soldiers. Who would dare go to war with a hostile country using disloyal soldiers? War is not the time to decide who is on your side? Faithful, loyal, dependable people are needed to advance the mission of the Church. When you know that you are fighting with soldiers who have stayed long enough to prove that they been faithful in previous battles, it makes a huge difference. Your long-term loyalty makes a huge difference in the confidence of your leaders. There is much to be said in regard to simply being faithful. Faithful people comfort church leaders. Their jobs are very difficult in a world where God's Word has promised "a great falling away" (see 2 Thessalonians 2:3). Your loyalty combined with your longevity empowers the leaders in your church. Longevity founded in loyalty is the greatest gift you can give any pastor. The dozens of people who started with me fifteen years ago are my heroes. They have proven their commitment through many troubles and trials. It is one thing to be called a soldier of Christ;

it is another thing to prove it by sticking in the same battle with the same leader on the same mission until the job is completed!

### Wisdom Point F:
*Loyal people sail the seas of adversity with great faithfulness.* While longevity is a good characteristic of loyal people, there are times that people desert you after having a close relationship with you. Paul talks about a man named Demas in Colossians 4:14 and Philemon 1:24. Paul calls him a companion during his first Roman imprisonment. This native of Thessalonica eventually deserted the apostle Paul (2 Timothy 4:10). Paul called him a "fellow worker" (Colossians 4:10-14). This is a Greek word which means to work with, labor, and toil with another human being. Demas was close to Paul, he was involved; he acted on Paul's behalf. In 2 Timothy 4:10, Paul says that Demas "deserted" him. This Greek word means, "To abandon, forsake, to leave while there are troubling times." The New Testament places a great emphasis on being faithful to the cause during times of great trouble. Paul tells Timothy in 2 Timothy 1:15: "All those in Asia have turned away from me, including Phygelus and Hermogenes." The word for desertion is the same one used in 2 Timothy 4:4 and Titus 1:14 for doctrinal apostasy. These people have not only deserted Paul but also the gospel that he was following. Loyalty involves conduct.

According to the famous author on loyalty, Josiah Royce, loyalty begins in childhood. He writes, "While the beginning of loyalty extends far back into the life of childhood, its full development must belong to mature years."[5] This insight into loyalty points us toward the difference between the young growth of the seeds of loyalty and the mature branches of the oak of loyalty. Consider these questions:

- Are you a sapling of loyalty or an oak of loyalty in your local church?
- Does your church leadership see you as a twig easily broken by the conflict of storms, or do they see you as strength protected by deep roots of aged loyalty?

To know who is loyal, look at those people who have been through difficult times with you. Watch what they do, and take note of the people who are absent during times of crisis. The greatest proof of loyalty is those people who have proven their loyalty through multiple storms. Faithfulness requires endurance. Endurance is earned by faithfulness and implies resistance. Loyal people are those people who have made it through great times of resistance and are still standing with you.

**Wisdom Point G:**

*Loyal people are characterized by defending the weakness of their leaders.* No leader is perfect. Paul said he struggled with a "thorn in his flesh" (2 Corinthians 12:7-10), and he tells us: "I do not practice what I want to do, but I do what I hate" (Romans 7:15). All leaders have faults and shortcomings. The old saying "familiarity breeds contempt" is so true. When you see your pastor only from the pulpit, you can accidently assume that your pastor lives under that strong anointing Monday through Friday. He or she is a human being just like you. When you truly love someone, you defend them when their weakness is pointed out, because you deeply believe in their good. You believe in a cause. You value something deeply. I love my children even though I know that they are not always perfect. When I hear someone criticize them unfairly, I speak up. The same is true of your wife, friends, and church leaders. There is a difference between making an excuse for poor behavior and giving grace to imperfections! I stand up for my staff, and they stand up for me. Why? We value one another. I know they are not perfect, and they know I am not perfect. But I won't let my familiarity breed contempt. I consider it an honor to know someone so well that I am a friend to his or her weaknesses and successes. Loyal people protect the humanity of their leaders.

**Wisdom Point H:**

*Loyal people are open and analytical.* To be loyal does not mean that you don't keep an open mind. To be loyal does not mean that you are expected to never think for yourself. To be loyal does not mean that a difference of opinion is never welcomed. (Actually, Dag Heward-Mills wrote a brilliant book on loyalty that you can pick up at www. nbpar.com). This book points out this powerful point: Loyalty demands analysis. "Whenever your loyalty is tested, you will have to analyze several things to stay loyal. To analyze means to study and interpret the information set before you."[6] Dag Heward-Mills believes that analysis of loyalty requires four basic behaviors: (1) analysis of the past, (2) the individual, (3) their words, and (4) the Word. First, loyal people always analyze the past behavior of the individual. Before you believe the worst about a church leader, ask yourself what kind of behavior they have previously modeled in the past. The best predictor of future behavior is past behavior. Second, take a good look at the behavior of the individual, listen to what is being said, and determine if his/her words and actions are aligned. Loyal people speak with loyal language. Loyal people act consistently. Loyal people consistently speak words of loyalty. Paul told Timothy, "Hold on to the pattern of sound teaching that you have heard from me" (2 Timothy 1:13). Third, if you listen closely enough, a person will tell you who he/she really is! Listen and believe the person the first time he/she says something. While it is possible to clean the outside of the cup and then externally look presentable, it is not possible to clean the inside of the cup with self-control (Matthew 23:25). The Word of God further points out: "The mouth speaks from the overflow of the heart" (Matthew 12:34). One's mouth is eventually going to say what the heart is feeling. Fourth, take a good hard look at what the Word of God says about any situation—it is the Book of Life. The writer of Hebrews said: "The Word of God is living and effective and sharper than any double-edged sword, penetrating as far as the separation of soul, spirit, joints, and marrow. It is able to judge the ideas and thoughts of the heart" (4:12). The psalmist said, "Your word is a lamp for my feet and a light on my path!" (Psalms 119:105). Luke says in Acts 17:11: "The people here were more open-minded than those in Thessalonica, since they welcomed the message with eagerness and examined the Scriptures daily to see if these things were so."

Being loyal does not mandate that you spend the rest of your life as a non-thinking human being. It actually means to be the direct opposite. Loyalty requires analytical thinking while we properly bring analysis to the situation before us. Loyalty is a form of intelligence. It is having the intelligence to weigh the matter that is before us and then to live by its principles.

### Wisdom Point I:

*Loyal people pay the price for being loyal.* I am sure there were people in ancient Corinth who were troubled at the "member" who reported poor behavior among them to the apostle Paul. Shaming someone in that culture was a huge issue. It certainly and most directly went against the cultural cues of their day. Shame and honor were paramount values in that society, so to shame someone was an act of bravery. This person literally had to make a decision of loyalty—loyalty to the individual or loyalty to the greater body of Christ and its spiritual authority. That courageous act of loyalty may have saved the Corinthian church from internal destruction. A loyal soldier supports the leadership and his fellow soldiers. You see, loyalty defines your allegiance. It is proof of your convictions. Loyalty does not waver during the times of troubled seas; it is actually strengthened by such adversity.

> This year I have stood before the actual gravesites of several of the original disciples of Jesus Christ. I stood by the tomb of Saint Philip at Hierapolis, looking at the slab where they laid him—only feet from the ground where they martyred him. As I stood there, I couldn't help but think of the moment directly after the crucifixion when the disciples all ran from their faith. My mind raced as I thought about the troubled mind and distressed heart that they must have experienced during those three long days. I suddenly realized that I was now standing directly in front of their final answer.

There are times that you will let your closest friends down. However, failure makes great fertilizer. All of them composed themselves and anchored the troubled seas of their frightened hearts and exhausted minds. They took up their crosses and began to follow Him daily once again. In the end, they paid a price for loyalty. I know, I am an eyewitness to their final answer.

One thing never makes a loyal person, but it's the sum total of a consistent clear-valued life. Loyal people are not perfect, but they are consistent. One fall or slip should never disqualify the loyal associate. Let one's entire life speak to you. There are many ways that people can show themselves loyal to you or the cause of the local church. So, keep watch on the consistency of the person's behavior, not just the talk of being loyal.

## PRECEPT FOUR:
### Disloyalty Is a Process.

It is an interesting fact that disloyal people actually grow into being disloyal. Few betrayers ever wake up and say, "I think I will be disloyal today." It is a chronological process in their lives that often happens unconsciously. Dag Heward-Mills, in his book, *Loyalty and Disloyalty*, describes this process better than anyone else I have read, and I want to use his structural insights into disloyalty because he hits the nail on the head.

> Recently, a person I dearly loved became extremely disloyal to me. I was shocked, hurt, angered, and ashamed. Many people warned me, but I didn't listen. Since then, I have spent countless nights rolling over in my mind why I couldn't see his disloyal actions coming straight at me. The good news is, I could have if only I had known the wisdom I am about to share with you from Dag Heward-Mills. Disloyal people walk through stages; no one just becomes disloyal.

### Wisdom Point A:
*Stage One: The Independent Spirit.* This stage is subtle because it is actually an attitude within an individual. In 2 Samuel 3:20-21, King David decided to make peace with one of his commanders named Abner. David planned a great feast for him as a token of renewed friendship. David had another close commander named Joab who did whatever he wanted, no matter what King David said. In 2 Samuel 3:26-29, the writer tells us that Joab was actually angered at the peace agreement. David had instructed him to be kind to Abner, yet Joab ignored the wishes of the king and killed Abner. The independent spirit of Joab endangered the entire well-being of Israel. A person begins disloyalty with an independent spirit.

In 2 Samuel 18:5, (notice the repetitive behavior) Joab was told by David not to harm his son Absalom. Then, one day someone told Joab that they had seen Absalom hanging in a tree by his hair. Second Samuel 18:11 records Joab's words to the person reporting Absalom's whereabouts: "'You just saw him!' Joab exclaimed. 'Why didn't you strike him to the ground right there?'" Joab had an independent spirit; he ignored the wishes of godly authority. In fact, he brushed off any idea that his independent spirit would bring danger to many other lives in the kingdom of David. While 2 Samuel 18:12 tells the tale of a loyal servant of David, 2 Samuel 18:14 again shows the disloyalty of an independent spirit as Joab kills Absalom. Independent people are dangerous during times of war or peace. Loyalty requires a cause greater than we are.

Watch independent spirits in your church. I am not talking about self-starters, highly motivated people, or those who properly think analytically. I am talking about those people in your church who never hang out with the masses or engage in acts of community. I am talking about the kinds of people who plan backyard cookouts when the rest of the church is celebrating at the park.

> The first church I ever helped to plant taught me a great lesson. We found a building for them, signed for a loan, and gave them manpower. I could never figure out why they worked so hard at distancing themselves from us. No fellowship, no accountability, no warmth—they were only taking from us. Then, one day I discovered that the pastor was not only having an affair but also planning to separate the congregation from its life-giving mother church. What selfishness, and needless to say, this church folded.

It takes loyalty to build something great. Deuteronomy 32:30 asks, "Could one man pursue a thousand, or two put ten thousand to flight?" Watch independent spirits, because it's the first stage of disloyalty.

## Wisdom Point B:

*Stage Two: Offense.* Disloyal people begin by being independent spirits and move from there to having offended spirits. They become disgruntled with you, the leader, or someone in authority. Disloyal people become disloyal by cultivating a disloyal spirit and harboring an offense. I heard a former mentor of mine preach a message titled: "Don't Pick Up Another Person's Offense." That title has stuck with me over the years. Wounded people betray other people. They live with the bitterness of the wrong they perceive being done to them. They ignore Matthew 18 and let their offense fester. Behind every act of disloyalty, one can find an offensive blister. This sore refuses to heal; therefore, it contains a dangerous infection. This offense fuels the progressive nature of disloyalty. They sit and stew in their offense rather than gain the maturity to confront them in love and work out their problems (Matthew 18).

## Wisdom Point C:

*Stage Three: Passivity.* Disloyal people are independent spirits who carry offenses while passively standing by your critics. Disloyal people will go from being offended to a season of being uninvolved. In 2 Samuel 13:22, we see where Absalom, after being offended at his father, became indifferent, and this led to murder. Ancient rabbis saw slander as a form of murder. Passive people who let an offense happen IN THEM will always give birth to a murdering form of slander. When a wound is ignored, it gets worse. Passivity is the Enemy's way to birth slander and disloyalty.

## Wisdom Point D:

*Stage Four: The Critical Stage.* Disloyal people are never passive forever. Eventually, the wound festers until it is out of control. They literally hold their mouths until they

THE LAW OF LOYALTY

cannot hold their tongues another minute. Their wound festers into criticism. They see only the imperfections of people. Criticism is a poisonous pill that can wound the spirit deeply. However, we don't often think about how criticism wounds the person who criticizes. The soul is sick, and the heart is jealous. The person is eaten up with bitterness and wrath. Passivity breeds the fourth stage of disloyalty—criticism. There is a gap as huge as the Grand Canyon between constructive criticism spoken in love and a critical spirit. Miriam had a critical spirit against her brother, Moses. Paul writes to us in Romans 14:10-13 and says, "But you, why do you criticize your brother? Or you, why do you look down on your brother? For we will all stand before the tribunal of God. . . . Therefore, let us no longer criticize one another. Instead decide never to put a stumbling block or pitfall in your brother's way." The Greek here is actually saying "Why do you, the weaker brother, criticize?" Passive, disloyal people will become obsessed with criticism and fault-finding. The difference between constructive criticism and criticism is that the first builds up while the second one tears down. It is often rooted in a person who doesn't know his/her identity in Christ. During the passive stage, former friends who now lie awake in bed struggling with the favor of God on their lives, suppress negative feelings. Their insecurity is actually a sign of their immaturity. As they stew, they will become political in nature against the other person. It's a process that is inevitable, if not stopped by the maturity of the Scripture and conviction of the Spirit.

**Wisdom Point E:**

*Stage Five: The Political Stage.* As a disloyal person moves from being critical to political, he/she begins to operate in the power of people's opinions. He/she deeply desires to be the hero of the day. Absalom's life is such a perfect picture of this sad process. He was passive, analytical of David's policies, eventually becoming critical, and then political. In 2 Samuel 15:3-4, it says, "Absalom said to him, 'Look, your claims are good and right, but the king does not have anyone to listen to you.' He added, 'If only someone would appoint me judge in the land.'" Passive people move to criticism, and then use their criticism to engage political warfare against leadership. Just like Absalom, they first subtly question the humanness of your leadership, your blind spots, and rather than hide them as a loyal person would, they expose you secretly to those whom you lead every week. Disloyal people love to discuss your short-comings! And just like Absalom, they drag innocent people into the discussion. As Dag Heward-Mills writes, "He wants to gather a following and make people believe that he has identified a real problem that must be addressed."[7] I have learned to watch those who sit outside an elders meeting or a deacons gathering with all of the solutions before and after the meeting, but remain silent during the meeting! Mark them! Many associates and church leaders deceive themselves "into thinking that his more frequent interaction with the people makes him a better pastor (elder, deacon, or volunteer), and therefore is to be chosen over or preferred over the senior."[8] They undermine authority and suggest that leadership is really incompetent. Thank God for loyal assistants who love their leaders. They guard the kingdom of God. They ensure that the Enemy's forces shall not move the Church into atrophy, betrayal, or the great shame of disloyalty.

The political stage is particularly dangerous because the disloyal use these gaps or lies about other people's leadership to establish their own kingdom. Second Samuel 15:6 says to us: "Absalom did this to all the Israelites who came to the king for a settlement. So Absalom stole the hearts of the men of Israel." Few people can handle the power of great delegated authority. If you are in authority, don't trust it to just anyone. Trust it only to the humble and the proven. Absalom used this delegated authority to gain confidence. Had he not held delegated authority and had he not been trusted by the king, he would have never had the opportunity to steal the kingdom. "Much will be required of everyone who has been given much" (Luke 12:48); it works both ways. There is no good outcome of any human in biblical history who defined his/her life by betraying the trust of former friends. God's people need to remind themselves to be faithful to trusted leadership. Satan is, after all, called "The accuser of our brothers" (Revelation 12:7-12). The disloyal use this political stage to maneuver people to their cause, which always points to deception.

**Wisdom Point F:**

*Stage Six: The Deceptive Stage.* The first stage of deception begins when the disloyal begin to deceive themselves. Jesus said in John 14:12: "I assure you: The one who believes in Me will also do the works that I do. And he will do even greater works than these, because I am going to the Father." And yet, this same Jesus said, "I assure you: A slave is not greater than his master, and a messenger is not greater than the one who sent him" (John 13:16). I love what Dag Heward-Mills said: "The obstinate insurgent thought that within six months he could achieve things that take many years of experience to attain."[9] Somehow, a little press goes to people's heads very quickly.

> I remember one time when we were having a week of convocation at Covenant Community Church. We had asked several well-known guests to speak to our region, and I had asked a "rising star" to speak as well. He was so rude that I almost asked him to leave before he ever entered into my pulpit. I remember thinking to myself: *If this is all of the fame, power, and authority you can handle, then you are in huge trouble already.*

Disloyal people deceive themselves first.

Second, they work hard at deceiving the people. During my more than thirty-three years in ministry, I have watched disloyal people work. I know where they hide, talk, speak, write, and how they live their lives. They do it as prophetic martyrs. They consider themselves wavers of the banner of order and righteousness while they completely ignore the laws of community. They often lie. I have finally learned that not everyone who carries a Bible is a Bible believer! Test those around you. Absalom, Lucifer, Judas, Joab—all were deceivers! Proverbs 12:22 says, "Lying lips are detestable to the Lord, but faithful people are His delight." Proverbs 10:9 says, "The one who lives with integrity lives securely, but whoever perverts his ways will be found out." Now that is good news. There is a saying in Kentucky: "You can't win the Kentucky Derby riding a donkey!" You also need to be reminded that if you give a donkey enough rope, he will eventually hang himself! As one of my spiritual fathers once told me, "Sit still, and watch the rats come out of hiding." Disloyal people are deceptive, and deceptive people work in the dark!

**Wisdom Point G:**

*Stage Seven: Open Rebellion.* The deceptive stage intermingled with the preceding political stage gives the disloyal person a false sense of security. False confidence and deception will fool disloyal people into thinking that they have rallied enough people to their cause, and if not, the cause emboldens their sinful insight. Joab, Absalom, Lucifer, and Judas all have their star in the walk of shame—they are the disloyal elite. Jesus is against them all. First Samuel 15:23 says, "For rebellion is like the sin of divination, and defiance is like wickedness and idolatry." Divination means that one serves anti-godly demonic powers. Pretty strong words! Rebellion and defiance are like serving false gods. When we rebel, we are voluntarily rejecting God's authority. Disloyal people wait for their moment of potential fame, and then they ambush unsuspecting leaders. I have watched many people rebel against their leaders and local churches. I have seen none of them prosper in the long term. The Bible is clear as to the future of disloyal people.

## Wisdom Point H:

*Stage Eight: The Execution Stage:* Lucifer thought he had started a coup in heaven. But the prophet Isaiah records this pronouncement: "Shining morning star . . . you have fallen from the heavens! You destroyer of nations, you have been cut down to the ground." (Isaiah 14:12). A disloyal person is executed in their execution. In the end, they deceive themselves. Lucifer did so. Revelation 12:9 promises us that his ending will not be good. Second Samuel 18:15 reminds us that Absalom died a horrible death. Also, Matthew 27:5 tells us that Judas met a horrible ending directly related to the guilt of his great disloyalty. Be very careful what revolt you join. Think twice about believing any accusation against leadership that is not established by two to three witnesses (1 Timothy 5:19). Pray hard about attacking the church with your tongue or aligning yourself with people who speak evil without hearing the other side of a matter completely. If you have allowed disloyalty to spring up in your heart, you will be executed in your execution. God deals swiftly with disloyal people. Ask Lucifer.

Disloyalty is a process that starts with an independent spirit that harbors an offense. This offense marinates in passivity until it festers a bitter stew. Eventually, the passivity boils over to a critical stage. The fire is out of control. This critical stage leads to self-deception when the disloyal engage in church politics. When deception has ripened on the tree of offense, it breeds a false confidence, which engages in open rebellion. This rebellion to strike your leader, to wound the one who loved you, will be the burial ground for all disloyal people. The law of loyalty demands that disloyal people be removed from authority. Their immaturity demands it, the Scripture requires that leaven and small foxes spoil the entire mission, and common sense knows it must be done. To those who have been disloyal, repent and ask the Lord to forgive you. To the loyal, your character and strength, coupled with your consistency and longevity will bring you through every storm the Enemy may throw at your church. Ironically, the process of disloyalty is the stages of backsliding against God. Repent, and fall in love with Him again. The deeper the roots the less likely you are going to be blown over.

## PRECEPT FIVE:
### How the Law of Loyalty Guards Your Church

If the Church is going to overcome the gates of hell, it is going to have to be an airtight community. Satan has always used a traitor to destroy the work of God. He is a traitor to God first and mankind second through Adam and Eve. Traitors have littered the long road of history, and they all come from the exact same place—within. These disloyal people breed discontentment, strife, hatred, and murmuring. It all began in the Garden with the original betrayer, Lucifer. To see his work, you have to look only at the pages of Genesis. It was a perfect environment of loyalty. You see, loyalty is first a choice. The two trees demanded that a choice be made. As I make a choice by not eating of this particular tree, I am making a conscious choice to be loyal to God. But when man chose to be disloyal to God, he reaped the fruit of disloyalty, hatred, strife, murmuring, and eventually death. God has always dealt a blow of justice to the disloyal. However, He greatly rewards the loyal, but remember that loyalty involves conduct.

## Wisdom Point A:

*God needs you to be an example of loyalty in your local church.* Josiah Royce said, "Much of the art of loyalty, consequently, depends upon training yourself to observe the loyal who are all about you, however remote their cause is from yours, however humble their lives."[10] First Corinthians 4:2 says, "In this regard, it is expected of managers that each one of them be found faithful." Don't be tossed to and fro, hop from church to church like an inebriated rabbit. Again, Paul says in 1 Corinthians 10:21, "You cannot drink the cup of the Lord and the cup of demons. You cannot share in the Lord's table and the table of demons." Your church leadership will be greatly encouraged when you make a vocal stand of loyalty.

## Wisdom Point B:

*Your loyalty encourages other people.* To be loyal is to be moral. It takes a conscious effort to be a loyal person. God needs for all these things together—our personal friends who inspire us to the service of our own causes; the hosts of the loyal about whom we know so little, but who constitute the invisible church of those who live in the Spirit; the many griefs that teach us the glory of what our human vision has lost from its fields; the imagination that throws over all the range of human life with its idealizing light; the labors that leave us breathless; the crushing defeats that test our devotion—these are only the means and the ministers whereby we are taught to enter the realm of spiritual truth. Your life teaches other lives what loyalty actually looks like. We should all be encouraged by the potential future words of Christ: "Well done, my good and FAITHFUL servant" (Matthew 25:21 NLT). When you are a loyal member of your local church, you are manifesting eternity. Loyalty assumes unity. Christ's prayer was, "that they may be one as We are [one]" (John 17:11 NKJV), and that needs to be your prayer for your local church today.

**Wisdom Point C:**

*Loyalty manifests the eternal.* "Loyalty is the will to manifest the eternal in and through the deeds of individual selves."[11] How can unsaved people ever see the goodness and faithfulness of God when His church remains so unfaithful to one another? When a world sees the kindness of God, (Jeremiah 28–29) they will see Him through our faithfulness. Have you ever wondered why we celebrate faithfulness? When we retire, we celebrate forty years with a gold watch. We are honoring faithfulness. When we remain faithful, we grow. No plant can be plucked up every time there is a storm and replanted somewhere else, thus expecting to survive, not to mention thrive. But our individual faithfulness and loyalties point men to the One who will never let us down. He is called Faithful and True. Don't we use the words, "He is a true friend"? In fact, the Bible says, "A man with many friends may be harmed, but there is a friend who stays closer than a brother" (Proverbs 18:24). John 13:1 tells us that Jesus loved us to the end. Our loyalty manifests the faithfulness of God to the world.

Loyalty will bring more value to your church than $10 million. It builds an environment of trust, consistency, longevity, and deep commitment. Be committed to one local church. Love the Lord enough to dig some roots and develop some loyalties. As we have seen, loyalty is a law; it requires an environment and has characteristics. Whereas, disloyalty flows through a process, loyalty guards the house of God. As a pastor, I know that loyalty is the greatest gift anyone can give to church leadership. It empowers the mission of the church and it shows people in this world that God is faithful. Dig your roots down deep, navigate your walk with Christ by the laws of community, and watch the power of loyalty empower your mission.

# END NOTES

## Chapter 12
## The Law of Loyalty

[1] Josiah Royce, *The Philosophy of Loyalty* (New York: The McMillian Company, 1908), 17.

[2] Royce, *The Philosophy of Loyalty*, p. 59.

[3] Ibid., pp. 256-57.

[4] Dag Heward-Mills, *Loyalty and Disloyalty: Dealing with Unspoken Divisions Within the Church* (Franklin, Tenn.: Carpenter's Son Publishing, 2013), p. 57.

[5] Royce, *The Philosophy of Loyalty*, p. 259.

[6] Heward-Mills, *Loyalty and Disloyalty*, p. 64.

[7] Ibid., p. 28.

[8] Ibid.

[9] Ibid., p. 34.

[10] Royce, *The Philosophy of Loyalty*, p. 287.

[11] Royce, p. 377.

# CHAPTER THIRTEEN

# THE LAW OF HOSPITALITY

 **The Knowledge Box**

**The Law of Hospitality** is the friendly reception and treatment of both strangers and people within the community of Christ. It is a willingness to share, with godly discernment, the resources God has given us.

**The Precepts:**
1.  The Theology of Hospitality as a Way of Life
2.  Leadership Is to Lead in the Example of Hospitality.
3.  The Church Is to Have a Reputation of Hospitality in the Community.

> Luella Duncan, my grandmother, broke the mold when God was dispensing the grace of hospitality. She had the ability to make the most uncomfortable guest feel like he/she had just reclined at home. It didn't hurt that she could cook like the greatest of all grandmothers. I know what "made from scratch" really means, because I watched her do it for dozens of years. She was a believer, and I have often wondered if she ever realized her gift of hospitality and how the Holy Spirit was using it to work within her. I love to be hospitable, but I get a little stressed out being a "Martha" in a "Mary" world. My wife is the "Mary," as she loves to converse and focus on the relationships at hand. It takes both to operate in the grace of hospitality. When you have the love for hospitality, you have to guard your heart. There are always busloads of people waiting to take advantage of your generosity.

Hospitality is a grace, not a gift, because all believers are called to hospitality.

## PRECEPT ONE:
### The Theology of Hospitality as a Way of Life

Some, Christians are uniquely empowered by God to excel at hospitality. Others must work on the expert delivery of this grace in their lives. The word *hospitality* originally meant "fond of strangers." This kind of hospitality requires a special kind of love that will mark the local church. Hospitality should serve as a verb, since it requires action. *Hospitality* can be defined as "the reception and treatment of strangers" (Hebrews 13:2). Hospitality played an important part in the Old Testament (Genesis 19:2-3; 24:32:33), as well as the New Testament (Luke 7:36; 9:3-5; 10:38; 14:1). Jesus relied heavily on the grace of hospitality and emphasized its importance in the life of the mission of the church (Mark 1:29; 2:15; 14:3; Luke 10:34;

11:5; 14:12-14). The early church crafted itself as a master of hospitality (Romans 12:20-21; 1 Peter 4:9). The Bible especially admonished widows to use the grace of hospitality (1 Timothy 5:9-10). The travel conditions of an ancient Mediterranean world have changed from its first-century demands, yet this Scripture is profitable and applicable for us in the twenty-first century, or the Holy Spirit would not have preserved it in the Holy Canon. We still need the grace of hospitality today in our churches. In the Scripture, hospitality isn't an office, practice, or simply a gift; it is a way of life. It is, in many ways, an ethic in the early church. Today, it is rather difficult to find good writings about the gift of hospitality in the church. Ironically, the business world is full of books and research regarding the power of hospitality. The following discussion is a look at hospitality in the Scriptures.

### Wisdom Point A:

*The key to Christian hospitality is the sacred process of how to change a stranger into a guest.* Both the Old and New Testaments are filled with stories of how strangers where turned into guests and then eventually close family! Some examples include Moses being received in a basket, Rahab welcoming spies, and Paul's acceptance within the Christian community. The Book of Isaiah even notes that hospitality is greater than fasting! Hospitality is the process of turning strangers into guests.

### Wisdom Point B:

*Hospitality is an ethic for everyone.* First Peter 4:9 says, "Be hospitable to one another without complaining." It is truly one of the distinguishing marks of Christianity. (Romans 12:13; 1 Timothy 3:2; Titus 1:8; Hebrews 13:2). Nowhere in the Scriptures is the practice of hospitality regulated to one office or believer. The act of welcoming a stranger or visitor is a moral act in Christianity; in fact, it is the foundation of our identity and faith practice. In the ancient world, Christianity was distinguished by its acts of love for the stranger, widow, orphan, and guest. To practice hospitality is to place a high worth on humanity. Asking strangers to sit at our table is to acknowledge their dignity.

**Wisdom Point C:**

*The Incarnation was an act of hospitality.* In the unpublished manuscript, "Christian Hospitality—A Way of Life" by Jason Foster, he acknowledges this fact: "Incarnation, following the example of Jesus as given to us in John 1 and Philippians 2, is the act of proactively entering into the world of others. . . . Hospitality is the flip side of "Incarnation." Hospitality is the act of inviting other people into our world, in order to accomplish the same things."[1]

**Wisdom Point D:**

*Hospitality is an eternal issue.* Hospitality doesn't end on this side of heaven. The first event in heaven is the Marriage Supper of the Lamb (Revelation 19). In our culture, there isn't a great picture of hospitality. At best, hospitality could be placing your best foot forward, entertaining guests, and the marriage of two individuals. Jesus said he was going to "prepare us a home." In heaven, community is everywhere, and unspoiled.

**Wisdom Point E:**

*Christ was once a stranger.* In Matthew 25:34-46, Jesus said, "I was a stranger and you took Me in" (v. 34 NKJV). We must understand that the practice of hospitality is rooted in Jesus Christ himself. In Matthew, service to strangers was equated with service to Christ himself. Notice in Matthew that there is an eternal reward for being hospitable to strangers—you inherit the Kingdom! Hospitality is so important to Christology that Christ himself gives a reward or punishment based on our success or failure at being hospitable. To Christ, hospitality is the mark of a true believer.

**Wisdom Point F:**

*Christ was a guest.* Mark 2:15-17 says, "While He was reclining at the table in Levi's house, many tax collectors and sinners were also guests with Jesus and His disciples." Jesus identifies with the stranger who knew no one and needed a friend to invite Him into fellowship, and He knew what it was to enter deeper fellowship as He moved from stranger to guest. The Scriptures are full of times where Jesus was the guest in the presence of the "elite" and the "impoverished." He welcomed fellowship with all of humanity, not just one social group.

**Wisdom Point G:**

*Jesus was a host.* The very first miracle Jesus performed was turning the water into wine at a wedding so that the host would not be embarrassed. Hosting was important to Christ. In Luke 9:10-17, five thousand people stood before Him hungry. "Hospitality is extended to the masses without regard for their spiritual condition or any other distinctive. . . . It is through this miraculous feeding that Jesus sets the stage for one of His most striking teachings—Jesus himself is the Bread of Life (John 6:35-40, 48-51).[2] Jason Foster points out in his manuscript that "Hospitality is the grid through which the miraculous comes to visit us, and we see God at work in unique ways. There is a supernatural component to Christian hospitality that we abandon or minimize to the detriment of the Kingdom."[3]

We see Jesus as a host everywhere in Scriptures! He does so in John 7 as He attends the Feast of Tabernacles. What a powerful metaphor of Christ living with us daily! We see Him as host in the Last Supper (Mark 14:12-16) and at the Marriage Supper of the Lamb (Revelation 19). Jesus is . . .

- A selfless host.
- A humble host.
- A host that blesses His guests.
- An impartial host.
- A proactive host.
- A courteous host.
- A host even to His enemies.
- A tolerant host.
- The master host.

## Wisdom Point H:

*Hospitality transmits the gospel message.* Our church leaders must realize that hospitality is a tool to transmit the gospel of Jesus Christ to people who do not know Him (strangers). Gentile conversion began with the act of hospitality (see Acts 10:24-48). Cornelius invited people into his personal home as strangers. "They represent different cultures, different allegiances, different histories, and different people. Yet, hospitality is the bridge that overcomes these differences and becomes the avenue through which God's salvation begins extending to the Gentiles in force. Hospitality is the setting through which the Gospel spreads."[4] We see this process repeated in Acts 16:11-15; 16:29-34; 17:1-9; and 18:24-28. In the Garden of Eden, God provided the food and fellowship, and then He asked man to join Him daily in a walk through the Garden. In Revelation, God meets us again, but this time at a supper table. He told us that He was going away to prepare us a "place." In the beginning, we started with fellowship; and in the end of the book, we end with fellowship. It must be pretty important to God.

Great hospitality doesn't happen without planning. The personal attention, the food, drink, and the atmosphere, are all part of the hospitality process. If it is so important to Jesus, then it should be just as important to your church leaders! In the local church today, the first place the grace of hospitality must originate may surprise you. It is not in the ladies ministries, but rather in the top tier of biblical leadership—your local church.

## PRECEPT TWO:
### Leadership Is to Lead in the Example of Hospitality

Isn't it interesting that of all of the graces an elder or deacon would need to effectively execute their positions, hospitality is at the top of the list. In 1 Timothy 3:2, it says, "An overseer (elder), therefore, must be . . . hospitable." Titus 1:7 says, "For an overseer as God's administrator, must be . . . hospitable." The early church depended upon the hospitality of their members to spread the gospel because of their constant travel and oftentimes lack of resources. I doubt that the Holy Spirit inspired the New Testament writers to place this word "hospitality" in the characteristics for church leadership as only a reference to the first century A.D. In ancient times, the church was taught hospitality because of the apostolic nature of early Christianity. Itinerant preachers traveled from city to city relying on the hospitality of members of the local church. Christianity was being persecuted, the roads were unsafe, and times demanded the reliance upon "others" as resources. Luke gives us the Lord's instruction on the ancient practice of hospitality. "Take nothing for the road," He told them, "no walking stick, no traveling bag, no bread, no money; and don't take an extra shirt. Whatever houses you enter, stay there and leave from there. If they do not welcome you, when you leave that town, shake off the dust from your feet as a testimony against them" (Luke 9:3-5). They were told not to take a bag (used as an overnight bag), bread, or money, which was originally silver. The instructions imply their expected reliance upon the hospitability in the local churches. The philosophers of their day went from house to house—a contrast to the disciples who embraced the practice of staying at one house. The same references to traveling that we find here were also mentioned in the ancient church administration document called the Didache. Clear instructions were given as to how we are to "receive" guests in our churches. It literally says, "Deal with them as if you were receiving the Lord" himself (Didache 11-12).

While times have changed and hotel accommodations and cultural demands have morphed, there is still a biblical need today for hospitality among church leadership. However, today there are far too many abuses by church leaders as they visit local congregations. Any good pastor knows that you have to be careful lest one of them fleece the flock for their own benefit. For example, some manipulate local church members by challenging them to place on a credit card what they do not have in their bank accounts as "their step of faith." Even international evangelists have lied about orphans, and they possess egos that refused to "come" unless their exuberant demands were met. All of this, however, does not release us from the spirit of hospitality, or show true "honor" to men and women of God as they enter our churches. As we have previously learned in the laws of community, we are to be His ambassadors. Such a realization challenges us to master the grace of hospitality in His name and on His behalf.

### Wisdom Point A:
*Leaders show the way in loving the stranger.*

> I was speaking to a pastor friend of mine who is trying to change a very traditional church culture. He was telling me how he had nineteen visitors for a baby dedication for a new family. During this time of celebration, a woman who had been in the church for many years exclaimed: "Why are they coming around here?"

Unfortunately, that is the case for too many believers in our local churches; strangers are seen as intruders. You can't manufacture community, and you can't fool a visitor; either you truly love them or you don't. Many churches assume they are friendly, when in reality, they are friendly only to people who look, act, and behave just like them. Church leaders must lead the way in showing love and care for the visitors and the hospitality to the saints.

> One of the leaders in our church recently found a bill-fold on the floor with $2,000 in cash inside. This man of God tracked down the person who had lost the billfold and strategically asked him to meet him at the church to claim back his billfold. He wanted this "stranger" to know that God's people are still honest and caring for other people. The man was overcome by emotion when his money and cards were returned to him.

Leaders lead the way in establishing care and authentic love for strangers and disciples. There is an art to receiving strangers or visitors into the church. We need leaders who know how to show our congregation the art of welcoming a stranger.

### Wisdom Point B:

*Leaders lead the way in the etiquette of hospitality.* I love being around great men and women of God—people who have scaled the mountain of success and reached its peak. I love to sit quietly in their presence to learn and watch their lives up close. It is the greatest of all classrooms. Really good leaders know how to make you feel at ease in their presence. People who have accomplished great things, those who wield tremendous power, know how to make you feel like you're in the presence of your oldest and dearest friends. One of the greatest gifts you can have as a church leader is the knowledge regarding the etiquette of hospitality.

1. *Common Courtesies.* Great hospitality in your local church begins when its members learn to extend common courtesies. If any place in the world should be welcoming, it should be the house of God. It is tragic when the unsaved, or strangers, are treated poorly in a local church; it is infallible proof that a local congregation has lost its way. The Christian faith is a journey, not an event. We need to allow individuals the grace to seek God further, ask the tough questions, and experience God with us as we worship, feed the poor, or commune with one another. Not allowing a person of this postmodern generation to do so, only assures the end of any kind of searching for the existence of God. My friend actually had a member tell him that "unless you're saved, you should not even be allowed to mow the grass at the church!" The core to common courtesies is love. Matthew 25:34-46 reminds us that when we are courteous to the "least of these" we have been courteous to God. You see, courtesy is an internal issue, as well as an external issue. God's love flows from the inside to the outside, and so does courtesy. When we show kindness to strangers, we do so because the kindness of God has shined within our hearts. "It is evangelical charity enthroned in the soul."[5] Our manners should be suited to the character of the One we serve.

2. *The grace of hospitality is used by God to soften young hearts.*

> Years ago, I engaged in a word-by-word exegetical study on the first fifteen chapters of the Book of Proverbs. Social-rhetorical criticism, which is a method of interpreting Scripture, had taught me to step back, line up the multiple words in a passage, and see the trees despite the forest. The key that I found in Proverbs showed me clearly that wisdom in the life of our children, and raising a

child to fear the Lord, begins with teaching them
how to respect, not only human life but also the
property of other people.

Unless we learn to be kind to other people, we will never learn to fear the Lord. How can we respect the stranger if we don't respect the Divine Being? How we treat humanity is an insight into the true soul of a man. How could this be so? It's quite simple. We have a recession all right, but it's not a recession of materialism; it's a recession of the heart. How can a twelve-year-old child stab another twelve-year-old child? How does a young adult drive around in a BMW at the age of twenty-one and justify shooting six people? What causes a mother to abandon her children or a father to leave his home and never return? The answer is, "their hearts." When we reject a visitor or become unkind to a stranger, it is a mirror of the poverty within our own hearts. When you love and fear God, you will love the unlovable, feed the unfed, clothe the naked, and embrace the broken. When the local church rejects the stranger, fails in showing love, acceptance, and hospitality to others, they have proven their sickness. The lack of hospitality is a heart problem.

## PRECEPT THREE:
### The Church Is to Have a Reputation of Hospitality in the Community.

In Matthew 5, it says, "For if you love those who love you, what reward will you have? Don't even the tax collectors do the same? And if you greet only your brothers, what are you doing out of the ordinary? Don't even the Gentiles do the same? Be perfect, therefore, as your heavenly Father is perfect" (vv. 46-48). Archbishop William Temple said, "The church is the only cooperative society in the world that exists for the benefit of its non-members."

This passage is calling all of us to press beyond our comfort zones of reciprocal love. How do you build a church with hospitality in the twenty-first century?

**Wisdom Point A:**

*Community begins when we prepare the outside and inside of our churches.* Your property speaks to visitors. There is a great deal of research that suggests a visitor will decide to return to your church within the first twelve minutes of their first visit. There has been much criticism toward those churches that have reinvented the basic environments in a church. There is a reason why Cornell University offers a Ph.D. in hospitality management. Such students will study a wide variety of subjects such as architectural design, operations management, property development, communication, and making capital investments. Such researchers point toward a visitor's immediate observation of your facilities, people, and activities for their families as a barometer for whether or not they will return. Additional researchers have pointed to the lobby, the restrooms, and the nursery as leading indicators of a return visit. Visitors will assume that if you "sweat the small stuff," then you can be trusted with the moral instruction of their families. Postmodern visitors are actually judging our churches on a spirit of excellence in the smallest of places.

**Wisdom Point B:**

*Visitors are looking for a sign.* That sign is an inviting environment. You don't need a $10 million building to attract the lost, but you will need a clean, well-organized, friendly, creative environment. If you don't believe me, then think deeply about the restaurants you choose and why. We choose them based on environment and atmosphere as much as we do the taste of the food. Long before we notice the way our steaks are seasoned, we are drawn by their landscapes and creative, warm designs inside.

> We are surrounded by a world of objects and events, and with apparently no conscious effort we sense their presence. Indeed, it seems so natural and almost effortless to be aware of the environment that, generally, we tend to take sensation and perception for granted...While perhaps less than a miracle, it is quite a feat, especially when we consider that virtually everything we are aware of about the environment is based on a pattern of physical energies that directly affects our sensory receptors. For example, what we smell is based on a complex chemical reaction taking place in the inner reaches of the nasal cavity, what we see is the result of a changing pattern of radiant energies cast upon the back of the eyeball, and what we hear comes from a varying pattern of airborne vibrations conveyed to the receptors of the inner ear.[6]

Billboards along the highways in the United States often contain a phrase that says, "If you are looking for a sign from God, here it is!" Visitors are looking for direction. Proper signage that clearly states where each ministry is located is crucial. Make your ministries easy to identify and locate. Ensure a well-kept environment that feels warm and inviting. These are the signs of a hospitable church.

### Wisdom Point C:

*Extend a welcoming hand:* We assume that most average visitors have already been to church, know their way around, and understand our verbiage (sanctuary, vestibule, Royal Rangers). This simply is no longer predominantly true. Great hospitality begins with a welcome, and it can't look manufactured or forced. Visitors are actually our guests, and great hospitality escorts them to the Information Center, the right classrooms, and restrooms. Nothing turns me off to a restaurant any quicker than a rude host who seats me. Health care is never more aggravating than when a physician or a nurse does not possess little social skills. Nothing turns a person off to the possibility of exploring the realities of God faster than an unfriendly church.

The concept of reception is peppered throughout Scripture. Take some time and notice how much preparation God has gone through in awaiting our arrival in heaven. He said, "I go to prepare you a place..." (John 14:3). In Revelation 19:9, the writer tells us of a great marriage feast—"The Marriage Supper of the Lamb." Revelation 21 speaks about the gift of a new city for all of us. Think about the fact that there isn't a day in our culture where more preparation takes place than our marriages. It is a celebration in every sense. Excellence in your church is an extension of additional invitations to the celebration of a coming marriage.

**Wisdom Point D***:*

*It's the smile that speaks a thousand messages.* Major hotel chains have hired only those people who smiled more than four times. A smile goes a long way. As a matter of fact, new research shows that "a child's smile creates as much pleasure as 2,000 chocolate bars or $25,000 in cash." This same report found that we can detect a smile from more than three hundred feet away. In one study, Swedish researchers found that "a smile is also contagious."[7] If hotels, restaurants, department stores, and scientists all know the power of a smile, then surely the house of God can too.

**Wisdom Point E:**

*Hospitality requires the mastering of the art of transitions.* Many people expect a smile and a greeter at the front door. How many are looking for such warm behavior in the parking lot? At Covenant Community Church (CCC), we meet them at their cars on a golf cart. We carry their baby bags, help them out of the rain, and walk them to the door. It's a great time to discover interests and needs of visiting people.

**Wisdom Point F:**

*Build a Welcome/Information Center:* My mentor in church growth, Dr. Owen Weston, drilled into my head the truth that "First impressions are lasting impressions." New families will be looking for information like where the nursery is located and how to go about signing the children in for children's church. Such a center provides another avenue for an intimate touch of hospitality.

**Wisdom Point G:**

*Acknowledging guests during worship is very important:* Many years ago during the seeker-sensitive church explosion, leaders thought that visitors did not want to be formally recognized. While that may have been true years ago, today times have changed. People are looking for ways to connect with your church. Today, churches are finding out that there really is an art to being hospitable during worship. At CCC, we ask for our visitors to sit while our regular members stand. This immediately takes the pressure off everyone staring at them! We have also trained our congregation to look for people they don't know, for people who might feel alone, and "old friends" last. An inviting atmosphere is created on purpose. True hospitality doesn't wait to see if people feel welcomed; it takes personal responsibility of leading the way.

**Wisdom Point H:**

*How a church can successfully track growth.* One of the most successful models of inviting guests to become family is a reception for new members and/or a growth-track teaching class designed to get to know the church better. Our church used both, and studies show great results when new visitors are offered a free reception with the church leadership. Every Sunday, we invite people to our guest-relations room where they meet the different pastors, staff, and elders.

## Wisdom Point I:

*Hospitality is not possible without love.* People know a fake smile when they see one. People know when you really care about them and their families. Clement of Alexandria called hospitality a form of love. Throughout the years, I have met many hurting people. One such lady stands out in my mind as a testimony to our church's reputation for reaching out in love/hospitality to hurting people. A woman had recently been released from prison. She had accepted Christ in a prison fellowship. Upon her release, she began to attend her childhood church again. One day in the hallway, several members confronted her and told her she didn't "belong" at their church. Their church wasn't the "right" place for a woman like her. As she stood in the hallway crying, a deacon walked up to her and said, "I heard about a church that will accept you. I think you should go there." It was our church. What kind of hospitality is your church known for? Jesus was a "friend of sinners" (Mark 2:13-17). While there are clearly laws in community that require abstaining from certain relationships, they are there for the purpose of discipleship.

> Recently, I fell apart amidst high blood sugar, acute diverticulitis, extreme carpal-tunnel, gouty arthritis, and a very broken new health care system. My body simple gave out. As a pastor, I am a constant roller-coaster of emotions. I have led hundreds through tragedy during this year alone. I should have known that eventually my heart/spirit would give out from giving out! I knew that I was sick and needed some help. An employee at a health care facility treated me poorly, actually my Hipaa Laws were violated, and through rudeness, abuse of power, and the lack of intelligence, my spirit finally broke. In the midst of my

> brokenness, a professional lady spoke kindness to my soul. She listened, apologized, and promised confidentiality. Another man sat by my bedside in the hospital and just listened. All of these things created an environment that began the healing of my tired soul; however, it was the realization that kindness can go a long way to healing hurtful events. It is a powerful antidote to an uncaring world.

Is your church kind? Does your church love and show the kindness of God to those you don't know? How kind are you to strangers? It is something to think seriously about today, because it does make a big difference.

**Wisdom Point J:**

*Hospitality is a sign of a true believer.* Paul tells the church of Colosse that conversion begins with the heart and the mind (Colossians 3:1-4). He tells the church that their "life is hidden" (Colossians 3:3). But this life is revealed when we "put on" the new man (baptism language in the first century: Colossians 3:10). This new man is being "renewed in the knowledge"—a renewal that comes only from God himself. What is so interesting is what Paul uses as proof of the Christian life. It is not shouting, tongues, gifts, clothing, etc., rather, it was "heartfelt compassion, kindness, humility, gentleness, and patience, accepting one another. . . . Above all, put on love—the perfect bond of unity" (Colossians 3:11-14). These are many of the disciplines required to excel in hospitality. The phrase, "the perfect bond of unity" is actually an old Greek word for a garment that holds all the other pieces of our attire together. Love surely holds hospitality together!

At the end of the day, hospitality is overlooked and misunderstood by most believers. We fail to grasp the weight of hospitality to a believer. In Scripture itself, it is a mark of our distinction. Paul told Timothy that in the last days, people would become "lovers of self . . . ungrateful, unloving" (2 Timothy 3:1-5). These are marks of inhospitable people. I want to encourage your local church to love the unlovable, reach out to the hurting, heal the brokenhearted, and give out water and clothes in His name; because when you have been hospitable to the least of these, you are actually being hospitable to Christ himself.

# END NOTES

Chapter 13
The Law of Hospitality

[1] Jason Foster, "Christian Hospitality—A Way of Life: Practical Christian Living Sunday School Class" (unpublished manuscript, Winter 2008), p. 3, Microsoft Word file.

[2] Foster, "Christian Hospitality," p. 15.

[3] Ibid.

[4] Ibid., p. 21.

[5] George Winfred Hervey, *Principles of Courtesy* (New York: Harper and Brothers Publishers, 1852), Introduction.

[6] Harvey Richard Schiffman, *Sensation and Perception: An Integrated Approach*, 4th edition (New York: John Wiley and Sons, Inc., 1996), p. 1.

[7] "Surprising Facts About Smiling," Yahoo Health, December 19, 2011, www.health.yahoo.net/experts/dayin-health/science-smiles.

# CONCLUSION

Revival has to be protected by a foundation in the local church, and the local church is to be protected by the laws of community. After all, God the Father has given us clear instructions about a host of different topics ranging from sex, family, money, pastors, apostles, the rich, the treatment of the poor, and so forth. He then gave us clear instructions regarding the institution He gave His life for—the local church.

I have studied revivals for over thirty-three years. Sadly, what I found was a littered history of good people who just couldn't get along for any quality length of time. Many revivals sputter out because of the same stronghold. Over and over again, one finds a deadly relational virus. Revival can't happen unless people are involved. Revival will not continue unless a profound sense of community protects it. There is a deep reason why the wisdom of Christ compelled the disciples and new converts of Christianity to the Upper Room. I believe it was the wisdom of Christ that community was needed before the outpouring of the Holy Spirit could come, lest it survive only one generation. Peter clearly remarked that this promised revival fire was "for you and for your children, and for all who are far off, as many as the Lord our God will call" (Acts 2:39). Revival requires community. It is not the shouting or miraculous signs that sustain any revival that has the power to "turn the world upside down" (Acts 17:6). In Acts 4:32, it says: "Now the multitude of those who believed were of one heart and soul; neither did anyone say that any of the things he possessed was his own, but they had all things in common" (NKJV). God wants to bless the local church with a powerful contextualized gospel. He will continue to pour His Spirit out, with fresh renewing power; the greater question, however, is: Can we love one another deep enough, long enough, and maturely enough to carry those fires to the uttermost parts of the world?

# BIBLIOGRAPHY

Banks, Robert, J. *Paul's Idea of Community: The Early House Churches in Their Cultural Setting* (Peabody, Mass.: Hendrickson Publishing, 2009).

Bilezikian, Gilbert. *Reclaiming the Local Church as Community of Oneness* (Grand Rapids: Zondervan Publishing, 1997).

Borchert, Gerald L. *The New American Commentary, John 12-21: Volume 25B,* ed. E. Roy Clendenen (Nashville: Broadman & Holman, 2002).

"Can or Should Christians Judge One Another?" bibleteacher.org. www.bibleteacher.org/Judging.htm.

Chaleff. *The Courageous Follower: Standing Up, to and for Our Leaders.* 2nd ed. (San Francisco: Berrett-Koehler Publishers, 2002).

Chinnock, Edward J. *A Few Notes on Julian and a Translation of His Public Letters* (London: David Nott, 1901).

Collins, Jim. *Good to Great: Why Some Companies Make the Leap . . . and Others Don't* (New York: HarperCollins, 2001).

Delio, Ilia. *Franciscan Prayer* (Cincinnati, Ohio: St. Anthony Messenger Press, 2004).

Delio, Ilia, O.S.F. *The Humility of God: A Franciscan Perspective* (Cincinnati: St. Anthony Messenger Press, 2005).

deSilva, David A. *Honor, Patronage, Kinship & Purity: Unlocking New Testament Culture* (Downers Grove, Ill.: InterVarsity Press, 2000).

"Detecting Deception." *American Psychological Association* (December 16, 2013) www.apa.org/monitor/julaug04/detecting.aspx.

Dickson, John. *Humilitias: A Lost Key to Life, Love, and Leadership* (Grand Rapids: Zondervan, 2001).

Dorff, Elliot N. (Rabbi). *Tikkun Olam: Repairing the Broken World* (Woodstock, Vermont: Jewish Lights Publishing, 2007).

Elwell, Walter A., ed. *The Bible Knowledge Background Commentary: Acts-Philemon.*

Elwell, Walter A. and Phillip W. Comfort, eds. *The Tyndale Bible Dictionary* (Wheaton, Ill.: Tyndale Publishing, 2001).

Foster, Jason. "Christian Hospitality—A Way of Life: Practical Christian Living Sunday School Class" (unpublished manuscript, Winter 2008). Microsoft Word file.

Gardner, Jake. "The Doctrine of Divine Judgment" (accessed: December 26, 2013; December 1, 2013) www.thedoctrineofdivinejudgment.com.

Grenberg, Jeanine. *Kant and the Ethics of Humility: A Story of Dependence, Corruption, and Virtue* (New York: Cambridge University Press, 2005).

Hall, Douglas. *The Steward: A Biblical Symbol Comes of Age* (Grand Rapids: William B. Eerdmans Publishing, 1990).

Hanson, Paul D. *The People Called: The Growth of Community in the Bible* (San Francisco: Harper and Row Publishers, 1986).

Harris, Murray J. *The Second Epistle to the Corinthians: A Commentary on the Greek Text* (Grand Rapids: William B. Eerdmans Publishing Company, 2005).

Hellerman, J.H. *The Humiliation of Christ in the Social World of Roman Philippie: Part One* (Bibliotheca Sacra, 2003).

Hellerman, Joseph. *Reconstructing Honor in Roman Christi as Curus Pudorum: Society for New Testament Studies Monograph Series* (New York: Cambridge University Press, 2005).

Hervey, George Winfred. *Principles of Courtesy* (New York: Harper and Brothers Publishers, 1852).

Heward-Mills, Dag. *Loyalty and Disloyalty: Dealing With Unspoken Divisions Within the Church* (Franklin, Tenn.: Carpenter's Son Publishing, 2013).

Hinson, E. Glenn. *The Early Church: Origins of the Dawn of the Middle Ages* (Nashville: Abingdon Press, 1996).

Hirsch, Alan and Dave Furgerson. *On the Verge: A Journey Into the Apostolic Future of the Church* (Grand Rapids: Zondervan, 2011).

Hirsch, Alan and Tim Catchim. *The Permanent Revolution: Apostolic Imagination and Practice for the 21st-Century Church* (San Francisco: Jossey-Bass, 2012).

Holl, Karl. *The Distinctive Elements in Christianity* (Edinburg: Clark, 1937).

"Humility." *Wikipedia, the Free Dictionary, n.a., 2008.* http://en.wikipedia.org/wiki/humility/ (accessed: October 28, 2008).

Keller, Tim. *Center Church: Doing Balanced, Gospel-Centered Ministry in Your City* (Grand Rapids: Zondervan, 2012).

Kelley, Robert. *The Power of Followership* (New York: Currency Doubleday, 1992).

Kierkegarrd, Soren. *Works of Love* (New York: Harper, 1963).

Kittel, Gerhard, Geoffrey William Bromiley, and Gerhard Friedrich. *Theological Dictionary of the New Testament.* Logos Software (Grand Rapids: Eerdmans, n.d.).

"Know Your Bible? Many Christians Don't." CBN (February 27, 2014; July 24, 2009) www.cbn.com/cbnnews/us/2009/June/Do-You-Know-Your-Bible-Many-Christians-Don't/.n

Lennick, Doug and Fred Kiel. *Moral Intelligence: Enhancing Business Performance and Leadership Success* (New Jersey: Wharton School Publishing, 2005).

Lohfink, Gerhard. *Jesus and Community* (Philadelphia: Fortress Press, 1934).

Louf, André. *The Way of Humility* (Kalamazoo, Mich.: Cistercian Publications, 2007).

Martyr, Justin. *Apology of Justin Martyr.* eds. Rev. Alexander Roberts, James Donaldson, and A. Cleveland Coxe (Tartow, Ohio: Suzeteo Enterprises, 2012).

Mathews, Kenneth A. *New American Commentary Volume 1A Genesis 1–11:26.* Logos Software, ed. E. Ray Clendenen (Nashville: Broadman and Holman, 1996).

Morris, Leon. *The Pillar New Testament Commentary: The Epistle to the Romans,* ed. D.A. Carson (Grand Rapids: William B. Eerdmans, 1988).

Morris, Leon. *The Pillar New Testament Commentary: The Gospel According to Matthew.* Logos Software, ed. D.A. Carson (Grand Rapids: William B. Eerdmans Publishing Company, 1992).

Murray, Andrew. *Humility* (Radford, VA.: Wilder Publications, 2008).

"Philippians Hymn, The (2:5-11)." *As an Early Mimetic Christological Model of Christian Leadership in Roman Philippi:* "Inner Reflections on Leadership." Corné Bekker (January 27, 2010; August 1, 2006) www.innerresourcesfor leaders.blogspot.com/.

"Psychology of Wellbeing: Musings on the Science of Holistic Wellness, The." *Psychology of Wellbeing* (March 6, 2014; September 4, 2012) www.psychologyofwellbeing.com.

Quotes About Truth Telling." *Goodreads.* www.goodreads.com/quotes/tag/truth-telling.;

Ritchhart, Ron. *Intellectual Character: What It Is, Why It Matters, and How to Get It* (San Francisco: Jossey-Bass, 2002).

Robertson, Archibald Thomas. *Word Pictures in the New Testament* (Nashville: Broadman Press, 1930) Electronic Version.

Royce, Josiah. *The Philosophy of Loyalty* (New York: The McMillian Company, 1908).

Scherman, Nosson and Meir Zlotowitz, (Rabbis), eds. *Bircas Kohanim: The Priestly Blessing: Background, Translations, and Commentary Anthologized From Talmudic, Midrashic, and Rabbinic Sources* (New York: Mesorah Publications, 1991).

Schiffman, Harvey Richard. *Sensation and Perception: An Integrated Approach.* 4th ed. (New York: John Wiley and Sons, Inc., 1996).

Siegel, Ronald D. ed. "Positive Psychology: Harnessing the Power of Happiness, Mindfulness, and Personal Strengths." *Harvard Health Publications* (Boston: Harvard Healthy Publishers, 2013).

"Small Churches Struggle to Grow Because of the People They Attract." The George Barna Group (February 10, 2014; September 2, 2003) www.barna.org/barna-update/article/5-barna-update/126small-churches-struggle-to-grow-because-of-the-people-they-attract#UwQLEHmklds.

"Surprising Facts About Smiling." Yahoo Health (December 19, 2011) www.health.yahoo.net/experts/dayin-health/science-smiles.

"Sustainable Traditions: Empire and Love" (December 24, 2013; January 01, 2013) www.sustainabletraditions.com/tag/Julian-the-apostate/.

"Tertullian Project, The" (December 10, 1999; December 26, 2013) www.tertullian.org/quotes.htm.

"Unity." KJV Dictionary Definition: *The King James Bible Page* (accessed: January 1, 2013) www.av1611.com/kjbp/kjv-dictionary/unity.html.

Varillon, Francois. *The Humility and Suffering of God* (New York: Alba House, 1905).

Vining, John Kie. *Servant Church: Drooling and Dreaming of the Milk and Honey of Church Relevance* (Cleveland, Tenn.: Derek Press, 2008).

White, James Emery. *You Can Experience . . . A Spiritual Life* (Nashville: Word Publishing, 1999).

"Wikipedia Community." Wikipedia. www.wikipedia.org/wiki/Community.

Worthington, Everett L. *Humility: The Quiet Virtue* (Philadelphia: Templeton Foundation Press, 2007).